M000268513

MAXIMUM
PERFORMANCE

SPORTS MEDICINE FOR ENDURANCE ATHLETES

Michael J. Ross, M.D.

VELO
press®

BOULDER, COLORADO

Disclaimer
The information in this book is intended for educational and instructional purposes. It is not intended to replace medical care, rather to be an adjunct to it.

Maximum Performance: Sports Medicine for Endurance Athletes
Copyright © 2003 Michael J. Ross, M.D.

All rights reserved. No part of this book may be reproduced, stored in a retrieval system, or transmitted, in any form or by any means, electronic or photocopy or otherwise, without the prior written permission of the publisher.

Printed in the United States of America.

10 9 8 7 6 5 4 3 2 1

Distributed in the United States and Canada by Publishers Group West.

International Standard Book Number: 1-931382-22-0

Library of Congress Cataloging-in-Publication Data

Ross, Michael J.
Maximum performance : sports medicine for endurance athletes / Michael J. Ross.
    p. cm.
  Includes bibliographical references and index.
  ISBN 1-931382-22-0
    1. Sports—Physiological aspects. 2. Muscle strength. 3. Physical fitness. 4. Physical education and training. I. Title.

RC1235 .R67 2003
612/.044—dc21

                                                                    2002044602

VeloPress®
1830 North 55th Street
Boulder, Colorado 80301–2700 USA
303/440-0601 • Fax 303/444-6788 • E-mail velopress@7dogs.com

To purchase additional copies of this book or other VeloPress® books, call 800/234-8356 or visit us on the Web at velopress.com.

Cover and interior design by Erin Johnson
Cover photo, Getty Images/EyeWire; back cover photo of mountain biker courtesy of K2, swimmer and runner photos, Photos.com

For Wendy, who provides me with inspiration
and encouragement to fulfill my dreams.

And Benjamin, although you have only been here a week,
you bring me joy and happiness every day.

CONTENTS

Acknowledgments vii

Introduction ix

PART ONE. Physiology

1. Athlete Physiology 3

2. Carbohydrate Metabolism 11

3. Protein Needs for Exercise and Training 23

4. Fat Metabolism and Weight Loss 29

5. Fluids, Electrolytes, and Hydration 39

6. Exercise Endocrinology for Maximal Recovery and Performance 51

7. Smarter Training for Injury Prevention 59

PART TWO. Medical Problems

8. Exercise-Induced Asthma 69

9. Road Rash 73

10. Acid Reflux: A Hard Problem to Swallow 79

11. Lower-GI Symptoms 85

12. Overtraining, Sleep, and Recovery 93

13. Sports Psychology 105

14. Exercise Immunology 115

15. Rhinitis, Sinusitus, and the Common Cold: It's All in Your Head . . . 127

16. Eating Disorders and the Female Athlete Triad. 133

17. Environmental Injury and Illness. 141

PART THREE. Overuse Injuries

18. Overuse Injuries of the Knee 155

19. Overuse Injuries of the Foot and Ankle 181

PART FOUR. Putting It All Together

20. Case Studies. 193

Index 199

About the Author 213

ACKNOWLEDGMENTS

Teaching is a noble enterprise. I hope that everyone who reads this book learns something. It would not be possible for me to have written this without all of the people who have taken time out of their lives to teach me a thing or two. I especially want to thank the following people:

My parents and family for teaching me how to ride a bicycle and that being a good person is its own reward.

Jack Angevine and Mike Fraysse who transformed a high-school student into a cycling enthusiast.

Amy Sorrells and Renee Jardine at VeloPress for all I learned about writing a book.

All those who have trusted their training to me and continue to have faith in me.

My friends, especially Team ReTRO for their enthusiasm, support and interest, particularly Steve, Andrew, Michele, and Eric. My models: Steve, Raphael, Kim, Karen, Carolyn, Art, and Kate. My beautiful photographer Wendy.

My friends at Threshold Sports. Cheryl, for her book-writing advice.

Everyone within the industry who has provided me with help: Skip Reyes at K2 Bikes, Richard Bryne at Speedplay, Sports Instruments, Graber Products, Oakley.

And to all of those who have helped me get to the happy place where I am right now, Thank You.

INTRODUCTION

Medicine in the United States has become a "patch kit" for health. People tend to use medical advice only when they are sick and injured. This has led to a society of doctor-patient relations not in health but in disease. Sports medicine has followed this path. Most young, healthy athletes seek medical advice only when they have been injured.

Perhaps the problem lies in the fact that athletes perceive themselves to be healthy, when in fact they are as susceptible to disease as is everyone else. It's true that athletes will suffer less from heart disease, high cholesterol, stroke, high blood pressure, and type 2 diabetes, but there are other medical problems they will face more frequently.

Part of the purpose of combining medicine with sport training is to create an environment in which the athlete can train in a healthy state and avoid some of the injury and disease patterns that can sideline endurance athletes. This dual approach is similar to the model developed in Europe, where athletes seek advice from doctors and "trainers" who look after the whole athlete and do not prescribe training sessions without taking into account physiology and fitness. By combining biomechanics, medicine, physiology, and training principles, this program develops a complete athlete and avoids the need to "patch" holes in health and training.

The key to successful athletic performance lies not solely in training nor solely in diet, but instead is embedded in a complex interaction of training, recovery, diet, and timing. The manipulation of these factors can lead to more efficient training and better performance.

The first part of this book will teach you some of the principles of exercise science, training, and diet and how they can be timed to maximize your effort. In Part II, I discuss the common medical issues associated with endurance sports to help you improve your performance by limiting the medical problems that can put an end to a hard athletic effort. The third part of the book examines overuse injuries that can occur even in a well-planned program. I am aware that getting back to activity is a priority for an athlete sidelined by overuse, and I offer some sport-specific strength and stretching exercises to help you return faster.

I was raised as a cyclist through a constant diet of long, steady distance rides early in the season, followed by a Tuesday, Wednesday, Thursday schedule of sprints, distance, and hills respectively. These three days were followed by a weekend of races.

Although this schedule got me into the best shape I had ever been in up to that point, it provided very little time for recovery and disregarded other physiological factors such as diet or timing needed to achieve physical optimization.

One example is the long, steady distance ride that many cyclists perform at low intensity for hours on end, in the belief that this will lead to increases in endurance. Steady endurance training can be done in half the time with dietary periodization and workouts that are timed to coincide with the natural ebb and tide of hormone release. Likewise, training the body to use fat as energy is done with dietary planning, exercise timing, and carefully selected workouts that use the environment in the best way for you to be successful.

The interaction of all of the elements is the key to developing as an athlete and achieving the fitness you want. The use of this book will help to get you there.

PHYSIOLOGY

ATHLETE PHYSIOLOGY

HEART

The heart is a muscular pump that will contract approximately three billion times in an average person's life. Roughly the size of your fist, the heart is divided into four chambers. Buried in its muscular walls is a complex system of conduction pathways that control the pacing of the heart. Blood returns from the body to the right side of the heart. The right side of the heart pumps blood that has been depleted of oxygen to the lungs, where it picks up oxygen; the left side receives the oxygen-rich blood and delivers it to the rest of the body.

Like any muscle that is used repetitively, the heart will adapt and change from exercise. This adaptation depends upon adjustment of several factors: As exercise load increases, the heart must pump out more blood to meet the muscles' increasing demands for oxygen. The amount of blood the heart can pump is called cardiac output (CO) and is dependent upon two factors: heart rate (HR) and stroke volume (SV). Heart rate is the number of times that the heart beats each minute and stroke volume represents the amount of blood the heart can pump with each beat. This can be represented by the equation CO = HR x SV. Therefore, to meet the increased blood and oxygen demands of exercise, the heart must either work faster or increase the amount that it pumps with each beat. Obviously the heart beats faster during exercise, but it also undergoes structural changes from the demands of increased blood volume circulating through it.

When increased volume demand is chronic, as in the trained endurance athlete, the diameter of the heart will increase (dilation) to accommodate the extra volume of blood being transferred. The heart then responds to dilation by thickening the wall of the ventricles.

These changes increase the heart's efficiency by increasing stroke volume. As the walls of the ventricles become larger and thicker, a larger stroke volume can be ejected (called ejection fraction) by a smaller contraction of the heart muscle fibers. This saves energy and leads to more efficient contractions. As the stroke volume increases, the heart rate can decrease to keep the overall cardiac output the same. More than half of trained endurance athletes have a heart rate of less than sixty beats per minute. In turn, they have a more forceful pulse due to the increased stroke volume. These changes occur rapidly after beginning training, with an increase in heart muscle mass seen within one week. After only four days of inactivity, however, these changes begin to reverse themselves, although stroke volume can remain elevated after three weeks of inactivity.

When a training session begins, the heart rate increases, the heart beats stronger, and there is an increase in catecholamines, which are the hormones responsible for increased activity. The heart rate will increase with increasing workload until the maximum heart rate is reached, at which point the accumulation of lactic acid will prevent further work. When charted as a graph of power and heart rate, the heart rate does not increase in completely linear fashion. In theory, the heart rate will plateau or have a deflection point at which the slope of the line changes. This point, known as the lactate threshold heart rate, is when blood lactate starts to increase and is the basis for the Conconi test (discussed later in this chapter). Many athletes do not have a deflection point, however, and the validity of the Conconi test is constantly debated in the research literature.

To become more effective, athletes undertaking cardiovascular fitness improvements should focus on improving power at the lactate threshold. This way, lactic acid does not accumulate as rapidly, and high-level exercise can be maintained for a longer period of time.

LUNGS

The lungs act as the intermediary between the outside environment and the energy we need to fuel our activity. By supplying the body with oxygen, the lungs are one of the primary organs of endurance exercise. The most widely used measure of heart-lung function in the endurance athlete is the VO_2max. This is the maximal oxygen consumption and is loosely related to the maximum heart rate. The maximum oxygen uptake by the body is a function of the minute ventilation (amount of air moving in and out each minute) and the amount of oxygen the body uses. At the VO_2max, an increase in workload will not increase oxygen uptake because the body is already using all of the oxygen that it can. At 100 percent of VO_2max, the amount of oxygen being used (expressed in liters per minute) depends upon lung capacity, breathing rate, and heart rate. Any further increase is achieved with the anaerobic energy system. The greater the VO_2max, the greater the athlete's endurance capacity.

At rest, we breathe at a rate of 10–14 times a minute. With exercise, however, the rate increases to 40–50 times a minute. During exercise, the volume of each breath also increases, such that the total ventilation (volume of inhaled air each minute) increases several fold. As exercise increases beyond 50–90 percent of VO_2max, the blood lactate concentration increases exponentially. The percentage of VO_2max at which there is a rise in lactic acid depends upon the condition of the athlete, with better-conditioned athletes having a delayed rise in lactic acid. As the blood lactate increases, the lungs compensate with a further increase in ventilation. This point at which the respiratory rate increases is known as the ventilatory threshold.

MUSCLE

The third component of the exercise performance triad is the skeletal muscle. This is what powers the limbs to move and propel the athlete forward. Muscle has two basic jobs: creating energy for the work and performing the work. For repeated contraction of a muscle to occur, the muscle must be able to meet the energy demands of repeated use. To achieve this, the muscle must increase the so-called oxidative enzymes from the different biochemical pathways that produce energy. There is an initial increase in these enzymes when a training program begins, but as the fast-twitch muscle fibers are transformed into the more efficient slow-twitch (endurance) muscle fibers, the enzymes do not need to be present in such high concentrations. Even after equilibration, athletes have these enzymes present at three times the rate sedentary people do. An increase in blood supply to the muscles also takes place, allowing for increased oxygen delivery.

An issue in exercise science is its relevance to training and competition and how the science can be applied to training programs. With regard to endurance training, the untrained athlete may see some increase of oxidative enzymes with light exercise (such as jogging or steady cycling), but the endurance athlete must train at 70–80 percent of VO_2max to experience the enzyme increases.

Unfortunately, there is no research in humans comparing oxidative enzymes and duration and intensity of exercise, but one study in rats can be used as a guideline. Rats were exercised daily at rates correlating with 60, 70, 80, 95, 105, and 115 percent of VO_2max. No additional enzyme increase was found after one hour of exercise for the first four rates. The two highest rates could not be sustained, so were performed intermittently (intervals) for 15 and 30 minutes respectively. The resulting changes in oxidative enzymes were the same or greater, depending upon the muscle, than with more exercise at lower intensities.[1] This same study also demonstrated that different muscle fiber types responded differently to different exertion levels. There is an activation threshold that must be reached before a training effect is seen. Once the threshold is reached, slow-twitch muscle fibers are activated. As the exercise workload is increased, there is further recruitment first of slow-twitch fibers followed by the different fast-twitch fibers.

Exercise at and above 80 percent of VO_2max is believed to recruit muscle fibers of all types, but fast-twitch glycolytic fibers that transform stored carbohydrate to energy are probably not fully activated unless very strenuous exercise is undertaken (100 percent or more or VO_2max). It follows that a sound training regimen includes exercise at 80–85 percent of VO_2max once the training foundation has been laid. Further intervals at and above the VO_2max are also recommended. High intensities will produce maximal fiber training in a shorter period of time.

Two months of training at high, submaximal intensity will also increase the capillaries feeding the muscle by 50 percent. This is important not only for oxygen supply but also for the delivery of fuel, in the form of glucose, to the muscle. As the muscle adapts to exercise, the molecules responsible for transporting glucose into the muscle are increased, which enables the body to use the increased glucose delivery.

FACTORS LIMITING MAXIMAL OXYGEN UPTAKE CAPACITY

In the interaction of heart, lungs, and muscles that determines the VO_2max, cardiac function is perceived to be the limiting factor. The muscles can accept a much larger volume of blood than the heart can deliver, even at maximal cardiac output.

During exercise, breathing is harder and may become labored, but unless the athlete has trouble breathing, the lungs are probably not the limiting factor. (Avoiding the limiting factors of the lungs that occur during exercise is discussed in Chapter 8.) Nevertheless, as exercise increases, the percentage of blood that is fully saturated with oxygen will drop from 100 percent to 97 percent, although this is not a significant decrease.

There is a group of researchers who feel that the muscle is the limiting factor. Even when an athlete is breathing 100 percent oxygen (ambient air contains only 21 percent oxygen), there is no appreciable increase in VO_2max. This suggests that the problem lies in the muscle's ability to extract oxygen from the blood. Maximizing oxidative enzymes by training above the lactate threshold will minimize the impact the muscle has as a limiting factor. The athlete should do intervals of 15–30 minutes of work above the lactate threshold heart rate or 85–90 percent of VO_2max. The length of the interval depends upon the duration of the power maintenance. Even if the heart rate is above the lactate threshold heart rate, if the power output drops, end the interval and work on increasing its duration.

Other factors affecting VO_2max include genetics, body composition, gender, age, and physical activity. Although most of these cannot be controlled, body composition and training should be mentioned.

Maximal oxygen uptake (VO_2max) is expressed two ways: as an absolute value (liters of oxygen per minute) or as a relative value (milliliters per kilogram per minute). Comparing different individuals requires using the relative value, which takes the athletes' weight into account. Decreases in body fat through dieting alone, without a change in exercise, will increase the relative VO_2max.

Endurance training will increase the VO_2max by up to 30 percent in two to three months in a previously untrained individual. Over the next year or two, the VO_2max can increase by 40–50 percent. In the trained athlete, there is a strong correlation between VO_2max and exercise frequency, duration, and intensity.

It follows that if these factors limit VO_2max , then increasing the delivery of oxygen from the lungs to the muscle would improve endurance exercise. One way to achieve this is through altitude training, which boosts the amount of oxygen delivered by increasing not only the number of oxygen-carrying red blood cells but also the presence of a molecule known as 2,3-DPG. This molecule facilitates the unloading of oxygen to the muscles. Both of these phenomena have been targeted by the illegal blood-boosting capabilities of EPO, blood doping, and RSR 13.[2] EPO (Erythropoetin) stimulates the growth and production of red blood cells. These methods provide the body with increased red blood cells and 2, 3-DPG to provide an advantage in oxygen delivery from the lungs to the muscles. Living in the oxygen-poor environment of high altitude causes the kidneys to increase the production of red blood cells. Environments that simulate the low-oxygen atmosphere, such as altitude tents or hypobaric chambers, will produce the same changes.

PUTTING IT ALL TOGETHER

As mentioned previously, the training effect is better attained with exercise at certain levels. Although most of the studies are performed at a certain percentage of the VO_2max, these are not values that the average person can achieve without having special equipment or incurring financial expense. Translating these numbers into more attainable values can be done with the Conconi test. This test, described initially by Francesco Conconi in 1982, can be performed by anyone with a treadmill or stationary bike and a heart rate monitor.

The lactate threshold (LT) is equal to approximately 90 percent of VO_2max.[3] This is the value around which a training program should be built. Power at the LT is the hallmark of the endurance athlete. In the former Soviet Union, the cyclists who were developed as champions were those who excelled at time trials. In this event, athletes exercise as hard as they can for about an hour. Since the lactate threshold corresponds to a level of exercise that can be sustained for one hour, power output at the lactate threshold is a good measure of endurance performance.

There are several protocols for testing, but some have had better results than others. If the test is not done properly, determining the LT will be difficult.

The initial Conconi test was performed on a track with runners increasing speed every 200 meters. The heart rate was plotted against power (speed), and the point at which the line flattened was the lactate threshold. This protocol was changed in favor of increasing speed or power at a fixed time interval instead of a fixed distance. Now most researchers use treadmill or stationary bicycle protocols with power (or speed) increases every 30 or 60 seconds (see Table 1.1 for examples). Sometimes a linear regression break-point analysis must be performed to find the deflection point, but it usually is sufficient to draw lines along the early, middle, and end segments of the curve and check the values at which they intersect.

Table 1.1

CONCONI TEST PROTOCOLS

Parameter	Cycling	Running
Start	40–60 watts	5.6 km/h
Increase	10 watts	1–2% incline
Alternate Increase	1 mi/h	1 km/h
Time	1 minute	1 minute

There are two important points to consider in lactate production. The first occurs as exercise intensity begins to increase and is the point at which lactate production first begins. The second is where lactate production greatly increases. This is the lactate (or anaerobic) threshold, where oxygen-utilizing aerobic exercise ceases and lactate-producing anaerobic exercise begins. As mentioned earlier, the ventilatory threshold is closely related to the lactate threshold. The ventilatory threshold is the point at which the respiratory rate increases and breathing begins to feel labored. Whoever is conducting the testing should note the point when breathing becomes labored, as this may be the only indication of LT.

Since the inception of the Conconi test, there have been many different protocols described and many studies suggesting the test is not valid.[4] With the protocol described here, however, the deflection in the heart rate should be more easily obtained.[5] Using a similar protocol, researchers found the heart rate deflection in 86 percent of subjects.[6] Variability may appear if the patient is tired or if glycogen reserves are depleted. Therefore, it has been suggested that the athlete should be well rested and should have eaten at least three hours previously.[7]

Sidebar 1.1

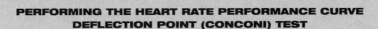

PERFORMING THE HEART RATE PERFORMANCE CURVE DEFLECTION POINT (CONCONI) TEST

1) *Warm up for 15 minutes.*
2) *Start at a low power or speed as defined in Table 1.1.*
3) *Every minute, increase power or speed, whichever you can measure. Power is a better measure if it is available. You can adjust stride, gearing, or cadence as you need.*
4) *Have someone record heart rate and power (or speed) every 60 seconds.*
5) *Continue as long as possible or until you are unable to increase power after two minutes.*
6) *On a graph, plot the heart rate on the vertical axis and the power (or speed) on the horizontal axis. (See Figure 1.1)*
7) *Using a ruler, draw straight lines along the initial, middle, and end segments of the curve. The heart rate values at which the lines intersect are the heart rates at the aerobic and anaerobic (lactate) thresholds. (See Figure 1.2)*

Figure 1.1

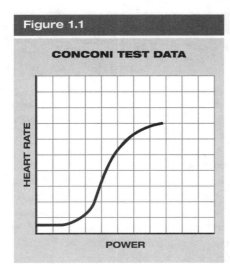

CONCONI TEST DATA

Figure 1.2

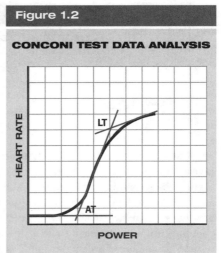

CONCONI TEST DATA ANALYSIS

Note: Lines drawn along the early, middle, and late part of the graph intersect at the heart rates for aerobic threshold (AT) and lactate threshold (LT).

MEASURING PHYSICAL PARAMETERS

Several devices to aid in testing are becoming available to athletes. These include heart rate monitors, power monitors for cyclists, and speedometers for runners. By using technology and smart training programs, the athlete can create a program that will enhance the exercise-induced training effect in the heart, lungs, and muscles and make the body better equipped to handle the demands of competition.

NOTES

1. G. A. Dudley, W. M. Abraham, R. L. Terjung. Influence of exercise intensity and duration on biochemical adaptations in skeletal muscle. *Journal of Applied Physiology* 1982, 228: 1029–33.

2. J. H. Horina, G. Schwaberger, H. Brussee, G. Sauseng-Fellegger, H. Holzer, G. J. Krejs. Increased red cell 2,3-diphosphoglycerate levels in haemodialysis patients treated with erythropoietin. *Nephrology Dialysis Transplant* 1993, 8(11): 1219–22.

3. A. Luci, J. Hoyos, J. L. Chicharro. Physiology of professional road cycling. *Sports Medicine* 2001, 31(5): 325–27.

4. J. A. Vachon, D. R. Bassett, S. Clarke. Validity of the heart rate deflection point as a predictor of lactate threshold during running. *Journal of Applied Physiology* July 1999, 87(1): 452–59
A. E. Jeukendrup, M. K. Hesselink, H. Kuipers, H. A. Keizer. The Conconi test. *International Journal of Sports Medicine* July 1999, 18(5): 393–96.

5. P. Hofmann, R. Pokan, S. P. von Duvillard, P. Schmid. The Conconi test. *International Journal of Sports Medicine* July 1997, 18(5): 397–99.

6. P. Hofmann, R. Pokan, S. P. von Duvillard, F. J. Seibert, R. Zweiker. Heart rate performance curve during incremental cycling. *Medical Science Sports Exercise* June 1997, 29(6): 762–68.

7. F. Conconi, G. Grazzi, I. Casoni, et al. The Conconi test: Methodology after twelve years of application. *International Journal of Sports Medicine* 1996, 17: 509–19.

OTHER REFERENCES

Bodner, M. E., E. C. Rhodes. A review of the concept of the heart rate deflection point. *Sports Medicine* July 2000, 30(1): 31–46.

Harries, M., C. Williams, W. D. Stanish, L. J. Micheli. *Oxford Textbook of Sports Medicine*. 2d ed. Oxford University Press, Inc., New York, 1998.

Myers, J., E. Ashley. Dangerous curves: A perspective on exercise, lactate, and the anaerobic threshold. *Chest* March 1997, 111(3): 787–95.

Pokan, R., P. Hoffmann, S. P. von Duvillard, G. Smekal, R. Hogler, et al. The heart rate turn point reliability and methodological aspects. *Medical Science Sports Exercise* June 1999, 31(6): 903–7.

Takaishi, T., T. Yamamoto, T. Ono, T. Ito, et al. Neuromuscular, metabolic, and kinetic adaptations. *Medical Science Sports Exercise* March 1998, 30(3): 442–49.

CARBOHYDRATE METABOLISM

Endurance exercise differs from its shorter, less demanding counterparts in length of activity. To provide energy for sustained activity, the body must call upon its energy reserves to function. These reserves are primarily stored carbohydrates that are converted to fuel in the form of ATP (adenosine triphosphate) to allow muscles to contract. The science of carbohydrate metabolism is complex and incorporates many different biochemical pathways to convert stored glucose to energy and deliver ATP to the exercising muscle. This chapter combines both the molecular science and the sports science to give strategies to optimize each so that your body has maximum energy to perform.

Consider feeding strategies of different athletes. All too often at the start line of an event many people devour energy gels and bars, a few sips of water, and a few sips of carbohydrate beverages. The people who ingest large volumes of carbohydrates at the start line are often those who begin to fade a few minutes into the race.

Consider the cyclist who drinks only water for a three-hour race. After about an hour and a half, he starts to fatigue and falls back from the pack on a series of small climbs.

One athlete ingests too much carbohydrate; one ingests too little. How much should you ingest before a race or when training? To answer this question about fueling your body for optimal endurance exercise, you need to examine the processes through which the body converts carbohydrate into fuel.

Glucose is a carbohydrate in its most basic form. Simple sugars such as glucose contain six carbon molecules attached to hydrogen and oxygen molecules, which exist in a 2 to 1 ratio. Because of the chemical structure containing only carbon, hydrogen, and oxygen, carbohydrate is frequently abbreviated as CHO or CH_2O.

Carbohydrates are our primary source of energy. One way of describing carbohydrates is by ranking them according to the glycemic index. This index describes the rate in which carbohydrates are absorbed into the blood and how the body responds with insulin. Foods with a high glycemic index produce a rapid rise in blood sugar with a rapid insulin response. Pure glucose has a glycemic index of 100 and is the reference against which other foods on the glycemic index are measured. A food with a high glycemic index is generally considered to be a simple carbohydrate; a food with a low index is a complex carbohydrate. (See Table 2.1 for the rating of some common foods.) Complex carbohydrates are found in less-processed foods and take longer to break down into glucose or other simple sugars that can be used during exercise. One is not necessarily better than the other, but there are times when each should be eaten. First, it is useful to understand how the body uses carbohydrates to fuel exercise.

When used as fuel, carbohydrate combines with oxygen to produce energy, creating

Table 2.1

GLYCEMIC INDEX OF COMMON FOODS

Percent	Grain	Vegetables, Legumes	Fruit	Beverage	Snack
> 100	Baguette Rice Corn flakes Millet	Parsnips Baked potato Carrots Fava beans	Dates		Honey
90–100	Corn chips Wheat shred Crackers Barley	Rutabaga	Apricots		Mars Bar
80–89	Rye bread Rice Oatmeal	Beets Corn		Banana	
70–79	Raisin Bran Graham crackers Bread	French fries	Watermelon	Gatorade	Skittles Gatorade
60–69	Taco shells Shortbread Pumpernickel Pasta Couscous Bulgur	Peas Baked beans	Grapefruit Cantaloupe Raisins Pineapple Orange	Orange juice Pineapple juice Soft drinks	Twix Ice cream Sucrose
50–59	Whole wheat Pita bread Sourdough Ravioli	Sweet potato Lima beans Pinto beans Lentils	Banana Kiwi Mango Papaya Apple		Clif Bar Power Bar
40–49	Chickpeas Kidney beans			Milk Soy milk	Milk chocolate
30–39	Barley	Soy beans Peanuts Vegetables (nonroot)	Cherries Plums		Fructose

carbon dioxide and water as by-products. This process is anything but simple, and the body employs several pathways to turn glucose into energy.

AEROBIC GLUCOSE METABOLISM

Glucose metabolism in the presence of available oxygen is known as aerobic metabolism. (When the body's energy requirements exceed oxygen delivery, the body switches to anaerobic metabolism.) Exercise is more efficient when performed during aerobic metabolism, which has six important pathways by which carbohydrates of different forms are transformed into ATP, the body's energy currency.

Glycolysis is the pathway where glucose from the diet or from glycogen is broken down via glycogenolysis and is converted to a molecule called pyruvate. During this process, two molecules of ATP are produced. In the presence of oxygen, pyruvate undergoes enzymatic changes and enters the citric acid cycle. Also known as the Krebs cycle and the TCA cycle, the citric acid cycle converts pyruvate to several intermediates and produces twelve molecules of ATP along the way. Aside from energy production, the citric acid cycle is important because amino acids can also be key players. In the absence of glucose, the body will supply the intermediates of the cycle from amino acids. Since the body's amino acids are proteins that are stored in the muscle, muscle breakdown occurs. Clinically, this can be recognized by the smell of ammonia coming from the body. If you smell ammonia when you ride, you are underfed and are destroying your muscle to provide you with energy. This is referred to as a catabolic state, and any weight loss that results comes not from fat metabolism but from muscle breakdown.

The hexose monophosphate pathway is a side path from glycolysis that results in several high-energy intermediaries that are used by other pathways for making ATP molecules. The most notable of these is the sugar-phosphate conversion of ribose to a high-energy ribose-phosphate bond that can store energy for later conversion into ATP. Ribose has recently shown some promise as an energy source for this reason.

The high-energy bonds, which are produced in glycolysis and the citric acid cycle, donate electrons to the electron transport chain. As the electrons are passed from carrier to carrier, they lose energy that is captured by the chain, creating ATP. The electron transport chain produces the most molecules of ATP per molecule of glucose but will function only in the presence of oxygen. Above the lactate threshold, the chain does not run, and the citric acid cycle backs up to glycolysis.

In the absence of oxygen, glucose is converted to pyruvate, which is immediately converted to lactate. This process of anaerobic glycolysis still produces two molecules of ATP, but there are no high-energy bonds formed for use by the electron transport chain. The lactate that results from anaerobic glycolysis in the muscle is transported back to the liver for the synthesis of glucose, which is released back into the circulatory system and delivered to the working muscles.

CARBOHYDRATE RESERVES AND GLUCONEOGENESIS

After being absorbed from the intestines into the bloodstream, glucose can be incorporated into long chains of glucose, called glycogen, or can be used directly as blood glucose. Glycogen is stored in the muscles (muscle glycogen) and in the liver (liver glycogen). How each type is used depends largely upon the athlete's level of fitness and the duration and intensity of the exercise.

When exercise is started, the body will increase the levels of blood glucose. This glucose comes from the breakdown of glycogen stores through a process called glycogenolysis. This process can fuel exercise for approximately ninety minutes. The depletion of glycogen stores explains the phenomenon of "hitting the wall" that elite marathon runners experience around mile eighteen. Muscle glycogen can release glucose only to the muscle, whereas liver glycogen can release glucose to the bloodstream. When all of the glycogen is used up, the athlete "hits the wall" or "bonks" as the process of gluconeogenesis takes over and blood sugar levels drop.

Another source of glucose production is from by-products of metabolism of glucose and protein, a process called gluconeogenesis. The ingredients for gluconeogenesis are lactate, pyruvate, the amino acid alanine, and glycerol from the metabolism of fat. Alanine, an amino acid the muscle releases during exercise, combines with pyruvate to transport it to the liver where the two are separated and the pyruvate is used for gluconeogenesis. Metabolism of fat produces fatty acids and glycerol. The muscle uses fatty acids as an energy source by feeding into the citric acid cycle, and the liver uses glycerol for gluconeogenesis.

The Cori cycle allows the recycling of lactate (lactic acid) back into something that can be used for energy. Working muscles that are using glycogen can be supplied lactate first from the working muscles and then from other muscles for gluconeogenesis via the Cori cycle. Gluconeogenesis is the most dependable energy production source for prolonged endurance exercise. It has been estimated that 60 percent of the energy used by the body comes from gluconeogenesis for three hours of exercise at moderate intensity (58 percent VO_2max). As exercise continues, the increase in gluconeogenesis requires the breakdown of the body's protein stores (muscle) for energy, although having adequate glycogen stores before exercise and providing exogenous glucose during exercise can mitigate use of protein by the body.

HORMONAL CONTROL OF CARBOHYDRATE METABOLISM

During the stress of acute exercise, the body produces and releases several hormones. Many performance-enhancing drugs try to replicate the effects of these hormones by increasing the circulating glucose.

As soon as exercise begins, epinephrine is released into the blood. Epinephrine acts on the muscle and liver to release glycogen and on the fat in muscle and adipose tissue to supply fuel for the exercising muscles.

Some performance-enhancing (ergogenic) aids will increase the hormonal response. Caffeine acts on the release of glucose without increasing circulating hormones. Ephedrine, pseudoephedrine, ma huang, phenylpropanolamine, country mallow, and amphetamines all bind to the same receptors as epinephrine, causing an increase in fuel for exercising muscles. These substances alone will not increase energy if the body does not have sufficient reserves of glycogen. The use of these substances is illegal for a number of reasons and can have serious health consequences, including seizures and heat-related illness.

Insulin levels, which will decrease circulating glucose and be counterproductive to glycogenolysis and gluconeogenesis, are kept low, whereas glucagon levels, which are increased in response to decreasing blood glucose levels, rise. Glucagon stimulates both glycogenolysis and gluconeogenesis to provide the body with energy.

Exercise itself has an insulin-like effect and causes glucose to enter the muscle without insulin secretion. If a large glucose load is ingested immediately (within 30–60 minutes) before exercise begins, there will be an insulin response, lowering the blood sugar. Fifteen minutes after exercise is started, its insulin effect can cause a further lowering of blood sugar, leaving the body without any energy until glycogenolysis begins.[1] Although the hypoglycemic effect of exercise is well described in the exercise physiology research, it is still unclear whether it has a significant effect on performance.

GLUCOSE STORAGE AND GLYCOGEN METABOLISM

Glycogen is the main storage form of glucose and exists in the body as long, branched chains of glucose molecules. The amount of glycogen (both muscle and liver) is never significantly more than the body ingests in a single day. Glycogen is most prevalent in the liver and can double in quantity after a carbohydrate-rich meal. In contrast, achieving top levels of muscle glycogen requires special attention, such as carbohydrate loading. Studies comparing groups that increased their glycogen concentrations had improved running and cycling performance, resulting in faster times and longer distances covered before fatigue set in.[2]

Muscle Utilization of Energy

Muscle glycogen is broken down at different rates, depending upon the intensity of the exercise session. Glycogen breakdown is about five times faster at 100 percent of VO_2max than at 50 percent of VO_2max. The time to fatigue, however, has more to do with initial glycogen levels than with the rate of utilization. Ingesting carbohydrates during exercise provides the body with another source of energy, sparing muscle glycogen and allowing exercise to continue longer.[3] During exercise, carbohydrate can be used at a rate of one gram per minute.[4] This would require ingestion of about sixty carbohydrate grams every hour, or slightly less if the body can call upon muscle glycogen.

The key to enhancing performance, therefore, is to fill glycogen reserves, reduce glycogen utilization and increase use of other energy reserves, such as fat. This leads to increased energy for later in the race, allowing the athlete to finish strong. One way to achieve this effect is to train for endurance exercise. Training just seven to ten days for two hours a day was found to increase the oxidative enzymes (fat burning, citric acid cycle) and reduce glycogen utilization and lactate-producing enzymes. This happens through an increase in the number of mitochondria, which are the energy producers of the cells.[5]

During exercise, the muscles should be fed glucose in a 6–8 percent solution. This has been shown to increase endurance performance and capacity. The athlete would need to ingest one liter every hour to keep up with the carbohydrate utilization.

GLYCOGEN WINDOW

Glycogen is easily depleted during two hours of moderate exercise (more quickly with intense exercise), but can be replaced only by glucose. Muscle glycogen can be replaced at a rate of 5–6 mmol/kg of muscle per hour to approximately 150 mmol/kg of muscle in trained athletes, or up to 200 mmol/kg for those who are able to supercompensate for used glycogen.

Several factors affect the body's ability to synthesize glycogen: the extent of glycogen depletion; the level of insulin (which controls the hormone responsible for synthesizing glycogen); and the amount and timing of carbohydrate intake after exercise. Of the glucose that is ingested after exercise, 90 percent is deposited as muscle glycogen. Greater depletion of muscle glycogen during exercise will contribute to improved rates of glycogen synthesis, as will high insulin levels. To maximize insulin levels, high glycemic index carbohydrate should be consumed after exercise.[6] Although fructose is good at replacing liver glycogen, glucose and sucrose are better at replacing muscle glycogen. The amount that you eat after exercise is more important than how you eat it. After exercise, the appetite is suppressed, and it can be difficult to eat large quantities. Snacking has been shown to be equal to four large meals over a twenty-four-hour replacement period.[7]

Timing is important too. The so-called glycogen window is a period in which muscle synthesis of glycogen is at maximal rates. Different times have been described for this phenomenon. In one study,[8] a four-hour period following exhaustive exercise showed that glycogen synthesis increased by 43 percent. In the same study, moderate, nonexhaustive exercise increased glycogen synthesis by only 13 percent. Studies have examined the importance of feeding extra carbohydrate at the time exercise begins as well as for two and four hours afterward. Analysis of muscle biopsies can indicate the presence of the glycogen-building enzymes (glycogen synthase) and the amount of glycogen. In a study comparing immediate ingestion of a carbohydrate solution with ingestion at two hours after exercise, the rate of glycogen storage declined 67 percent if feeding was delayed for two hours.[9] Even when feeding was started after the two-hour delay, the rate still remained 43 percent slower despite increased glucose and insulin levels. This demonstrates that muscle glycogen synthesis is highest within the first two hours after exercise. However, if the post-exercise feed is delayed until two hours after exercise, the rate of glycogen synthesis at eight and twenty-four hours is unaffected provided that adequate carbohydrate is supplied.[10] This assumes that in the twenty-four hours after exercise, none of the muscle glycogen is used. It is still best to feed immediately post-exercise and up to two hours afterward to ensure rapid glycogen replacement. Although timing is important, there does not seem to be any need to ingest more than 1.5 g/kg of carbohydrate.[11] Even if you consume large amounts of glucose during exercise, it will have no effect on glycogen synthesis, so post-exercise feeding is important.[12]

The addition of protein to the high glycemic carbohydrate solution has been researched with varied results. Some studies have found that the addition of protein does not have an effect on glycogen replacement,[13] but others seem to demonstrate a clear glycogen-enhancing effect.[14] When the addition of protein to post-exercise carbohydrate was initially described,[15] 40 grams of protein were added to 112 grams of carbohydrate with

GLYCOGEN MAXIMIZING QUICKSHEET

Pre-exercise
Eat familiar, high-carbohydrate meals.
Have moderate-size meals of easily digestible foods (avoid fat and protein).
Pack foods for travel; they aren't as greasy as what you will find on the road.
Four hours prior, ingest 4–5 grams CHO/kg. (Option: one hour prior, ingest 1–2 grams CHO/kg.)
For an event of 1 hour or less, concentrate on liquid carbohydrate/electrolyte solutions.

During exercise
Use carbohydrate foods and drinks that are easily digested and well tolerated during training.
Start ingesting early to spare glycogen stores.
Use a concentration of 6–8% (6 grams CHO in 100 ml of fluid).
Sodium aids absorption; use a drink with sodium or add a pinch of salt to the mix.
Drink 4–8 oz every 15–20 min. This will provide 0.5–1.0 liter of fluid and 30–60 grams
     of carbohydrate each hour.
To avoid overfeeding, use 0.15–0.3 grams of carbohydrate per pound of body weight every hour.

Post-exercise
Consume CHO at a rate of 6–10g/kg/day.
Periodize CHO intake with training: low volume, low intensity, low carbohydrate.
Glycogen stores are replenished in 1–4 hours; fluids are more digestible.
Adding protein in a ratio of 4 to 1 may help glycogen replenishment.
CHO intake of 1 g/kg after exercise and every two hours for 4–6 hours.

faster rates (39 percent) of muscle glycogen synthesis. The mechanism was thought to be insulin secretion. Further research questioned whether this increase was due to the effect of the extra calories the protein supplied. When the number of calories were maintained constant, the rates of glycogen storage were not different between glucose and glucose-protein solutions.[16] Despite the inconclusive nature of these studies, the addition of protein is important not only for the glycogen-building effect but also for replacing the protein from muscle breakdown that occurs during exercise. I therefore recommend adding it to the recovery diet.

Glycogen resynthesis after exercise clearly allows the athlete to recover faster for another day of training and racing. The enzyme responsible for replenishing glycogen from the dietary sugars is called glycogen synthase and comes in two forms: the less active version, glycogen synthase D, and the more active version, glycogen synthase I. The more glycogen present in the muscle, the less of the activated form exists. Exercise and insulin convert the less active D form to the more active I form. The larger insulin response from the higher glycemic index foods will enhance this effect. Despite this conversion, the activity of glycogen synthase I increases only 25 percent in response to glycogen depletion and returns to pre-exercise levels as glycogen levels increase. Glycogen resynthesis increases by 500–600 percent, so it is felt that the D form plays a large role in replenishing glycogen.[17] The D form is activated in the presence of glucose-6-phosphate (G6P), an intermediate in the glycolysis pathway. G6P is produced as glycogen and glucose enter the pathway.[18] Fructose, however, enters the pathway after G6P is produced, so it is not the ideal carbohydrate source for glycogen replenishment. Still, it can be an excellent source for maintaining caloric intake.

After exercise and resynthesis of the glycogen stores, the athlete nevertheless may not achieve maximal exercise. In one study, subjects were allowed to eat whatever they wanted to restore glycogen; their repeat treadmill tests were lower than the original tests.[19] I therefore recommend being scientific in the source of glycogen replenishment.

CHARGE: Muscle Glycogen Supercomposition (Carbo-loading)

CHARGE is a helpful acronym for endurance athletes to remember; it is derived from the phrase "consuming huge amounts requires glucose for endurance." Following are some recommendations that pertain to CHARGE.

Endurance athletes require a diet of 60 percent carbohydrate. For men, this is approximately 8–10 grams of carbohydrate per kilogram of body weight per day (g/kg/d); for women, this is roughly 6–8 g/kg/d.

Liver glycogen is responsible for maintaining blood glucose during the night and is consumed in the morning. Eating breakfast will replenish glycogen in an amount equaling 4–8 percent of the liver's weight. Therefore, I cannot overstate the importance of a high-carbohydrate morning meal to replace glycogen. This is true of both competition and training days. Like many people with hectic work schedules, athletes often forget to eat well in the days leading up to an event, so eating the morning of an event is paramount. Although you can eat the meal one to six hours before the event, two to three hours is probably a better time frame to prevent hunger before the event and gastrointestinal problems during exercise. If you are unable to eat before exercise due to anxiety, use liquid forms of carbohydrate to replace overnight glycogen losses.

One study[20] demonstrated that a pre-exercise meal of 5 grams of carbohydrate per kilogram of body weight supplemented with an 8 percent carbohydrate solution allowed cyclists to exercise harder and longer than when they ate only breakfast, and performance was even higher than when they ate only during exercise. All of these rates were greater than when exercise was undertaken in a fasting state and without supplementation. If eating causes gastrointestinal discomfort, liquid carbohydrate can be used.

Carbohydrate comes in many different flavors. Glucose is the primary carbohydrate molecule, but other single molecules and polymers (chains of single molecules) can be used for energy. Fructose is the sugar found in fruit and fruit juices and is also the main ingredient in high-fructose corn syrup. Although similar to glucose in structure, it enters the bloodstream more slowly than glucose and then is transformed into glucose by the liver. One study[21] failed to demonstrate that fructose would spare glycogen anymore than would drinking water before exercise. Fructose still contains 4 calories per gram and can contribute to glycogen stores and glucose levels when used in conjunction with other types of carbohydrate. However, due to the attenuated glycemic response to fructose alone, it does not replace glycogen as quickly as glucose or glucose polymers, but it will still raise blood glucose levels. Because fructose can cause cramping and diarrhea, it probably should be avoided during exercise.

Sucrose, also known as granulated (table) sugar, is a combination of two glucose molecules and rapidly raises the blood glucose levels. Glucose polymers, chains of many glucose molecules, are also rapidly absorbed in the gut to raise blood glucose levels. The molecular structure of glucose polymers has several advantages. Because these are larger molecules, they affect the concentration of a solution and will be emptied from the stomach faster, resulting in fewer upper-gastrointestinal side effects. They also taste less sweet than single glucose or sucrose molecules, making them more palatable at effective concentrations of 6–8 percent.

The form of carbohydrate ingested (liquid, gel, solid, or intravenous) produces similar results in maintaining blood glucose and glycogen stores, provided all forms have a similar number of calories.[22]

Whereas a high glycemic index carbohydrate is preferred for replenishing glycogen stores after exercise, a low glycemic index food is preferred for the pre-exercise meal. Traditional "carbo loading" was first described as a six-day regimen during which no carbohydrate was consumed for the first three days and then only carbohydrate was ingested for the next three days. This plan involved no exercise at all during the six days and interfered with training plans. To facilitate carbo loading, a three-day plan was developed, but it also involved zero physical activity during the load. More recently, a one-day plan has shown promise.[23]

The one-day plan capitalizes on the glycogen window after exercise but on a grand scale. In the twenty-four-hour period before a major event, the athlete performs a two-and-a-half-minute interval of exercise above the anaerobic threshold followed by an all-out thirty-second sprint. After the interval, and for the next twenty-four hours, the athlete ingests 12 grams of carbohydrate per kilogram of body weight. (If the percentage of body fat is known, 10 grams of carbohydrate per kilogram of lean weight can be used.) The results of this study were promising, and the high-intensity/low-volume workout fits in well with a taper.

CONCLUSION

Carbohydrates fuel exercise. Improving performance necessitates proper "tanking up" by filling glycogen stores and sparing them as much as possible by ingesting carbohydrate during exercise. After exercise, replenishing glycogen stores is possible with the proper ingestion of carbohydrate.

Anaerobic metabolism of carbohydrate is less efficient than aerobic metabolism and can be avoided by training to improve power at the lactate threshold.

NOTES

1. A. R. Coggan, S. C. Swanson. Nutritional manipulations before and during endurance exercise: Effects on performance. *Medicine and Science in Sports and Exercise* 1992, 24(9): S331–35.

2. C. Williams, J. Brewer, M. Walker. The effect of a high carbohydrate diet on running performance during a 30-km treadmill time trial. *European Journal of Applied Physiology* 1992, 65: 18–24.
J. J. Widrick, D. L. Costill, W. J. Fink, et al. Carbohydrate feedings and exercise performance: Effect of initial muscle glycogen concentration. *Journal of Applied Physiology* 1993, 74: 2998–3005.
L. Rauch, I. Roger, G. Wilson, et al. The effects of carbohydrate loading on muscle glycogen content and cycling performance. *International Journal of Sport Nutrition and Exercise Metabolism* 1995, 5:25–36.

3. B. B. Yaspelkis 3d, J. G. Patterson, P. A. Anderla, Z. Ding, J. L. Ivy. Carbohydrate supplementation spares muscle glycogen during variable-intensity exercise. *Journal of Applied Physiology* October 1993, 75(4): 1477–85.

4. Coggan and Swanson.. Nutritional manipulations.

5. R. J. Spina, M. M.-Y. Chi, M. G. Hopkins, et al. Mitochondrial enzymes increase in muscle in response to 7–10 days of cycle exercise. *Journal of Applied Physiology* 1996, 80: 2250–54.
A. Chesley, G. J. F. Heigenhauser, L. L. Spriet. Regulation of muscle glycogen phosphorylase activity following short-term endurance training. *American Journal of Physiology* 1996, 270: E328–35.

6. L. M. Burke, G. R. Collier, M. Hargreaves. Muscle glycogen storage after prolonged exercise: Effect of the glycemic index of carbohydrate feedings. *Journal of Applied Physiology* August 1993, 75(2): 1019–23.

7. L. M. Burke, G. R. Collier, P. G. Davis, P. A. Fricker, A. J. Sanigorski, M. Hargreaves. Muscle glycogen storage after prolonged exercise: Effect of the frequency of carbohydrate feeding. *American Journal of Clinical Nutrition* 1996, 64: 115–19.

8. A. Bonen, G. W. Ness, A. N. Belcastro, R. L. Kirby. Mild exercise impedes glycogen repletion in muscle. *Journal of Applied Physiology* 1995, 58: 1622–29.

9. J. L. Ivy, A. L. Katz, C. L. Cutler, W. M. Sherman, E. F. Coyle. Muscle glycogen synthesis after exercise: Effect of time of carbohydrate ingestion. *Journal of Applied Physiology* April 1998, 64(4): 1480–85.

10. J. A. Parkin, M. F. Carey, I. K. Martin, L. Stojanovska, M. A. Febbraio. Muscle glycogen storage following prolonged exercise: Effect of timing of ingestion of high glycemic index food. *Medicine and Science in Sports and Exercise* February 1997, 29(2): 220–24.

11. J. L. Ivy, M. C. Lee, J. T. Brozinick Jr., M. J. Reed. Muscle glycogen storage after different amounts of carbohydrate ingestion. *Journal of Applied Physiology* November 1988, 65(5): 2018–23.
P. C. Blom, A. T. Hostmark, O. Vaage, K. R. Kardel, S. Maehlum. Effect of different post-exercise sugar diets on the rate of muscle glycogen synthesis. *Medicine and Science in Sports and Exercise* October 1987, 19(5): 491–96.

12. J. J. Zachwieja, D. L. Costill, W. J. Fink. Carbohydrate ingestion during exercise: Effects on muscle glycogen resynthesis after exercise. *International Journal of Sports Nutrition* December 1993, 3(4): 418–30.

13. B. D. Roy, M. A. Tarnopolsky. Influence of differing macronutrient intakes on muscle glycogen resynthesis after resistance exercise. *Journal of Applied Physiology* 1998, 84(3): 890–96.
J. A. Carrithers, D. L. Williamson, P. M. Gallagher, M. P. Godard, K. E. Schulze, S. W. Trappe. Effects of postexercise carbohydrate-protein feedings on muscle glycogen restoration. *Journal of Applied Physiology* June 2000, 88(6): 1976–82.
B. B. Yaspelkis 3d, J. L. Ivy. The effect of a carbohydrate-arginine supplement on postexercise carbohydrate metabolism. *International Journal of Sport Nutrition and Exercise Metabolism* September 1999, 9(3): 241–50.

14. L. J. van Loon, W. H. Saris, M. Kruijshoop, A. J. Wagenmakers. Maximizing postexercise muscle glycogen synthesis: Carbohydrate supplementation and the application of amino acid or protein hydrolysate mixtures. *American Journal of Clinical Nutrition* July 2000, 72(1): 106–11.

15. K. M. Zawadzki, B. B. Yaspelkis 3d, J. L. Ivy. Carbohydrate-protein complex increases the rate of muscle glycogen storage after exercise. *Journal of Applied Physiology* May 1992, 72(5): 1854–59.

16. M. A. Tarnopolsky, M. Bosman, J. R. MacDonald, et al. Postexercise protein-carbohydrate and carbohydrate supplements increase muscle glycogen in men and women. *Journal of Applied Physiology* 1997, 83(6): 1877–83.
J. A. Carrithers et al. Effects of postexercise carbohydrate-protein feedings on muscle glycogen restoration.

17. J. L. Ivy. Muscle glycogen synthesis before and after exercise. *Sports Medicine* January 1991, 11(1): 6–19.

18. J. E. Friedman, P. D. Neufer, G. L. Dohm. Regulation of glycogen resynthesis following exercise: Dietary considerations. *Sports Medicine* April 1991, 11(4): 232–43.

19. H. Keizer, H. Kuipers, G. van Kranenburg. Influence of liquid and solid meals on muscle glycogen resynthesis, plasma fuel hormone response, and maximal physical working capacity. *International Journal of Sports Medicine* 1987, 8: 99–104.

20. D. A. Wright, W. M. Sherman, A. R. Dernback. Carbohydrate feedings before, during, or in combination improve cycling endurance performance. *Journal of Applied Physiology* 1991, 71: 680–87.

21. V. A. Koivisto, M. Harkonen, S. L. Karonen, P. H. Groop, R. Elovainio, E. Ferrannini, L. Sacca, R. A. Defronzo. Glycogen depletion during prolonged exercise: Influence of glucose, fructose, or placebo. *Journal of Applied Physiology* March 1985, 58(3): 731–37.

22. B. F. Hansen, S. Asp, B. Kiens, E. A. Richter. Glycogen concentration in human skeletal muscle: Effect of prolonged insulin and glucose infusion. *Scandinavian Journal of Medical Science Sports* August 1999, 9(4): 209–13.

23. T. J. Fairchild, S. Fletcher, P. Steele, C. Goodman, B. Dawson, P. A. Fournier. Rapid carbohydrate loading after a short bout of near maximal-intensity exercise. *Medicine and Science in Sports and Exercise* June 2002, 34(6): 980–86.

OTHER REFERENCES

Champe, P. C., and R. A. Harvey. *Biochemistry*. Philadelphia: J. B. Lippincott Co., 1994.

PROTEIN NEEDS
FOR EXERCISE
AND TRAINING

There are twenty different amino acids in the body (Table 3.1). Of these twenty, eight cannot be synthesized by the body and are referred to as essential amino acids. The other twelve can be found in food and are called nonessential amino acids. At the center of every amino acid is the amine group consisting of one nitrogen molecule combined with two hydrogen molecules.

Together, these amino acids are linked in various configurations by peptide bonds to make up proteins. A polypeptide structure that contains more than fifty amino acids is a protein. There are approximately 50,000 protein combinations in the human body.

Plants synthesize all of the necessary amino acids, but animals need to ingest most of their protein requirement. Proteins that have the entire complement of essential amino acids are complete proteins, whereas incomplete proteins lack one or more of the essential amino acids. A diet of incomplete protein will eventually lead to protein malnutrition.

The macronutrient (fat, carbohydrate, and protein) without an energy storage form, protein in the body is stored largely as muscle. Protein also exists as free amino acids, primarily as the amino acid glutamine that fuels the immune system.

Table 3.1

THE AMINO ACIDS

Essential	Nonessential
Branched-chain amino acids	Alanine
Isoleucine	Arginine
Leucine	Asparaginim
Valine	Aspartic acid
Lysine	Cysteine
Methionine	Glutamic acid
Phenylalanine	Glutamine
Threonine	Glycine
Tryptophan	Histidine
	Proline
	Serine
	Tyrosine

Protein role

Unlike fat (adipose tissue) or carbohydrate (glycogen), there are no reservoirs of protein in the body. Protein is stored in blood plasma, body tissue, and muscle, which account for 65 percent of total body protein.

Protein construction is a process known as anabolism. Anabolic activity is continuous in the body. Even when growth ceases, protein is constantly being broken down and rebuilt. Without adequate dietary intake of protein, there will not be sufficient building blocks for the anabolism to continue, and deficiency will result. Although too much protein will not enhance performance, too little protein will result in fatigue and infection.[1]

DNA, cell membranes, and structural elements of the cell are all made of protein. On a larger scale, the hair, skin, nails, bones, tendons, and ligaments are composed of collagen protein. Proteins in the blood plasma are responsible for blood clotting and buffering the lactic acid produced during exercise. Muscle proteins provide structure and function for the muscle cell, allowing them to contract and move the bones to which they are attached.

Metabolism and nitrogen balance

Nitrogen balance is the sum of total amino acids ingested in food minus the amino acids lost in urine, feces, and sweat.

$$\begin{array}{l} \text{Ingested protein} \\ \underline{-\ \text{Protein losses}} \\ \text{Nitrogen balance} \end{array}$$

If more amino acids are ingested than excreted, the body is in positive nitrogen balance. If the diet is deficient in amino acids, the body is in negative nitrogen balance. Positive nitrogen balance occurs during growth, recovery from illness, and resistance training. Muscle and liver protein are more plentiful in positive nitrogen balance and can be mobilized for energy metabolism.

In negative nitrogen balance, protein loss outweighs intake, which indicates that primarily muscle proteins are metabolized for energy and the used amino groups are excreted in the urine. Under sufficiently intense exercise, some amino acids are directly burned as fuel by incorporation into the citric acid cycle, while the liver uses others to create glucose. Protein can contribute up to 15 percent of total energy expenditure during exercise.[2] During fevers, growth, steroid use, or recovery from serious illness, negative nitrogen balance can occur. If inadequate carbohydrate energy is consumed, heavy training may lead to the use of protein as a primary energy source with a resultant loss of lean mass.

Although protein breakdown, also called catabolism, increases slightly with exercise, protein synthesis increases dramatically with recovery from endurance and resistance exercise. Anabolism during recovery increases up to 80 percent within four hours after exercise and remains elevated for up to forty-eight hours.[3]

Protein dynamics in exercise

Exercise increases the protein requirement in two ways: First, the use of amino acid as a muscle fuel increases; second, exercise causes muscle damage for which protein is needed to make repairs. During exercise, the group of amino acids called "branched-chain amino acids" (BCAA, so named because of their similar molecular structure) undergoes catabolism for energy. The amino group of the BCAA is used to make alanine or glutamate. Once formed, alanine is transported to the liver where it undergoes several changes and leaves the liver as glucose. This alanine-glucose cycle generates up to 15 percent of the total energy requirement. Generating glucose from the carbon atoms of other compounds is called gluconeogenesis and is increased with endurance training. The enzymes responsible for the change are located in the muscle and liver and are increased with training.

Glutamate, meanwhile, can be fed into the citric acid cycle. Glutamate enters the middle of the cycle to continue production of energy, but because it is not starting at the beginning of the cycle, it does not yield as much energy as glucose.

Not all exercise results in the use of protein for fuel. Different studies have found that protein use during endurance exercise is increased when the exercise is longer than 100 minutes at 60 percent of maximum when the athlete is well fed or after one hour in the case of carbohydrate depletion. When intensity is high, protein use is increased by 25 percent over resting levels. The enzymes responsible for BCAA degradation are intensity dependent.

Synthesis of new muscle protein decreases during exercise but increases afterward.

Protein needs

The increased need for protein during and after exercise means that athletes require more protein than do sedentary individuals. Nitrogen loss is further increased with low energy (carbohydrate) consumption. Dieters, in particular, will increase the use of protein for energy.

Too little protein will result in an adaptation with a reduction in protein turnover, catabolism, and nitrogen excretion.[4] During adaptation to exercise training, decreased protein turnover is detrimental to performance. With exercise, protein needs can increase 50–100 percent,[5] which would leave an athlete who adheres to the USDA's recommended daily allowance (RDA) for protein (0.8 g/kg/day) in a negative nitrogen balance, even with the 0.35 g/kg/day safety margin that has been incorporated into the RDA.

The protein needs for athletes are higher than for the general population.[6] However, most athletes eat more than twice the recommended level of protein.[7] Still, the key issue is not the recommended level but that the athlete is getting enough protein. When the focus is exclusively on high carbohydrate intake, protein is sometimes overlooked. However, the most important factor in protein adequacy is the amount of energy intake (carbohydrate);[8] if insufficient carbohydrate is consumed due to low calorie consumption, negative nitrogen balance could occur.

It is important that protein losses during exercise are matched with intake.[9] For this to occur in athletes, the recommended intake is 1.2–1.9 g/kg/day. One study concluded that a daily protein intake of 1.37 g/kg/day is sufficient for endurance athletes, whereas a sedentary individual needs only 0.73 g/kg/day, and a resistance-trained athlete requires 0.82 g/kg/day.[10]

Although most athletes consume enough protein, several groups are at higher risk of inadequate protein intake. These groups include dieters, women (in general, decreased intake), those starting new exercise programs, vegetarians, those with eating disorders, and the elderly.

In a study of athletes who kept a food diary, some were found to be consuming less protein than the RDA.[11] Even without a food diary, you can still recognize if you are in positive or negative nitrogen balance. During protein catabolism, the amino group is converted to ammonia and excreted. If you smell ammonia while exercising, you are definitely in negative energy and negative nitrogen balance.

Protein sources

Protein can be found in many food items, but consuming a full complement of amino acids can be challenging for someone who tries to fit work, family, and training into a hectic schedule. In a rating system known as biologic value, proteins are rated by quality based upon whether they contain all of the essential amino acids. Eggs have the optimal mixture of essential amino acids and are given the highest biologic value. Other food sources and their biologic value ratings are given in Table 3.2.

Table 3.2	
BIOLOGIC RATINGS FOR COMMON FOODS	
Food	**Rating**
Eggs	100
Fish	70
Lean meat	69
Milk	60
Brown rice	57
White rice	56
Soybeans	47
Whole-grain wheat	44
Peanuts	43
Dry beans	34
White potato	34

These ratings do not mean that to get all the amino acids you must consume a diet of eggs and meat; in fact, this would lead to a diet high in saturated fat and cholesterol. As long as you consume a variety of plant foods, you will get all twenty amino acids. The only plant-based protein source that is an exception is soy-protein isolate, which compares with animal protein.

An example of protein matching is the frequently paired beans and rice. Rice lacks the essential amino acid lysine, whereas beans contain lysine but lack methionine, which is abundant in grains. Such complementary sources of protein enable vegetarians to maintain adequate protein intake.

Vegetarian diets provide ample carbohydrate and adequate protein without the added fat and cholesterol found in animal sources. Animal-free protein sources are higher in nonessential amino acids than animal sources and should preferentially favor glucagon production. Glucagon is antagonistic to insulin and promotes enzymes that decrease fat synthesis and cholesterol synthesis.[12] This is further enhanced by a diet that is high in fiber and low in fat. A diet of animal-free proteins may also decrease insulin-like growth factor (IGF-1) and thus prevent cancer.

In short, protein sources can be a Trojan horse for introducing saturated fat and cholesterol into the diet; you can use Table 3.2 to select adequate alternatives to the higher-fat proteins. For instance, instead of high-cholesterol meat, choose fish that is rich in omega-3 fatty acids, and replace milk with brown and white rice to provide increased carbohydrate yet retain most of the protein value.

MAXIMIZING PROTEIN BUILDING

Insulin not only transports glucose into cells, but it also facilitates the transport of protein into cells and is particularly anabolic.[13] Insulin is increased by carbohydrate availability. If high glycemic index carbohydrate is available after exercise when protein synthesis is highest, there will be a decrease in amino acid excretion.[14] A carbohydrate drink of 1 g/kg of body weight immediately after exercise and again one hour later will be sufficient for this effect. Both carbohydrate and carbohydrate-protein drinks will increase the levels of insulin and growth hormone, two hormones with anabolic properties after exercise. The carbohydrate-protein drinks, however, result in higher insulin levels for eight hours after exercise.[15] Carbohydrate-protein drinks after strenuous exercise also decrease the amount of muscle damage when compared with carbohydrate-only drinks.[16]

The availability of amino acids while at rest has a direct effect on the rate of protein synthesis. After exercise, when protein synthesis is high, there is decreased muscle breakdown, and protein synthesis is doubled. The consumption of protein following exercise may be anabolic and is recommended, provided that protein consumption does not come at the expense of carbohydrate and does not exceed 2 g/kg.

NOTES

1. K. J. Kingsbury, L. Kay, M. Hjelm. Contrasting plasma free amino acid patterns in elite athletes: Association with fatigue and infection. *British Journal of Sports Medicine* March 1998, 32(1): 25–32.

2. G. L. Paul. Dietary protein requirements of physically active individuals. *Sports Medicine* September 1989, 8(3): 154–76.

3. M. J. Rennie, K. D. Tipton. Protein and amino acid metabolism during and after exercise and the effects of nutrition. *Annual Review of Nutrition* 2000, 20: 457–83.

4. N. R. Gibson, F. Jahoor, L. Ware, A. A. Jackson. Endogenous glycine and tyrosine production is maintained in adults consuming a marginal-protein diet. *American Journal of Clinical Nutrition* March 2002, 75(3): 511–18.

5. P. W. Lemon, D. N. Proctor. Protein intake and athletic performance. *Sports Medicine* November 1991, 12(5): 313–25.

6. M. H. Hargreaves, R. Snow. Amino acids and endurance exercise. *International Journal of Sport Nutrition and Exercise Metabolism* March 2001, 11(1): 133–45.

7. D. J. Millward. Optimal intakes of protein in the human diet. *Proceedings of Nutrition and Sociology* May 1999, 58(2): 403–13.

8. P. W. Lemon. Protein and amino acid needs of the strength athlete. *International Journal of Sports Nutrition* June 1991, 1(2): 127–45.

9. D. J. Millward, J. P. Rivers. The nutritional role of indispensable amino acids and the metabolic basis for their requirements. *European Journal of Clinical Nutrition* May 1988, 42(5): 367–93.

10. M. A. Tarnopolsky et al. Influence of protein intake and training status on nitrogen balance and lean body mass. *Journal of Applied Physiology* 1988, 64: 187.

11. J. Walberg-Rankin, C. E. Edmonds, F. C. Gwazdausdas. Detailed analysis of the diets and body weights of six female bodybuilders before and after competition. *International Journal of Sports Nutrition* 1993, 3: 87–102.

12. M. F. McCarty. Vegan proteins may reduce risk of cancer, obesity, and cardiovascular disease by promoting increased glucagon activity. *Medical Hypotheses* December 1999, 53(6): 459–85.

13. S. L. Miller, R. R. Wolfe. Physical exercise as a modulator of adaptation to low and high carbohydrate and low and high fat intakes. *European Journal of Clinical Nutrition* April 1999, 53 Suppl 1: S112–19.

14. G. L. Dohm. Protein nutrition for the athlete. *Clinical Sports Medicine* July 1984, 3(3): 595–604.

15. R. M. Chandler, H. K. Byrne, J. G. Petterson, et al. Dietary supplements affect the anabolic hormones after weight-training exercise. *Journal of Applied Physiology* 1994, 76: 839–45.

16. J. R. Wojcik, J. Walberg-Rankin, L. L. Smith. Effect of post-exercise macronutrient intake on metabolic response to eccentric resistance exercise. *Medical Science Sports Exercise* 1997, 29(Suppl): 294.

FAT METABOLISM
AND WEIGHT LOSS

After carbohydrates, fat is the most utilized source of energy during exercise. Athletes have shunned fat, however, fearing that it will add unnecessary weight to a lean frame. Too much dietary fat will indeed be stored in the fat tissue (adipose tissue, composed of adipocytes), but too little fat also has repercussions. In this chapter, I explain the different types of fat, how they affect the body, and how best to use the fat stores as energy.

Fat has several important roles in the function of the human body. The most calorie-dense macronutrient, fat contains nine calories of energy per gram, compared with the four calories contained in carbohydrate and protein. Adipose tissue is the main storage center for the body's fat supply. Even an endurance athlete with 10 percent body fat and adequate glycogen has nearly 100 times more energy from stored fat than from carbohydrate reserves.

Fat also surrounds many of the organs in the body, providing a cushioning, protective layer against trauma. Approximately 4 percent of the body's fat is used for this purpose. In addition to protecting against jarring, fat also protects against heat loss. A thin layer of fat beneath the skin provides insulation in cold conditions. If there is too much fat, though, the protective effect in the cold can contribute to overwhelming heat stress when the temperature rises.

There are also nutritionally important roles for fat. Without adequate fat intake, the fat-soluble vitamins A, D, E, and K will not be absorbed, and this can lead to deficiency in these nutrients. In addition, the satiety mechanism is regulated by fat. We feel full if there is some fat in the diet because it takes longer to empty from the stomach, which can prevent overeating.

Fat is easily recognizable on a piece of meat by its shiny, slippery nature. This is due to its molecular structure. Lipids, or fat, are composed of four molecules fused together. This structure is known as triglyceride because there are three fatty acid chains that are joined to a molecule of glycerol. Fatty acids are long chains of carbon and hydrogen molecules and exist as two basic varieties, saturated and unsaturated. Saturated fats are chains of carbon molecules in which all of the extra spaces are occupied by a hydrogen atom, resulting in straight fatty acid chains. Because the chains are straight, the fatty acids tend to take up less space and are therefore denser. Saturated fats exist as solids at room temperature. Unsaturated fats, in contrast, do not have all possible bonds attached to hydrogen atoms, so the fatty acid chains are kinked, resulting in fatty acid chains that do not fit closely together. Unsaturated fats are less dense and are liquid at room temperature.

Not all fats are bad. In general, the harmful effects of fat come from saturated fat. Replacing saturated fat with unsaturated (monounsaturated or polyunsaturated) fat is recommended. Long chain polyunsaturated fatty acids, such as those found in olive oil and fish (the so-called omega-3 fatty acids) actually confer health benefits.

The industrial process of hydrogenation adds hydrogen to an unsaturated fatty acid, giving it the density of a saturated fat. Hydrogenated oils (and the trans-fatty acids they produce) present all of the health problems that go hand in hand with a diet high in saturated fat.

The lipid molecule that is composed of three fatty acids and a glycerol is called a simple lipid. Compound lipids are made in the liver when a triglyceride joins with a protein molecule, resulting in a lipoprotein. Lipids are transported through the blood primarily as lipoproteins.

High-density lipoproteins (HDL cholesterol) contain a high percentage of protein and a low percentage of lipids and cholesterol. In contrast, low-density lipoproteins (LDL) have a higher amount of lipid and cholesterol. It is the LDL particles—the "bad" cholesterol—that become incorporated into the walls of arteries, causing damage and narrowing of the arterial space. HDL, however, has a protective effect by removing cholesterol from the arterial walls and transporting it to the liver where it is excreted in the intestines.

Hydrolysis (also called lipolysis) is the process by which lipid is broken down. It involves cleaving the fatty acids from the glycerol by the enzyme lipase. Four conditions maximize lipolysis: low to moderate exercise, restricted caloric intake, cold-weather exercise, and glycogen-depleting exercise. Once separated from glycerol, the fatty acids have two fates: They can be rejoined with glycerol into triglyceride, or they can leave the fat cell, combine with a protein, and be transported through the blood to different tissues in the body.

With light to moderate exercise, there is increased blood flow through the fat tissue, allowing increased free fatty acid uptake and delivery to the muscle. Once at the muscle, the fatty acids bind to proteins and cross into the energy factory of the cell, the mitochondria. The carnitine palmytoyl transferase system (CPT) is responsible for this transfer.[1] As exercise intensity increases, there is less release of fatty acid from the adipose tissue, causing increased reliance on glycogen.

Energy contribution from fat decreases with increased exercise intensity and is greatest in endurance-trained athletes. The relative availability of fat and carbohydrate will also affect the utilization of fat. If there are adequate carbohydrate stores available, carbohydrates will be used preferentially during high-intensity exercise because carbohydrates are available from stored energy 60 percent faster than fat. When glycogen reserves are depleted, fat supplies 80 percent of the total energy, but cannot sustain intensity.

Insulin, which inhibits lipolysis, drops with decreased carbohydrate availability. The result is fatty acid mobilization for energy. As this change in energy sources occurs, the intensity of exercise decreases to a level that is regulated by the ability to mobilize fat for energy.

Two steps in this process limit fat usage for energy: mobilization of the fatty acids from the fat tissue and transport of fatty acids into the mitochondria. Mobilization of fatty acids is inhibited by insulin. While not exercising, an athlete should avoid foods that are high on the glycemic index to decrease the insulin response. Insulin is secreted in response to increased blood glucose, which rises rapidly with high-glycemic sugars. Decreasing dietary intake of simple sugars also will result in a decrease in the ability to call upon circulating blood glucose rapidly.

An ultra-low-fat, high-carbohydrate diet will decrease use of fat as a fuel during exercise.[2] This is due to the insulin suppression and the decreased fatty acid transport into the muscle cell.

The intramuscular triglycerides are the major fat source used in exercise.[3] Once the fatty acids have been mobilized, they need to be incorporated into the mitochondria before they can be used as fuel. Endurance training can enhance the transport system for fatty acids into the mitochondria.[4] Still, several factors inhibit transport into the muscle mitochondria. As the fatty acid is transported, the molecule that helped to carry it through the blood is changed and left behind. The new form of this molecule is unable to transport fat and will limit further fatty acid uptake into mitochondria.[5] With increasingly intense exercise, the density of mitochondria within the muscle limits the use of fat.[6] As exercise becomes more intense, the use of fat as an energy source decreases as a *percentage* of energy used, but the *amount* of energy from fat remains constant.

Therefore, the concentration of the mitochondria within a muscle cell is the determining factor in how much fat will be used. After regular aerobic training, there is an increase in the use of fat as a percentage of energy compared with energy supply before training is begun.[7] Some causes of this change include

- Increased density of the mitochondria[8] within the muscle cell
- Increased transport of fatty acids into the mitochondria via the CPT system
- Increased transport of fatty acids into the muscle[9]
- Increased reliance on intramuscular triglycerides[10]
- Increased mobilization of fatty acids from the adipose tissue through improved blood flow and increased lipolysis.

A SCIENTIFIC LOOK AT WEIGHT LOSS

If I wanted a get-rich-quick scheme, I would create an infomercial aimed at the average overweight person who does not exercise but wants to lose weight quickly. Even among the fittest of athletes, a frequent question that I am asked is how to lose weight while maintaining a rigid training plan. The answer is simple: negative energy balance. Let me explain.

Excess dietary fat and carbohydrate are stored in the body as fat. Weight loss is a balance between using the stored energy (energy output) and consuming enough calories to fuel your exercise (energy intake). With a negative energy balance, the output is higher than the intake and weight loss occurs. An energy deficit of 500–1,000 calories a day will lead to a weight loss of one to two pounds a week. This gradual approach to weight loss is preferred.[11] The tricky part is maximizing weight loss while maintaining fitness as well as the intensity needed for competition.

Creating a negative energy balance involves diet modification as well as body modification. The body uses calories for energy at rest as well as during exercise. To increase output, the basal metabolic rate needs to be increased. Also important is exercising at the correct workload to use fat as energy. The second part of weight loss involves manipulating diet and training to optimize fat oxidation as fuel.

Diet

Negative energy expenditure can be achieved with diet or exercise. Endurance athletes have more success with creating a negative balance through dietary manipulation.[12] When they use exercise to attain a negative energy balance, weight loss is slower, although protein is conserved. Exercise-induced negative balance has been associated with a larger fat loss.[13]

Negative energy balance can be achieved with a diet that is either low or high in fat (40 percent).[14] However, a sensible low-fat diet uses monounsaturated fatty acids as the primary fat source for up to 20 percent of total calories. Monounsaturated fats are present in nuts, avocados, and extra-virgin olive oil. These can be used to augment whole grains (including pasta) and vegetables to keep the overall fat content low. Vegetables and whole grains in the diet also carry the health benefits of antioxidants. Saturated fats should be avoided.

Many people who are trying to lose weight will cut fat from the diet completely, but studies show no advantage in lowering fat intake to less than 15 percent of total calories.[15] Just as an ultra-low-fat diet is not recommended, there should be no attempt to restrict carbohydrates in your diet. Although this will result in weight loss, calorie restriction has been found to decrease power, strength, intensity, and energy levels, most likely due to a decrease in carbohydrate intake.[16] The same study also found that stress, anger, fatigue, depression, and confusion were increased with seven days of calorie restriction.

A study that restricted caloric intake but maintained either a normal or a high percentage of carbohydrate resulted in high use of fat during exercise. Weight loss was achieved, but maintenance of power output was achieved only with the high-carbohydrate diet.[17]

If caloric restriction results in insufficient energy to continue training, it may be useful to try a diet consisting of a higher percentage of calories from fat. Five days of a high-fat diet combined with high-intensity training results in a 100 percent increase in fat oxidation over baseline.[18] Five days of a high-fat diet followed by one day of a high-carbohydrate diet still resulted in increased fat oxidation for energy—even in the presence of carbohydrates.[19] Short-term exposure to a high-fat diet confers all of the benefits of increased fat burning without the health and training disadvantages of a long-term high-fat diet.

Table 4.1

HIGH-CARBOHYDRATE AND HIGH-FAT DIETS

Meal	High Carbohydrate	High Fat
Breakfast	Muselix (135 g) Skim milk (300 g) Whole-grain bread (2 slices) Orange juice (280 g)	Muselix (100 g) Milk (280 g) Milk shake (580 g)
Lunch	Chicken/vegetable soup (300 g) Large roll and margarine	Chicken/mushroom soup (230 g) Small roll and margarine
Dinner	Lasagna Salad and low-fat mayonnaise Garlic bread Large piece of cake	Lasagna Salad and Italian dressing Small piece of cake
Snack	Chocolate chip cookie	Carrot and celery sticks Avocado and yogurt dip French onion dip
Energy drink	Hyperosmolar solution	Low-carb solution

Dietary Totals				
Carbohydrate	698	(68% total cal)	203	(20% total cal)
Fat	87	(20% total cal)	309	(68% total cal)
Protein	127		121	
Calories	4,083		4,077	

Source: L. M. Burke, J. A. Hawley, D. J. Angus, G. R. Cox, S. A. Clark, N. K. Cummings, B. Desbrow, M. Hargreaves. Adaptations to short-term, high-fat diet persist during exercise despite high carbohydrate availability. *Medicine and Science in Sports and Exercise* January 2002, 34(1): 83–91.

The training was completed in athletes on both high-fat and high-carbohydrate diets, but the athletes on the high-fat diet experienced more fatigue. Examples of the high-fat and high-carbohydrate diets are outlined in Table 4.1.

The only way to gauge accurately how many calories you are ingesting is to keep careful records of what you eat using a food diary. By charting all the different foods you eat and tallying their total grams of fat, protein, and carbohydrate as well as total calories, you can get a sense of where excess calories are coming from or if you are consuming enough calories. This is harder when eating out, but you can get a general idea from your own meals. Some critics of food diaries argue that when people are keeping track of what they eat, they avoid high-fat foods, and thus the recording is unrealistic. Still, the food diary is a useful tool to see where the majority of calories are in the diet. It is important to monitor eating habits and patterns to ensure that adequate nutrition to sustain training is maintained.[20] It is equally important during weight loss to find where calories can be restricted. If someone is consuming large quantities of food between meals, meals can be smaller.

Dieting works to decrease weight, but if not properly monitored, it comes at the expense of power, strength, and intensity, not to mention the negative effects on mood. Dieting alone results in decreased vigorous activity and is likely to result in weight gain.[21] Exercise alone is a valuable modality for weight loss,[22] but combining proper diet (not necessarily dieting) and exercise work together to improve weight loss. In one study, people in a weight-loss program that combined diet and exercise experienced greater restraint and less hunger than those in a similar program that used only exercise.[23]

Exercise

Exercise is thought to achieve weight loss in three ways. First, there is a prolonged increase in caloric utilization after each exercise bout. Second, exercise training increases the basal metabolic rate.[24] Third, there is an increase in energy consumption during nonexercise activity.[25]

The continued consumption of calories following exercise will vary depending upon the magnitude of exercise. Exercise below 75 percent of VO_2max does not appear to have the same effect as does higher-intensity exercise.

Long, steady endurance exercise was once thought to be responsible for fat burning. Studies have shown that this may not be true.[26] Endurance exercise above a certain intensity uses primarily carbohydrates. Regardless of intensity, endurance exercise will contribute to maintenance of a desired weight due to an overall negative energy balance.[27] To oxidize fat as fuel requires knowing the appropriate intensity of exercise. One group of researchers found that maximum fat oxidation (fat_{max}) occurred at 74 percent (± 3 percent) of maximum heart rate. A fat_{max} zone has been identified as exercise performed at 68–79 percent of maximum heart rate.[28]

Resistance exercise has also been shown to be useful in weight loss when added to a diet and aerobic exercise program.[29] Lean muscle mass will increase the resting metabolic rate, because lean muscle mass requires more energy than fat tissue. In a study that used light resistance exercise as part of a weight-loss program, protein synthesis was associated with an increased metabolic rate.[30]

Diet and exercise

Diet and exercise can be combined to maximize fat burning for energy. As discussed before, maximal fat burning through lipolysis can be achieved in the absence of insulin. Maximal fat loss occurs within specific heart rate ranges. We eat carbohydrate to fuel exercise lasting longer than one hour. These three principles can be applied to maximize fat utilization.

For cycling rides of less than one hour, exercise two to three times a week in the fat_{max} zone described earlier. For this strategy to be effective, insulin levels must be low, so exercise in the morning before breakfast. To capitalize on this workout, have two cups of coffee or tea. The caffeine will mobilize fatty acids, allowing them to be burned for fuel.[31] Do not perform low-carbohydrate, low-insulin training for more than one hour, as this will lead to depletion of muscle glycogen and use of muscle protein for energy.

Supplements

The vitamin and supplement market is flooded with products that promote weight loss. Only a few supplements are worth mentioning for their ability to decrease fat mass.

Stimulants have long been used as weight-loss aids. Most of these have significant health consequences, but there are two that can be used safely. During decreased caloric intake, there is a 12 percent reduction in nonexercising energy expenditure;[32] stimulants, along with exercise, can help to overcome that reduction. Caffeine can provide the hormonal stimulus to stimulate lipolysis. Yohimbine, a stimulant affecting the sympathetic nervous system, can also aid in weight loss. One study found that when it was combined with a low-calorie diet, yohimbine (intake of 5 mg four times a day) stimulated weight loss through an effort-induced increase in metabolism. There was no effect on lipolysis.[33]

Chromium picolinate has been touted as an effective weight-loss supplement to exercise. Chromium has not lived up to that promise for individuals engaged in an exercise program,[34] although some benefit has been shown in animal studies. The underlying chromium status, diet, duration of use, and dose of chromium have so far only muddied the data.[35] Whatever benefits may exist are small compared with the effects of diet and exercise.

High-protein diets became popular with the soccer-mom and weightlifting crowd as a means to weight loss. The basis of these diets is decreased insulin and decreased energy stores, resulting in starvation on a cellular level. Protein diets are not recommended for athletes. The decreased carbohydrate levels cannot support endurance training. In addition, high-protein diets cause dehydration.[36]

Although high protein diets are not advisable while training for endurance sports, the use of protein can be helpful as a weight-loss adjunct during a weight training phase. In one study, a reduced-calorie diet in conjunction with weight training and casein protein (1.5 g/kg/day) resulted in decreased body fat, increased lean mass, and more strength than when subjects used whey protein or no protein at all.[37] The significant difference found between the protein types is because the amino acid components of the casein protein have more anticatabolic effects than available from whey protein.

Another protein supplement has been shown to maintain performance in the calorie-restricted athlete. Branched-chain amino acid supplements, in conjunction with a moderate energy restriction, induced significant fat losses but did not reduce high-level performance.[38]

Finally, creatine supplementation has been the subject of substantial press and scientific inquiry into its use for muscle building. Its role in weight loss, however, is due to caloric restriction. Creatine supplementation increased muscle creatine during short-term caloric restriction, but there was no effect on body fat and protein loss.[39]

In summary, successful weight loss involves frequent monitoring of food intake, adhering to a low-fat diet that includes monounsaturated (not saturated) fats, and engaging in regular exercise. This strategy will result not only in weight loss but also in maintenance of that weight loss.[40]

NOTES

1. A. E. Jeukendrup, W. H. Saris, A. J. Wagenmakers. Fat metabolism during exercise: A review. Part I: Fatty acid mobilization and muscle metabolism. *International Journal of Sports Medicine* May 1998, 19(4): 231–44.

2. E. F. Coyle, A. E. Jeukendrup, M. C. Oseto, B. J. Hodgkinson, T. W. Zderic. Low-fat diet alters intramuscular substrates and reduces lipolysis and fat oxidation during exercise. *American Journal of Physiology, Endocrinology, and Metabolism* March 2001, 280(3): E391–98.

3. W. H. Martin 3d. Effect of endurance training on fatty acid metabolism during whole body exercise. *Medical Science Sports Exercise* May 1997, 29(5): 635–39.

4. R. J. Tunstall, K. A. Mehan, G. D. Wadley, G. R. Collier, A. Bonen, M. Hargreaves, D. Cameron-Smith. Exercise training increases lipid metabolism gene expression in human skeletal muscle. *American Journal of Physiology, Endocrinology, and Metabolism* July 2002, 283(1): E66–72.

5. A. E. Jeukendrup. Regulation of fat metabolism in skeletal muscle. *Annual Proceedings New York Academy of Science* June 2002, 967: 217–35.

6. A. E. Jeukendrup, W. H. Saris, A. J. Wagenmakers. Fat metabolism during exercise: A review. Part II: Regulation of metabolism and the effects of training. *International Journal of Sports Medicine* July 1998, 19(5): 293–302.

7. B. Kiens. Effect of endurance training on fatty acid metabolism: Local adaptations. *Medical Science Sports Exercise* May 1997, 29(5): 640–45.

8. D. Cameron-Smith. Exercise and skeletal muscle gene expression. *Clinical Experiments in Pharmacology and Physiology* March 2002, 29(3): 209–13.

9. B. C. Bergman, G. E. Butterfield, E. E. Wolfel, G. A. Casazza, G. D. Lopaschuk, G. A. Brooks. Evaluation of exercise and training on muscle lipid metabolism. *American Journal of Physiology* January 1999, 276(1 Pt 1): E106–17.

10. W. H. Martin 3d. Effect of endurance training on fatty acid metabolism during whole body exercise.

11. D. S. Miles. Weight control and exercise. *Clinical Sports Medicine* January 1991, 10(1): 157–69.

12. R. G. McMurray, V. Ben-Ezra, W. A. Forsythe, A. T. Smith. Responses of endurance-trained subjects to caloric deficits induced by diet or exercise. *Medical Science Sports Exercise* October 1985, 17(5): 574–79.

13. A. Tremblay, J. P. Despres, C. Bouchard. The effects of exercise-training on energy balance and adipose tissue morphology and metabolism. *Sports Medicine* May–June 1985, 2(3): 223–33.

14. K. Z. Walker, K. O'Dea. Is a low fat diet the optimal way to cut energy intake over the long-term in overweight people? *Nutrition, Metabolism, and Cardiovascular Disease* August 2001, 11(4): 244–48.

15. Position of Dietitians of Canada, the American Dietetic Association, and the American College of Sports Medicine. Nutrition and athletic performance. *Canadian Journal of Dietary Practice Research* Winter 2000, 61(4): 176–92.

16. E. Filaire, F. Maso, F. Degoutte, P. Jouanel, G. Lac. Food restriction, performance, psychological state, and lipid values in judo athletes. *International Journal of Sports Medicine* August 2001, 22(6): 454–59. C. A. Horswill, R. C. Hickner, J. R. Scott, D. L. Costill, D. Gould. Weight loss, dietary carbohydrate modifications, and high intensity, physical performance. *Medical Science Sports Exercise* August 1990, 22(4): 470–76.

17. R. G. McMurray, C. R. Proctor, W. L. Wilson. Effect of caloric deficit and dietary manipulation on aerobic and anaerobic exercise. *International Journal of Sports Medicine* April 1991, 12(2): 167–72. M. Fogelholm. Effects of body weight reduction on sports performance. *Sports Medicine* October 1994, 18(4): 249–67.

18. C. E. Broeder, M. Brenner, Z. Hofman, I. J. M. Paijmans, E. L. Thomas, J. H. Willmore. The metabolic consequences of low and moderate intensity exercise with or without feeding in lean and borderline obese males. *International Journal of Obesity* 1991, 15: 95–104.

19. L. M. Burke, J. A. Hawley, D. J. Angus, G. R. Cox, S. A. Clark, N. K. Cummings, B. Desbrow, M. Hargreaves. Adaptations to short-term high-fat diet persist during exercise despite high carbohydrate availability. *Medical Science Sports Exercise* January 2002, 34(1): 83–91.

20. P. J. Ziegler, S. S. Jonnalagadda, J. A. Nelson, C. Lawrence, B. Baciak. Contribution of meals and snacks to nutrient intake of male and female elite figure skaters during peak competitive season. *Journal of American College Nutrition* April 2002, 21(2): 114–19.

21. A. C. King, B. Frey-Hewitt, D. M. Dreon, P. D. Wood. Diet versus exercise in weight maintenance: The effects of minimal intervention strategies on long-term outcomes in men. *Archives of Internal Medicine* December 1989, 149(12): 2741–46.

22. R. Ross, J. A. Freeman, I. Janssen. Exercise alone is an effective strategy for reducing obesity and related comorbidities. *Exercise and Sport Sciences Reviews* October 2000, 28(4): 165–70.

23. M. Kiernan, A. C. King, M. L. Stefanick, J. D. Killen. Men gain additional psychological benefits by adding exercise to a weight-loss program. *Obesity Research* December 2001, 9(12): 770–77.

24. A. M. Sjodin, A. H. Forslund, K. R. Westerterp, A. B. Andersson, J. M. Forslund, L. M. Hambraeus. The influence of physical activity on BMR. *Medicine and Science in Sports and Exercise* 1996 January, 28(1): 85-91.

25. E. T. Poehlman, C. L. Melby, M. I. Goran. The impact of exercise and diet restriction on daily energy expenditure. *Sports Medicine* February 1991, 11(2): 78–101.

26. W. J. Pasman, M. S. Westerterp, W. H. Saris. The effect of body weight changes and endurance training on 24-hour substrate oxidation. *International Journal of Obesity-Related Metabolic Disorders* December 1999, 23(12): 1223–32.

27. L. B. Bunyard, L. I. Katzel, M. J. Busby-Whitehead, Z. Wu, A. P. Goldberg. Energy requirements of middle-aged men are modifiable by physical activity. *American Journal of Clinical Nutrition* November 1998, 68(5): 1136–42.

28. J. Achten, M. Gleeson, A. E. Jeukendrup. Determination of the exercise intensity that elicits maximal fat oxidation. *Medical Science Sports Exercise* January 2002, 34(1): 92–97.

29. W. J. Kraemer, J. S. Volek, K. L. Clark, S. E. Gordon, S. M. Puhl, L. P. Koziris, J. M. McBride, N. T. Triplett-McBride, M. Putukian, R. U. Newton, K. Hakkinen, J. A. Bush, W. J. Sebastianelli. Influence of exercise training on physiological and performance changes with weight loss in men. *Medical Science Sports Exercise* September 1999, 31(9): 1320–29.

30. T. Doi, T. Matsuo, M. Sugawara, K. Matsumoto, K. Minehira, K. Hamada, K. Okamura, M. Suzuki. New approach for weight reduction by a combination of diet, light resistance exercise, and the timing of ingesting a protein supplement. *Asia Pacific Journal of Clinical Nutrition* 2001, 10(3): 226–32.

31. P. J. Arciero, A. W. Gardner, J. Calles-Escandon, N. L. Benowitz, E. T. Pochiman. Effects of caffeine ingestion on NE kinetics, fat oxidation, and energy expenditure in younger and older men. *American Journal of Physiology* June 1995, 268(6 Pt 1): E1192–98.
P. J. Arciero, C. L. Bougopoulos, B. C. Nindl, N. L. Benowitz. Influence of age on the thermic response to caffeine in women. *Metabolism* January 2000, 49(1): 101–7.

32. P. Webb. Direct calorimetry and the energetics of exercise and weight loss. *Medical Science Sports Exercise* February 1986, 18(1): 3–5.

33. C. Kucio, K. Jonderko, D. Piskorska. Does yohimbine act as a slimming drug? *Israeli Journal of Medical Science* October 1991, 27(10): 550–56.

34. L. K. Trent, D. Thieding-Cancel. Effects of chromium picolinate on body composition. *Journal of Sports Medicine and Physical Fitness* December 1995, 35(4): 273–80.

35. R. A. Anderson. Effects of chromium on body composition and weight loss. *Nutrition Review* September 1998, 56(9): 266–70.

36. W. F. Martin, D. R. Bolster, P. C. Gaine, L. J. Hanley, M. A. Pikosky, B. T. Bennett, L. E. Armstrong, N. R. Rodriguez. Increased dietary protein affects hydration indices in endurance runners. FASEB 2002, 16(4): A613.

37. R. H. Demling, L. DeSanti. Effect of a hypocaloric diet, increased protein intake, and resistance training on lean mass gains and fat mass loss in overweight police officers. *Annual Review of Nutrition and Metabolism* 2000, 44(1): 21–29.

38. A. Mourier, A. X. Bigard, E. de Kerviler, B. Roger, H. Legrand, C. Y. Guezennec. Combined effects of caloric restriction and branched-chain amino acid supplementation on body composition and exercise performance in elite wrestlers. *International Journal of Sports Medicine* January 1997, 18(1): 47–55.

39. J. A. Rockwell, J. W. Rankin, B. Toderico B. Creatine supplementation affects muscle creatine during energy restriction. *Medical Science Sports Exercise* January 2001, 33(1): 61–68.

40. R. R. Wing, J. O. Hill. Successful weight loss maintenance. *Annual Review of Nutrition* 2001, 21: 323–41.

FLUIDS, ELECTROLYTES, AND HYDRATION

luid consumption during endurance exercise is perhaps the single most important aspect of such activity. Maintaining adequate hydration improves performance on many levels.[1] Dehydration in an athlete, even as little as 2 percent, can lead to a significant decline in performance. Maintaining hydration has numerous performance advantages, including decreased body temperature, heart rate, and perceived exertion and, possibly, decreased reliance on carbohydrate as a fuel source.[2]

The total amount of body water accounts for approximately 60 percent of total body weight. Of this substantial volume of water, about two-thirds resides in the body's cells. The remaining one-third is divided between the plasma, which is the liquid part of the blood, and the interstitial fluid that floats between the cells.

The regulation of these compartments requires an intricate balance of hormones to maintain the volume of extracellular fluid, specifically the plasma volume. Although the plasma accounts for only one-fifteenth of the total body water, it must be maintained or blood pressure will ultimately decrease and blood will not be delivered to the exercising muscles; as a result, performance will decrease. Maintaining plasma volume also maintains cardiac output, which helps to maintain blood flow to the skin; this in turn keeps body temperature lower, lowers the perceived effort, and prevents a rise in heart rate.[3]

When an athlete is dehydrated, the power at lactate threshold is decreased, and lactate threshold occurs at a lower percentage of VO_2max.[4] These physical effects are accompanied by decline in mental function and mood as well. Perception, thought, short-term memory, and estimation of fatigue are all negatively affected by dehydration.[5]

During exercise, the body's metabolic rate increases approximately fifteen- to twenty-fold that of the at-rest rate.[6] The amount of heat produced also increases. This heat must be dissipated to avoid heat illness. One of the main cooling mechanisms used by the body is evaporation of sweat. To experience an example of this, apply rubbing alcohol to the skin and feel the cooling effect as it dries. The body uses similar mechanisms by having the sweat evaporate, thus promoting a decreased temperature.

Sweat, however, comes from the body's store of fluid, specifically from the plasma part of the extracellular fluid. With exercise, sweat rates can approach three liters per hour[7] and can increase by another liter per hour in the heat.[8] Even in the cold, however, there is a significant reduction in exercise tolerance.[9] The decrease of the plasma leads to decreased flow to the kidneys, which triggers the activation of the renin-angiotensin system in the kidneys.[10] Renin is a hormone secreted by the kidneys in response to decreased plasma volume and decreased flow to the kidneys. Renin, in turn, activates the angiotensins, which cause the blood vessels to constrict, effectively shrinking the plasma compartment to match the decreased plasma. Angiotensin stimulates thirst. The renin-angiotensin system is effective after approximately twenty minutes. If thirst is the barometer by which an athlete starts to drink, then the onset of thirst will delay hydration by at least twenty minutes. In a hot and humid environment, this could result in a fluid deficit greater than one liter before thirst sets in.

As dehydration sets in, angiotensin also causes the secretion of aldosterone from the adrenal gland. Aldosterone is responsible for the retention of sodium (an electrolyte) by the kidney. Water follows the salt, and the body is able to retain water, resulting in more concentrated urine. The blood concentrations of the hormones rise significantly during exercise as the body fights to retain fluid.[11]

In addition, the pituitary gland in the brain secretes a substance called antidiuretic hormone to further conserve water by causing water retention in the kidney. The more concentrated urine appears as a darker yellow. Trainers advise athletes to use urine color and concentration as ways to judge hydration status and remember to drink.[12] If the urine is dark or measures more concentrated than it should be, more fluid should be consumed.

Body water can also be lost through breathing. As air is inhaled, it is warmed and humidified in the lungs. Upon exhalation, the moistened air leaves the body, carrying the water vapor with it. This loss increases with the increased breathing rate of exercise. At rest, respiratory losses are negligible, but as the breathing rate increases with exercise, the loss of fluid from the lungs is a major factor for water loss.[13]

As soon as exercise begins, there is an immediate shift of fluid from the plasma to the interstitial fluid. This shift does not continue to increase with prolonged exercise, due to the body's attempts at maintaining plasma volume.[14] Beginning an exercise session or competition in a state of normal or mild dehydration will worsen hydration status almost immediately. It is better to start with an increased plasma volume to maintain hydration even after the initial drop in plasma volume.

The mechanisms for adaptation to the heat are known as acclimatization. This is a process that allows for a decreased heart rate, body temperature, and perceived exertion during exercise. Acclimatization is also responsible for increased plasma volume and increased sweat rate. Aldosterone and antidiuretic hormone are also increased during acclimatization to preserve fluid and promote electrolyte retention. Athletes with a higher maximal power will acclimatize faster.[15]

To enhance acclimatization, exercise should be performed at an intensity greater than 50 percent of VO_2max for ten to fourteen days.[16] To prevent loss of acclimatization, do not remain inactive for more than a few days; inactivity will lead to decay of the protective changes over a few days to a week.

An increase in plasma protein results in the shift of fluid into the plasma.[17] This mechanism operates only during endurance exercise and helps the body to adapt to exercise and, more significant, to exercise in the heat. This is responsible for the bloating that athletes feel during ultra-endurance events. During an Ironman® triathlon, plasma volume increased despite an overall fluid deficit.[18]

Fluid status is the amount of fluid ingested minus the fluid losses from urine, sweat, and respiration. In order for the ingested fluid to count toward overall fluid status, the fluid must be absorbed into the bloodstream. This occurs after the fluid leaves the stomach, in the first half of the small intestine.[19] The process through which the stomach delivers fluid to the small intestine is known as gastric emptying and will be covered in detail later in this chapter.

Hydration during recovery from exercise is as important as hydration during exercise. Not maintaining adequate hydration will result in decreased exercise performance and physiologic function in subsequent training sessions.[20] Dehydration can affect recovery because the hormone responsible for performance enhancement after exercise, growth hormone, is related to the amount of extracellular fluid.[21] Depleted extracellular volume will cause a decrease in the secretion of growth hormone.[22]

HYDRATION RECOMMENDATIONS

Almost all of the research into hydration points to replacing fluid, electrolytes, and carbohydrate for exercise sessions lasting longer than 40–60 minutes. The following are the pooled recommendations divided into volume, electrolyte amounts, and carbohydrate.

Volume

The basic principle of fluid loss and hydration is simple: The fluid intake must be matched with the fluid output. There are three times to drink—before, during, or after exercise.

Drinking before exercise will ensure hydration at the start of the ride. The suggested amount is around 500 ml within two hours before exercise.[23] This amount will not only ensure that the fluid stores are optimal, but it will also allow the kidneys to regulate volume and electrolyte concentration. Avoid the temptation to become hyperhydrated before exercise. Although it may seem easier to drink before exercising and to drink less when exercising, overdoing it before the start does not confer improved performance[24] and may lead to the development of "side stitch."[25]

During exercise, the goal is to replace fluid to keep up with sweat loss. Measuring body weight before and after exercise and calculating the difference in the two weights can give an estimate of the amount of sweat lost during a workout. Carefully tracking the weight differences can give the athlete feedback as to whether enough fluid is being consumed.

The same strategy can be used following a workout to ensure that fluid replacement is equal to 1.5 times the losses. Fluid replacement should occur as rapidly as possible following exercise.[26]

Although sweat rates can vary depending upon the environment, plan on consuming 500–1,200 ml of liquid every hour.[27] This can be achieved by drinking 150–300 ml every fifteen to twenty minutes.

Electrolytes

Sodium is the major electrolyte lost in sweat. Additionally, because water follows sodium when it is reabsorbed in the kidney, sport scientists recommend adding sodium to the exercise beverage. Sodium is the most important electrolyte in terms of fluid ingestion. Although sodium ingestion is generally not necessary if there is adequate dietary intake, during the first few days in a hot environment or when an athlete has decreased dietary intake due to depressed appetite from hard training or decreased calorie consumption, supplementation may be necessary.[28]

How much sodium to ingest has been the topic of many scientific studies. Most sports drinks contain sodium in a concentration of 10–25 mmol per liter; however, more sodium may be required for optimal rehydration.[29] When tested, drinks that contained either 25 or 50 mmol of sodium per liter did not keep up with sodium losses. In contrast, sodium and fluid balances were maintained with a sodium content of 100 mmol per liter.[30] Although this research may not result in a palatable drink, it highlights the need for sodium if there is not a dietary source. Thus, a final recommendation is to drink a beverage that has 50–100 mmol per liter of sodium.[31] It is important to watch sodium, but it is more important to maintain fluid balance. Water is effective in replacing plasma volume,[32] but without optimal sodium, much of the water will not be retained and will be lost in the urine.[33]

A condition known as hyponatremia has garnered much attention. During exercise, the body's sodium levels can drop, especially if there has not been adequate dietary intake. Hyponatremia can result in weakness and fatigue and even lead to altered mental status, seizures, and coma. One theory is that hyponatremia arises from replacing fluid losses from sweat with plain water that lacks sodium. However, a person would have to drink two to three liters of water before hyponatremia would become symptomatic.[34] It is more likely that hyponatremia results from abnormal fluid retention.[35]

Other electrolytes in addition to sodium that are important include magnesium and potassium. These must not be overlooked for an athlete hydrating for endurance exercise. Magnesium is important as a player in the utilization of energy stores, with approximately 80 percent of cellular adenosine triphosphate (ATP)-forming complexes with magnesium. ATP is the muscle's fuel, which is created from glucose and oxygen metabolism. Magnesium has been found to decrease with exercise[36] and is deficient in most endurance athletes.[37] Ingesting magnesium during exercise has not been shown to replace body stores, but an increase has been found when magnesium supplements are taken daily (212mg/day).[38] Although magnesium does not show much promise for improving performance, it has some effect in one area: In one study, exercise following sleep deprivation was improved after magnesium supplementation.[39] This use for magnesium could be significant for those who are training and racing hard after a tiring week of work and family commitments. The dose was 100 mg of magnesium a day for a month, but up to 500 mg a day was used in some studies.[40]

Potassium, when deficient, can cause muscle aches and weakness. After sodium and chloride, potassium is the most common electrolyte lost in sweat. Recommendations for potassium supplementation are 2–5 mmol per liter.[41]

Carbohydrates

Although drinking during exercise has a performance-enhancing effect, adding carbohydrates to the fluid further aids performance.[42] The addition of carbohydrates to fluids ingested during exercise serves a few purposes: to spare glycogen, to enhance fluid absorption, and to maximize recovery.

Providing the body with extra carbohydrates enables the muscles to use the exogenous carbohydrates while sparing the glycogen stored in the muscle. By decreasing the muscle glycogen utilization by 22 percent during interval exercise,[43] carbohydrates can delay the onset of fatigue. Although ingested carbohydrates contribute to the overall glucose used during exercise, muscle glycogen is not spared during constant exercise at anaerobic threshold.[44] At lower intensities, however, ingested carbohydrates are useful in sparing the muscle glycogen.[45]

Exercise at different intensities clearly affects the use of muscle glycogen, but sparing of the liver glycogen is constant. The liver glycogen is responsible for maintaining a certain level of blood glucose and preventing problems encountered when blood glucose is depleted, such as decreased concentration, fatigue, and the "bonk." Ingested carbohydrates spare the use of liver glycogen during exercise and delay exercise-induced fatigue, mental status changes, and "bonking."[46]

Ingested carbohydrates help with absorption of fluid and also help to maintain levels of performance in the heat. During an experimental triathlon, the use of a 7 percent carbohydrate solution (7 grams of carbohydrate per 100 ml of water) allowed the athletes to exercise harder for a longer time than those using water alone.[47] The extra carbohydrates do not impair fluid replacement;[48] in fact, it helps to maintain hydration in a hot environment better than water does alone.[49]

Finally, carbohydrates are important in replenishing glycogen stores after exercise. With replaced glycogen, subsequent exercise is more effective and fatigue can be delayed.[50]

For carbohydrates to be effective in a sports drink, it must be in the right concentration and consumed in adequate quantities. The recommended concentration is 3–8 percent.[51] If the hydration amount previously discussed is used (150–300 ml every fifteen to twenty minutes), approximately one gram of carbohydrate will be delivered to the body every minute. Because the body uses glucose less in the first hour of exercise, the carbohydrate concentration should be at the lower end of the range during the first hour and should increase after that.

The type of carbohydrate used is not as important. Glucose, sucrose (table sugar), fructose, or maltodextrin are effective if used in a concentration of less than 10 percent.[52]

FACTORS AFFECTING HYDRATION

Hydration can be approximated by the amount of water ingested minus the amount of water lost in sweat and urine. For water to be used effectively by the body, it must pass through the stomach and be absorbed in the small intestine. The rates at which fluid leaves the stomach (gastric emptying) are important when considering what type of beverage to use.

Two main factors affect gastric emptying: volume and carbohydrate content. Increased volume speeds emptying, and increased carbohydrate slows emptying.[53] Other factors of lesser importance are decreased temperature and increased exercise intensity.

Once out of the stomach, the fluid is absorbed in the early part of the small intestine. Water follows gradients—that is, it flows from areas of low concentrations to high concentrations. Water is also absorbed along with sodium and glucose, so the addition of these nutrients will facilitate transport of water from the intestine into the body.

Dilute solutions are more readily absorbed than more concentrated solutions. If a solution is more concentrated than the fluid in the body (hypertonic), fluid moves from the body into the intestine, resulting in a net water loss. Hypertonic drinks also decrease gastric emptying,[54] making them even less effective as exercise replacement drinks.

If left to their own devices, athletes typically do not drink enough fluid to replace their losses, a concept defined by the term "voluntary dehydration." To overcome voluntary dehydration, athletes need a palatable fluid and will prefer flavored drinks over plain water as a way to maintain better hydration.[55] Athletes will consume more of a beverage that is both flavored and sweetened.[56] As exercise progresses, even an unpalatable beverage will become more acceptable, but once exercise is started with a drink that won't be consumed, voluntary consumption will be insufficient to maintain hydration.

Aside from flavor and sugar, salt and temperature also increase palatability. The use of less salt than optimal in sports drinks is probably due to taste issues; most drinks do not offer the ideal salt concentration for retention of fluid.[57] Cool beverages, aside from increasing gastric emptying, also enhance palatability. The issue of palatability is of special importance for the master athlete.[58] As we age, there is an alteration in the control of taste mechanisms, so beverages must be optimized for taste.

It takes practice to overcome voluntary dehydration. When you are training, practice drinking at regular intervals. Rehearsing drinking during training can increase tolerance to fluid ingestion; this response allows you to overcome voluntary dehydration, especially during running when fluid ingestion is not well tolerated.[59]

Since fluid balance equals fluid in minus fluid out, fluid can be ingested to limit the effects of urine loss. Although urine output is a measure of hydration, retention of fluid in the plasma volume is the ultimate goal. If urine output is increased due to caffeine ingestion, clear urine cannot be used as a measure of hydration. There is a misconception that large amounts of water will produce more urine and thus not contribute to hydration. In fact, ingestion of large quantities of plain water will result in clear urine in the first few hours after hydration, but overall, more fluid will be retained than if small amounts of water were consumed.[60]

SUMMARY

For hydration to be effective, fluid and electrolytes must be consumed in the right quantities. Within two hours prior to exercise, drink 500 ml of fluid to ensure that exercise is started while you are hydrated. During exercise of one hour or more, consume a carbohydrate-electrolyte solution at a rate of approximately 1,200 ml every hour. This solution should contain 3–8 percent carbohydrate and 0.5–0.7 grams per liter of sodium and 2–5 mmol per liter of potassium. For an exercise session of less than one hour, drink water at a rate of 1.5 times sweat loss, or approximately 1,200 ml per hour (or more in the heat).

NOTES

1. D. J. Casa, C. M. Maresh, L. E. Armstrong, S. A. Kavouras, J. A. Herrera-Soto, F. T. Hacker Jr., T. P. Scheett, J. Stoppani. Intravenous versus oral rehydration during a brief period: Stress hormone responses to subsequent exhaustive exercise in the heat. *International Journal of Sport Nutrition and Exercise Metabolism* December 2000, 10(4): 361–74.
R. J. Maughan. Food and fluid intake during exercise. *Canadian Journal of Applied Physiology* 2001, 26 Suppl: S71–78.

2. S. I. Barr. Effects of dehydration on exercise performance. *Canadian Journal of Applied Physiology* April 1999, 24(2): 164–72.
J. E. Greenleaf, R. Looft-Wilson, J. L. Wisherd, M. A. McKenzie, C. D. Jensen, J. H. Whittam. Pre-exercise hypervolemia and cycle ergometer endurance in men. *Biology of Sport/Institute of Sport* 1997, 14(2): 103–14.
S. N. Cheuvront, E. M. Haymes. Thermoregulation and marathon running: Biological and environmental influences. *Sports Medicine* 2001, 31(10): 743–62.
C. M. Burge, M. F. Carey, W. R. Payne. Rowing performance, fluid balance, and metabolic function following dehydration and rehydration. *Medicine and Science in Sports and Exercise* December 1993, 25(12): 1358–64.
S. J. Montain, E. F. Coyle. Influence of graded dehydration on hyperthermia and cardiovascular drift during exercise. *Journal of Applied Physiology* October 1992, 73(4): 1340–50.

3. T. D. Noakes. Fluid replacement during exercise. *Exercise and Sport Sciences Reviews* 1993, 21: 297–330.

4. A. Moquin, R. S. Mazzeo. Effect of mild dehydration on the lactate threshold in women. *Medicine and Science in Sports and Exercise* February 2000, 32(2): 396–402.
J. Gonzalez-Alonso, R. Mora-Rodriguez, P. R. Below, E. F. Coyle. Dehydration reduces cardiac output and increases systemic and cutaneous vascular resistance during exercise. *Journal of Applied Physiology* November 1995, 79(5): 1487–96.

5. C. Cian, P. A. Barraud, B. Melin, C. Raphel. Effects of fluid ingestion on cognitive function after heat stress or exercise-induced dehydration. *International Journal of Psychophysiology* November 2001, 42(3): 243–51.

6. R. J. Maughan. Fluid balance and exercise. *International Journal of Sports Medicine* October 1992, 13 Suppl 1: S132–35.

7. C. A. Horswill. Effective fluid replacement. *International Journal of Sport Nutrition and Exercise Metabolism* June 1998, 8(2): 175–95.

8. N. J. Rehrer. Fluid and electrolyte balance in ultra-endurance sport. *Sports Medicine* 2001, 31(10): 701–15.

9. H. Rintamaki, T. Makinen, J. Oksa, J. Latvala. Water balance and physical performance in cold. *Arctic Medical Research* 1995, 54 Suppl 2: 32–36.

10. F. Fallo. Renin-angiotensin-aldosterone system and physical exercise. *Journal of Sports Medicine and Physical Fitness* September 1993, 33(3): 306–12.

11. L. Rocker, K. A. Kirsch, B. Heyduck, H. U. Altenkirch. Influence of prolonged physical exercise on plasma volume, plasma proteins, electrolytes, and fluid-regulating hormones. *International Journal of Sports Medicine* August 1989, 10(4): 270–74.
B. D. Roy, H. J. Green, M. Burnett. Prolonged exercise following diuretic-induced hypohydration effects on fluid and electrolyte hormones. *Hormone and Metabolic Research* September 2001, 33(9): 540–47.

12. L. E. Armstrong, J. A. Soto, F. T. Hacker Jr., D. J. Casa, S. A. Kavouras, C. M. Maresh. Urinary indices during dehydration, exercise, and rehydration. *International Journal of Sport Nutrition and Exercise Metabolism* December 1998, 8(4): 345–55.
S. M. Shirreffs. Markers of hydration status. *Journal of Sports Medicine and Physical Fitness* March 2000, 40(1): 80–84.

13. J. B. Leiper, Y. Pitsiladis, R. J. Maughan. Comparison of water turnover rates in men undertaking prolonged cycling exercise and sedentary men. *International Journal of Sports Medicine* April 2001, 22(3): 181–85.

14. V. A. Convertino. Fluid shifts and hydration state: Effects of long-term exercise. *Canadian Journal of Sport Sciences* 1987, 12(Suppl 1): 136S–39S.

15. L. E. Armstrong, C. M. Maresh. The induction and decay of heat acclimatisation in trained athletes. *Sports Medicine* November 1991, 12(5): 302–12.

16. N. Terrados, R. J. Maughan. Exercise in the heat: Strategies to minimize the adverse effects on performance. *Journal of Sports Sciences* Summer 1995, 13 Spec No: S55–62.

17. Rocker et al. Influence of prolonged physical exercise on plasma.

18. D. B. Speedy, T. D. Noakes, N. E. Kimber, I. R. Rogers, J. M. Thompson, D. R. Boswell, J. J. Ross, R. G. Campbell, P. G. Gallagher, J. A. Kuttner. Fluid balance during and after an ironman triathlon. *Clinical Journal of Sports Medicine* January 2001, 11(1): 44–50.

19. R. J. Maughan, J. B. Leiper. Limitations to fluid replacement during exercise. *Canadian Journal of Applied Physiology* April 1999, 24(2): 173–87.

20. S. M. Shirreffs, R. J. Maughan. Rehydration and recovery of fluid balance after exercise. *Exercise and Sport Sciences Reviews* January 2000, 28(1): 27–32.
S. M. Shirreffs. Restoration of fluid and electrolyte balance after exercise. *Canadian Journal of Applied Physiology* 2001, 26 Suppl: S228–35.

21. J. F. Monnier, A. A. Benhaddad, J. P. Micallef, J. Mercier, J. F. Brun. Relationships between blood viscosity and insulin-like growth factor I status in athletes. *Clinical Hemorheology and Microcirculation* 2000, 22(4): 277–86.

22. C. Peyreigne, D. Bouix, C. Fedou, J. Mercier. Effect of hydration on exercise-induced growth hormone response. *European Journal of Endocrinology* October 2001, 145(4): 445–50.

23. C. V. Gisolfi, S. M. Duchman. Guidelines for optimal replacement beverages for different athletic events. *Medicine and Science in Sports and Exercise* June 1992, 24(6): 679–87.

24. M. N. Sawka, S. J. Montain, W. A. Latzka. Hydration effects on thermoregulation and performance in the heat. *Comparative Biochemistry and Physiology—Part A: Molecular and Integrative Physiology* April 2001, 128(4): 679–90.

C. M. Maresh, M. F. Bergeron, R. W. Kenefick, J. W. Castellani, J. R. Hoffman, L. E. Armstrong. Effect of overhydration on time-trial swim performance. *Journal of Strength and Conditioning Research* November 2001, 15(4): 514–18.

25. B. T. Plunkett, W. G. Hopkins. Investigation of the side pain "stitch" induced by running after fluid ingestion. *Medicine and Science in Sports and Exercise* August 1999, 31(8): 1169–75.

26. B. Melin, M. Cure, C. Jimenez, N. Koulmann, G. Savourey, J. Bittel. Effect of ingestion pattern on rehydration and exercise performance subsequent to passive dehydration. *European Journal of Applied Physiology and Occupational Physiology* 1994, 68(4): 281–84.

27. V. A. Convertino, L. E. Armstrong, E. F. Coyle, G. W. Mack, M. N. Sawka, L. C. Senay Jr., W. M. Sherman. American College of Sports Medicine position stand. Exercise and fluid replacement. *Medicine and Science in Sports and Exercise* January 1996, 28(1): 1–7.

28. W. A. Latzka, S. J. Montain. Water and electrolyte requirements for exercise. *Clinics in Sports Medicine* July 1999, 18(3): 513–24.

29. L. M. Burke. Nutrition for post-exercise recovery. *Australian Journal of Science and Medicine in Sport* March 1997, 29(1): 3–10.

30. S. M. Shirreffs, R. J. Maughan. Volume repletion after exercise-induced volume depletion in humans: Replacement of water and sodium losses. *American Journal of Physiology* May 1998, 274(5 Pt 2): F868–75.

31. R. J. Maughan, J. B. Leiper, S. M. Shirreffs. Factors influencing the restoration of fluid and electrolyte balance after exercise in the heat. *British Journal of Sports Medicine* September 1997, 31(3): 175–82.
L. M. Burke, Nutrition for post-exercise recovery.

32. B. Sanders, T. D. Noakes, S. C. Dennis. Water and electrolyte shifts with partial fluid replacement during exercise. *European Journal of Applied Physiology and Occupational Physiology* September 1999, 80(4): 318–23.

33. S. M. Shirreffs, A. J. Taylor, J. B. Leiper, R. J. Maughan. Post-exercise rehydration in man: Effects of volume consumed and drink sodium content. *Medicine and Science in Sports and Exercise* October 1996, 28(10): 1260–71.

34. T. D. Noakes. The hyponatremia of exercise. *International Journal of Sports Nutrition* September 1992, 2(3): 205–28.

35. D. B. Speedy, J. R. Rogers, T. D. Noakes, S. Wright, J. M. Thompson, R. Campbell, I. Hellemans, N. E. Kimber, D. R. Boswell, J. A. Kuttner, S. Safih. Exercise-induced hyponatremia in ultradistance triathletes is caused by inappropriate fluid retention. *Clinical Journal of Sport Medicine* October 2000, 10(4): 272–78.
D. B. Speedy, T. D. Noakes, J. R. Rogers, I. Hellemans, N. E. Kimber, D. R. Boswell, R. Campbell, J. A. Kuttner. A prospective study of exercise-associated hyponatremia in two ultradistance triathletes. *Clinical Journal of Sport Medicine* April 2000, 10(2): 136–41.

36. P. A. Deuster, A. Singh. Responses of plasma magnesium and other cations to fluid replacement during exercise. *Journal of the American College of Nutrition* June 1993, 12(3): 286-93.

37. I. Casoni, C. Guglielmini, L. Graziano, M. G. Reali, D. Mazzotta, V. Abbasciano. Changes of magnesium concentrations in endurance athletes. *International Journal of Sports Medicine* June 1990, 11(3): 234–37.

38. E. W. Finstad, I. J. Newhouse, H. C. Lukaski, J. E. McAuliffe, C. R. Stewart. The effects of magnesium supplementation on exercise performance. *Medicine and Science in Sports and Exercise* March 2001, 33(3): 493–98.

39. K. Tanabe, A. Yamamoto, N. Suzuki, N. Osada, Y. Yokoyama, H. Samejima, A. Seki, M. Oya, T. Murabayashi, M. Nakayama, M. Yamamoto, K. Omiya, H. Itoh, M. Murayama. Efficacy of oral magnesium administration on decreased exercise tolerance in a state of chronic sleep deprivation. *Japanese Circulation Journal* May 1998, 62(5): 341–46.

40. I. J. Newhouse, E. W. Finstad. The effects of magnesium supplementation on exercise performance. *Clinical Journal of Sport Medicine* July 2000, 10(3): 195–200.

41. G. W. Mack, M. F. Bergeron. Hydration and physical activity: Scientific concepts and practical applications. *Gatorade Sport Science Roundtable #26* 1996, 7(4).

42. P. R. Below, R. Mora-Rodriguez, J. Gonzalez-Alonso, E. F. Coyle. Fluid and carbohydrate ingestion independently improve performance during one hour of intense exercise. *Medicine and Science in Sports and Exercise* February 1995, 27(2): 200–10.

43. C. W. Nicholas, K. Tsintzas, L. Boobis, C. Williams. Carbohydrate-electrolyte ingestion during intermittent high-intensity running. *Medicine and Science in Sports and Exercise* September 1999, 31(9): 1280–86.

44. M. J. Arkinstall, C. R. Bruce, V. Nikolopoulos, A. P. Garnham, J. A. Hawley. Effect of carbohydrate ingestion on metabolism during running and cycling. *Journal of Applied Physiology* November 2001, 91(5): 2125–34.

45. R. J. Maughan, T. D. Noakes. Fluid replacement and exercise stress: A brief review of studies on fluid replacement and some guidelines for the athlete. *Sports Medicine* July 1991, 12(1): 16–31.

46. E. F. Coyle, S. J. Montain. Benefits of fluid replacement with carbohydrate during exercise. *Medicine and Science in Sports and Exercise* September 1992, 24(9 Suppl): S324–30.

47. M. Millard-Stafford, P. B. Sparling, L. B. Rosskopf, B. T. Hinson, L. J. DiCarlo. Carbohydrate-electrolyte replacement during a simulated triathlon in the heat. *Medicine and Science in Sports and Exercise* October 1990, 22(5): 621–28.

48. D. S. Seidman, I. Ashkenazi, R. Arnon, Y. Shapiro, Y. Epstein. The effects of glucose polymer beverage ingestion during prolonged outdoor exercise in the heat. *Medicine and Science in Sports and Exercise* April 1991, 23(4): 458–62.

49. A. J. Clapp, P. A. Bishop, J. F. Smith, E. R. Mansfield. Effects of carbohydrate-electrolyte content of beverages on voluntary hydration in a simulated industrial environment. *AIHAJ: A Journal for the Science of Occupational and Environmental Health and Safety.* Sept–Oct 2000, 61(5): 692–99.
S. D. Galloway, R. J. Maughan. The effects of substrate and fluid provision on thermoregulatory and metabolic responses to prolonged exercise in a hot environment. *Journal of Sports Science,* May 2000, 18(5): 339–51.

50. J. L. Bilzon, A. J. Allsopp, C. Williams. Short-term recovery from prolonged constant pace running in a warm environment: The effectiveness of a carbohydrate-electrolyte solution. *European Journal of Applied Physiology* July 2000, 82(4): 305–12.
S. H. Wong, C. Williams, N. Adams. Effects of ingesting a large volume of carbohydrate-electrolyte solution on rehydration during recovery and subsequent exercise capacity. *International Journal of Sport Nutrition and Exercise Metabolism* December 2000, 10(4): 375–93.

51. S. C. Dennis, T. D. Noakes, J. A. Hawley. Nutritional strategies to minimize fatigue during prolonged exercise: Fluid, electrolyte, and energy replacement. *Journal of Sports Sciences,* June 1997, 15(3): 305–13.
American College of Sports Medicine. Position stand on exercise and fluid replacement. *Medicine and Science in Sports and Exercise* 1996, 28(1): 1–7.

52. J. M. Davis, W. A. Burgess, C. A. Slentz, W. P. Bartoli. Fluid availability of sports drinks differing in carbohydrate type and concentration. *American Journal of Clinical Nutrition* June 1990, 51(6): 1054–57.

53. R. J. Maughan, J. B. Leiper. Limitations to fluid replacement during exercise. *Canadian Journal of Applied Physiology* April 1999, 24(2): 173–87.

54. N. J. Rehrer, F. Brouns, E. J. Beckers, F. ten Hoor, W. H. Saris. Gastric emptying with repeated drinking during running and bicycling. *International Journal of Sports Medicine* June 1990, 11(3): 238–43.

55. M. R. Minehan, M. D. Riley, L. M. Burke. Effect of flavor and awareness of kilojoule content of drinks on preference and fluid balance in team sports. *International Journal of Sport Nutrition and Exercise Metabolism* March 2002, 12(1): 81–92.

56. D. H. Passe, M. Horn, R. Murray. Impact of beverage acceptability on fluid intake during exercise. *Appetite* December 2000, 35(3): 219–29.

57. L. M. Burke, R. S. Read. Dietary supplements in sport. *Sports Medicine* January 1993, 15(1): 43–65.

58. W. L. Kenney, P. Chiu. Influence of age on thirst and fluid intake. *Medicine and Science in Sports and Exercise* September 2001, 33(9): 1524–32.

59. P. B. Sparling, D. C. Nieman, P. J. O'Connor. Selected scientific aspects of marathon racing: An update on fluid replacement, immune function, psychological factors, and the gender difference. *Sports Medicine* February 1993, 15(2): 116–32. T. D.
Noakes. Fluid replacement during exercise. *Exercise and Sport Sciences Reviews* 1993, 21: 297–330.

60. E. M. Kovacs, R. M. Schmahl, J. M. Senden, F. Brouns. Effect of high and low rates of fluid intake on post-exercise rehydration. *International Journal of Sport Nutrition and Exercise Metabolism* March 2002, 12(1): 14–23.

EXERCISE ENDOCRINOLOGY

FOR MAXIMAL RECOVERY AND PERFORMANCE

Successful athletes realize that training hard is the key to improved performance. Of equal importance is recovery. Intense training without adequate recovery will lead to overtraining. Recovery without intensity will still confer the positive effects of training as discussed in Chapter 1.

Of the many hormones in the human body, two have received much attention as performance-enhancing supplements: growth hormone and testosterone. Athletes have touted both of these hormones for promoting lean muscle mass, decreasing body fat, and increasing recovery through muscle building and repair.

The illegal use of these hormones has increased because their alleged performance-enhancing qualities appeal to athletes seeking an edge in competition. Taking growth hormone and testosterone supplements is unethical and shows no performance-enhancing effect.[1] Nevertheless, natural secretion of them can be maximized through careful diet and training modifications, resulting in improved strength, recovery, and performance.

GROWTH HORMONE

Human growth hormone (HGH) is secreted by the anterior pituitary gland at the base of the brain. The hormone is released in a pulsatile manner in response to exercise, stress, sleep, and diet. Maximal release of HGH normally occurs during the slow-wave stages of sleep, stages three and four, with other pulses coming at several-hour intervals during the day. The largest pulse of HGH is the first release during sleep. HGH affects muscle and bone as well as fat metabolism. Natural secretion of HGH is responsible for the growth and development of bone, cartilage, tendons, and ligaments. This quality is important, but it is how HGH can improve performance and muscle and, more important, how it can help recovery that should guide training.

The effect of HGH on the muscle is anabolic. The hormone increases the transport of amino acids into the muscle cells, and this enhanced concentration leads to an increase in the size and number of muscle fibers. After exercise-induced secretion of HGH, recovery is aided as muscles are repaired and new muscle is synthesized.

In addition, HGH enhances fat catabolism, resulting in increased free fatty acids for use as an energy source. The increased use of fat as a fuel supply preserves muscle and glycogen.

GROWTH HORMONE PHYSIOLOGY

Secretion of HGH from the anterior pituitary is controlled by a hormone that governs release of HGH (known as growth hormone releasing hormone). Once HGH is in the bloodstream, it is bound to a protein (GH-binding protein) and transported to the growth hormone receptor. Growth hormone, in turn, releases insulin-like growth factor (IGF-1), which exerts its effects on muscle.

Release of growth hormone is prevented by a mechanism called negative feedback. Once the levels of IGF-1 are increased, a signal is sent to the pituitary to stop producing HGH. Other hormones also exert negative feedback on HGH, including insulin and the regulatory hormone somatostatin.

GROWTH HORMONE AND EXERCISE

The anabolic effects of growth hormone at first do not seem to contribute to improved endurance exercise. However, the influence on lipolysis results in increased free fatty acids, which provide a virtually inexhaustible source of fuel for exercise. Furthermore, the exercise-induced release of growth hormone can have effects up to four hours after exercise stops, which will increase recovery by allowing muscles to repair themselves through the anabolic effects.

The secretion of HGH depends upon the type and intensity of exercise. Aerobic and anaerobic exercise affect HGH release differently. The threshold for release of growth hormone during exercise is at 30 percent of VO_2max, but release increases substantially with exercise intensity, especially with anaerobic exercise.[2] These features enable athletes to tailor training plans to maximize recovery through modulation of HGH release. Other factors that have an influence on HGH release are listed in Table 6.1 and Table 6.2.

Table 6.1
FACTORS INCREASING GROWTH HORMONE SECRETION
Increased intensity
Previous exercise
Aerobic fitness
Training at or above lactate threshold
Estrogen
Luteal phase of menstrual cycle
Protein after exercise
Circulating amino acids

Table 6.2
FACTORS DECREASING GROWTH HORMONE SECRETION
Increased body fat
High-fat diet
Insulin
Somatostatin

The types of exercise—endurance, anaerobic, resistance—and their effect on secretion of HGH are described in the next sections.

Endurance exercise

Prolonged endurance aerobic exercise has been shown either to have no effect on or to decrease the exercise-induced release of HGH. However, three thirty-minute intervals of steady-state aerobic training separated by one hour will increase growth hormone secretion after exercise.[3]

Exercise affects the increased release in growth hormone at two stages. The first occurs within ten minutes of exercise onset and lasts for the duration of exercise. The second effect is during nighttime release. Because the nocturnal secretion provides the body with the majority of growth hormone, it is equated with the twenty-four-hour HGH release.

Prolonged endurance training lasting 2.5 to 4.5 hours blunts the HGH spike that occurs immediately following sleep onset, but it can increase the production of HGH release in the second half of sleep.[4] This factor significantly diminishes the restorative property of sleep during the time when catabolic hormones (cortisol) are at their lowest.

After two weeks of training, the basal levels of HGH and IGF-1 in one study were increased by 37 percent.[5] However, another study found that after three weeks of endurance exercise, there was a decrease in the exercise-induced release of HGH.[6]

Gender also plays a role in the release of HGH. Women training at or above their lactate threshold will have increased secretion of HGH during and up to one hour after exercise but will not have a significant change in the twenty-four-hour secretion compared with a sedentary day. For men, training will increase growth hormone secretion by 82 percent. This highlights the importance of immediate post-exercise ingestion of protein for use by the circulating growth hormone.

Anaerobic exercise

Although it is generally believed that anaerobic exercise (exercise above the lactate threshold) and lactic acid will increase the exercise-induced release of growth hormone, research on interval sessions has produced conflicting results. Three ten-minute intervals of exercise above lactate threshold separated by one hour of recovery decreases the post-exercise rise in HGH. One theory that explains the drop is a decrease of HGH receptors with continuous exposure to HGH. With constant exposure, the receptors sense that there is too much hormone, so they regulate the effects of HGH by decreasing the number of receptors to which the hormone can bind. Perhaps a shorter interval or less recovery time would not result in the same negative trend.

Running at or above the lactate threshold three days a week increases the release of HGH, increases fat-free mass, and decreases percentage of body fat.[7]

Resistance exercise

Resistance exercise typically employs a short, intense effort that is similar in energy utilization to anaerobic exercise. Lifting protocols in the muscle hypertrophy phase, which include high repetitions and short rest periods, rely upon the anaerobic system and maximize the HGH response. For women, this type of exercise is needed to produce any HGH response at all to resistance training.

The production of lactate during anaerobic and resistance training is thought to stimulate HGH release during exercise.[8] However, the twenty-four-hour HGH levels do not change with exercise.

OTHER CONSIDERATIONS

Frequent, short aerobic rides and anaerobic training will increase HGH release, but these effects can be hampered or enhanced depending upon other lifestyle factors.

Certain dietary manipulations can enhance the release of HGH. A high-fat meal forty-five minutes before high-intensity exercise will decrease release of HGH by 54 percent compared with a noncaloric meal. Clearly, high-fat pretraining meals should be avoided. This may be due to the HGH release of fatty acids. If dietary fatty acids are already present in the circulation, HGH is not needed to release them and the growth hormone release will be blunted.

However, high-fat diets consumed for the ninety-six hours prior to an extended exercise session increased the release of HGH during exercise. This finding is perhaps related to a decrease in concentration of glucose, which can regulate the HGH response to exercise. Similarly, insulin decreases the HGH release. A high-carbohydrate meal before bed will lessen the spike of HGH that occurs just after sleep onset. For the anabolic effects of HGH to be maximally effective, the release should occur when the catabolic effects of cortisol are at a low. Cortisol release is low during the late night but increases with intense or exhausting exercise. A glucose load before sleep will increase insulin and decrease HGH release, which will decrease the anabolic activity during sleep. To maximize recovery following intense exercise, avoid high-fat, high-carbohydrate foods within three hours of sleep. Limiting caloric intake while maintaining a high percentage of carbohydrate will allow for continued exercise and training and enhance the exercise response of growth hormone.[9]

The dietary manipulations further stress the need for fat metabolism during exercise. If weight loss or improving endurance is a goal, focus on two workouts to improve HGH secretion.

Lipolysis training serves the purpose of increasing the enzymes responsible for metabolizing fat. Exercise should be performed after a prolonged fast, preferably in the morning. The research indicates that thirteen hours of fasting is sufficient;[10] at this time, the glucose and insulin levels are low, and previous dietary fat will not affect HGH release. Your exercise should be below the anaerobic threshold and should last no longer than one hour. Afterward, consume a glucose and protein meal to replace glycogen and provide amino acids for the anabolism of growth hormone.

Anaerobic training above the lactate threshold also increases release of growth hormone. Intervals should be less than 10 minutes and greater than 1.5 minutes to stimulate exercise-induced growth hormone. To capitalize on the hormonal response, consume a carbohydrate and protein meal immediately following exercise.

TESTOSTERONE

Testosterone is the hormone responsible for increased muscle mass (anabolic) as well as male sex characteristics (androgenic). The secretion of testosterone follows a cascade of hormones that starts in the hypothalamus. The hypothalamus secretes gonadotropin releasing hormone, which stimulates the pituitary to secrete luteinizing hormone (LH). In men, LH acts on the testicles to produce testosterone. Although the range of effects on the body is broad, the influence of testosterone on muscle accounts for the usefulness for exercise. Testosterone acts on the muscle to increase nitrogen retention, lean body mass, and fat-free body weight. Testosterone builds strength in a dose-dependent manner: As testosterone levels increase, so does strength. The effect is due to the increased size of muscle.[11] Androgens do not appear to affect endurance or aerobic capacity, but they can have a major effect on strength when combined with intense exercise and a high-protein diet.[12] The use of testosterone supplements is fraught with health risks, yet some athletes praise the androgenic and anabolic effects of testosterone and call it a "wonder drug."[13] Nevertheless, learning to build strength while causing the body to naturally secrete testosterone will lead to better training and strength gains.

MAXIMIZING TESTOSTERONE

Finding the right type of exercise to maximize testosterone secretion is more difficult than manipulating growth hormone. The main reason is that athletes with different levels of training respond differently to exercise. Research has shown that experienced athletes have a decreased testosterone response to the same exercise that increases testosterone in less-trained athletes.[14] In this study, the exercise impulse was brief (400-meter run) and was not as important as the level of experience. The athletes with eight years of training had a decreased testosterone response compared with those who had been racing for four years.

Another workout that has been effective in increasing testosterone levels is a 20-second exercise burst at maximum intensity followed by 100 seconds of recovery repeated until exhaustion (on average eight cycles will be completed). After five weeks of high-intensity training, testosterone levels were increased with this workout.[15]

Whereas altitude training increases the production of red blood cells that will certainly benefit performance, training below sea level increases testosterone levels.[16] It is believed that the increase in barometric pressure may be responsible for this change. Training at low altitude, or at least doing power workouts when there is a high barometric pressure, may be useful for strength gains.

Resistance training also affects testosterone levels. Lifting at the three-repetition maximum (3-RM) for squats and front squats and at the six-repetition maximum (6-RM) for leg extensions induces a higher exercise-induced testosterone release than the same exercises at 70 percent of resistance.[17] Exercise at this intensity will develop strength and short-term (i.e., sprinting) power. It is important to note that resistance training in younger athletes (age fifteen) will induce a significantly smaller increase in testosterone.[18]

Testosterone pitfalls

Insufficient recovery and repeated endurance exercise decrease testosterone levels.[19] Exercise stress suppresses the secretion of LH and testosterone.[20] This is illustrated by a study of testosterone levels during the three-week Tour of Spain bicycle race. After three weeks of daily racing, the athletes' testosterone levels were decreased.[21] One theory is that prolonged exercise causes the pituitary to reset its levels, resulting in decreased (or sometimes increased) secretion.[22]

Women can benefit from the natural secretion of testosterone as well. Increased secretion is observed immediately following exercise, but testosterone returns to pre-exercise levels within ninety minutes,[23] limiting the recovery window for post-exercise protein ingestion.

Training recommendations

Growth hormone maximizes recovery and is useful for all athletes. Those who prefer that an event will be determined in a sprint should aim to optimize testosterone secretion. Manipulating training and diet to achieve maximal body adaptation to exercise can give the careful athlete the competitive edge he or she seeks.

- Endurance training should not exceed two to three weeks at a time. Steady-state riding in the aerobic zone should also be less than 2.5 hours at a time.
- Multisport athletes tend to favor dual sessions of exercise in a single day. If this is your workout schedule, make recovery and HGH secretion a priority. The key to dual sessions is to keep intensity low and to maintain a heart rate below the lactate threshold.
- Women should capitalize on the one-hour increase in HGH by ingesting protein and carbohydrate to facilitate anabolism immediately following exercise.
- If you must eat before bed, avoid fat and carbohydrate. Choose high-protein or low-calorie snacks.
- One-minute intense intervals of exercise may benefit the less experienced athlete with testosterone-induced gains in strength.
- Trained athletes achieved increased testosterone levels with 20 seconds of exercise at maximum intensity followed by 100 seconds of recovery. These intervals should be repeated to exhaustion.

NOTES

1. C. A. Bradley, T. M. Sodeman. Human Growth Hormone; its use and abuse. *Clinics in Laboratory Medicine* September 1990, 10(3): 473–77.

H. Dean. Does exogenous growth hormone improve athletic performance? *Clinical Journal of Sport Medicine* July 2002, 12(4): 250–53.

2. P. J. Jenkins. Growth hormone and exercise. *Clinical Endocrinology* 1999, 50: 683–89.

3. J. A. Kanaley, J. Y. Weltman, A. D. Rogol, M. L. Hartman, A. Weltman. Growth hormone response to repeated bouts of aerobic exercise. *Medicine and Science in Sports and Exercise* 1996, 28: S25.

4. W. Kern, B. Perras, R. Wodick, H. L. Fehm, J. Born. Hormonal secretion during nighttime sleep indicating stress of daytime exercise. *Journal of Applied Physiology* 1995, 79: 1461–68.

5. C. A. Roelen, W. R. de Vries, H. P. Koppeschaar, C. Vervoorn, J. H. Thijssen, M. A. Blankenstein. Plasma insulin-like growth factor–1 and high affinity growth hormone-binding protein levels increase after two weeks of strenuous physical training. *International Journal of Sports Medicine* 1997, 18: 238–41.

6. J. N. Roemmich, A. D. Rogol. Exercise and growth hormone: Does one affect the other? *Journal of Pediatrics* 1997, 131: 1(part 2): S75–S80.

7. A. Weltman, J. Y. Weltman, R. Schurrer, W. S. Evans, J. D. Veldhuis, A. D. Rogol. Endurance training amplifies the pulsatile release of growth hormone: Effects of training intensity. *Journal of Applied Physiology* 1992, 72: 188–96.

8. S. E. Gordon, W. J. Kraemer, N. H. Vos, J. M. Lynch, H. G. Knuttgen. Effect of acid-base balance on the growth hormone response to acute high-intensity cycle exercise. *Journal of Applied Physiology* 1994, 76: 821–29.

9. R. G. McMurray, C. R. Proctor, W. L. Wilson. Effect of caloric deficit and dietary manipulation on aerobic and anaerobic exercise. *International Journal of Sports Medicine* April 1991, 12(2): 167–72.

10. L. Wideman, J. Weltman, A. A. Carmines, M. L. Hartman, A. Weltman. Effect of diet on exercise-induced growth hormone release (abstract). *Medicine and Science in Sports and Exercise* 1995, 27: 1057–62.

11. M. Sheffield-Moore. Androgens and the control of skeletal muscle protein synthesis. *Annals of Medicine* April 2000, 32(3):181–86.

12. C. J. Bagatell, W. J. Bremmer. Androgens in men-uses and abuses. *New England Journal of Medicine* March 1996, 334(11): 707–15.
S. Bhasin, L. Woodhouse, T. W. Storer. Proof of the effect of testosterone on skeletal muscle. *Journal of Endocrinology* July 2001, 170(1): 27–38.

13. A. B. Corrigan. Dehydroepiandrosterone and sport. *The Medical Journal of Australia* August 1999, 171(4): 206–8

14. M. Slowinska-Lisowska, J. Majda. Hormone plasma levels from pituitary-gonadal axis in performance athletes after the 400 m run. *Journal of Sports Medicine and Physical Fitness* June 2002, 42(2): 243–49.

15. H. Pitkanen, A. Mero, S. S. Oja, P. V. Komi, H. Rusko, A. Nummela, P. Saransaari, T. Takala. Effects of training on the exercise-induced changes in serum amino acids and hormones. *Journal of Strength and Conditioning Research* August 2002, 16(3): 390–98.

16. I. Bani Hani, F. El-Migdadi, A. Shotar, R. Abudheese, N. Bashir. Stress from exercise in the below sea level environment causes an increase in serum testosterone levels in trained athletes. *Endocrine Research* Feb–May 2001, 27(1–2): 19–23.

17. T. Raastad, T. Bjoro, J. Hallen. Hormonal responses to high- and moderate-intensity strength exercise. *European Journal of Applied Physiology* May 2000, 82(1–2): 121–28.

18. T. Pullinen, A. Mero, E. MacDonald, A. Pakarinen, P. V. Komi. Plasma catecholamine and serum testosterone responses to four units of resistance exercise in young and adult male athletes. *European Journal of Applied Physiology and Occupational Physiology* April 1998, 77(5): 413–20.

19. O. Ronsen, E. Haug, B. K. Pedersen, R. Bahr. Increased neuroendocrine response to a repeated bout of endurance exercise. *Medicine and Science in Sports and Exercise* April 2001, 33(4): 568–75.

20. L. Di Luigi, L. Guidetti, C. Baldari, A. Fabbri, C. Moretti, F. Romanelli. Physical stress and qualitative gonadotropin secretion: LH biological activity at rest and after exercise in trained and untrained men. *International Journal of Sports Medicine* July 2002, 23(5): 307–12.

21. A. Lucia, B. Diaz, J. Hoyos, C. Fernandez, G. Villa, F. Bandres, J. L. Chicharro. Hormone levels of world class cyclists during the Tour of Spain stage race. *British Journal of Sports Medicine* December 2001, 35(6): 424–30.

22. A. M. Viru, A. C. Hackney, E. Valja, K. Karelson, T. Janson, M. Viru. Influence of prolonged continuous exercise on hormone responses to subsequent exercise in humans. *European Journal of Applied Physiology* October 2001, 85(6): 578–85.

23. A. Kochanska-Dziurowicz, V. Gawel-Szostek, T. Gabrys, D. Kmita. Changes in prolactin and testosterone levels induced by acute physical exertion in young female athletes. *Fiziologia Cheloveka* May–June 2001, 27(3): 100–103.

SMARTER TRAINING FOR
INJURY PREVENTION

TRAINING PRINCIPLES

The most important aspect of injury prevention is proper training. There are many books devoted to developing a training plan, and this chapter does not attempt to replace them. Rather, I describe here several principles for you to follow to create an effective training plan that will get you through the season without injury. Adhering to these principles will help prevent overtraining and enable you to reach increased intensity without sustaining injury.

For training to progress with improvement in fitness, you must overload different systems. These systems can be energy systems (e.g., aerobic, anaerobic), strength, or power. Two elements of the training program can be overloaded: volume and intensity. Volume can be subdivided into frequency and repetition. Volume is the amount of time spent in an activity; frequency is the number of efforts followed by recovery. Repetition refers to the number of efforts in a set. Intensity is the difficulty of each session. A session is the period of exercise followed by recovery.

To increase volume, more time must be spent doing the activity. When volume is being overloaded, intensity must be less. Intensity can be increased either by increasing the effort in each session or by decreasing recovery time between efforts. Skill development, like fitness, should be pushed as well. Overload should occur in only one element at a time. Increasing more than one element at a time can lead to overtraining and injury.

The principle of specificity states that training must be specific to the sport for which the athlete is training. Cyclists train on the bike, runners train on the road, and so on. Although crosstraining helps to maintain freshness, competition without proper training is a recipe for disaster.

If proper training plans are followed, the body will respond with adaptation to become more efficient. In order to adapt, you must follow the concept of progression in training. A progressive training program will move through weeks with increasing volume/intensity, with each element changing in a manner consistent with improvement. The rule of thumb is to increase volume or intensity by no more than 10 percent a week.

Workouts should be continued to build and maintain fitness. Otherwise, loss of fitness—known as reversibility—will start to occur after seven to ten days of inactivity, but changes might not be felt for up to three weeks.[1] The amount of fitness lost is variable, but depends upon the level of fitness you have achieved. Although this principle implies you should stay active year-round, you should still have a rest period after every three to five weeks. A rest period taken after several weeks of heavy exercise (either in volume or intensity) will not result in a loss of fitness but instead will give you the benefits of overreaching by allowing your body to recover and become stronger.

If injury does occur, it should be treated with care. The loss of fitness through reversibility will be much greater if an injury is ignored and becomes worse than if it is caught at an early stage and damage is minimized.

THE PHASES

"He's moving!"

The punch line of a joke is not nearly as funny when it stands alone as when it follows a well-told joke that is properly delivered. Much as you wouldn't tell a joke by blurting out only the punch line, you shouldn't train without a properly built training schedule.

To tell a joke well, you start by setting the stage for the joke to come. *A cyclist, a runner, and a triathlete are having a conversation....* Similarly, in a training plan, you start by establishing a base of fitness. This base can initially come from crosstraining but should include sufficient training time in your primary sport. The base is usually at a low to moderate level of effort. I recommend adequate training time so that you can exercise for a period of time that is equal to the length of competition. For a professional cyclist, this might be six hours at a time. For a fun runner, this might be forty minutes. This part of the plan will develop endurance and will overload the aerobic system.

After the base is established, you are ready to progress through the training plan by moving into more specialized areas of fitness, such as sprinting, hill climbing, or further endurance. Specialized training can be more exhausting than the comparatively easy base training. As the intensity of the training escalates, the volume both in hours and miles must decrease. This part of the training program is the body of the joke:

The three athletes are discussing what they would like people to say about them at their funerals. The runner says, "I want people to look at me and remember my commitment to serious training." The triathlete says, "I want people to say he was a great athlete and beat his PR every year in the Ironman." The cyclists thinks carefully and says, "I want people to look at me and say, 'He's moving!'"

By giving the punch line at the start of this chapter, I ruined the way the joke unfolds later. The same principle holds true for starting a training program with the workouts that should be prepared for later in the season.

As the racing season approaches, the intensity of competition increases and volume decreases further. This competition period will bring the pinnacle of effort and fitness you have been building toward over the previous weeks and months. You can maintain this high level of fitness for approximately six weeks before you will need to rest and repeat the specialized training. When you repeat specialized training in the same season, your workouts can be harder than they were the first time around. In between blocks of specialization, however, you should plan for some rest. Rest and recovery will make the competition season seem less hectic and extended.

STRETCHING

For endurance athletes, the most important fitness factor is endurance capacity. There are three components to fitness that will not only enhance performance but prevent injury as well. Building endurance capacity through a periodized training program using the principles of progression previously outlined is the first step toward injury-free fitness. The second step is incorporating stretching into the training program.

When treating overuse injuries, I frequently put athletes on stretching programs. Through chronic strength building and endurance use, the muscles become less flexible. The tighter a muscle becomes, the more it can pull the body in a particular direction. An example of this is the hamstrings, the strongest muscles in the body for their size. As they tighten up and lose flexibility, they can pull on the lower back muscles and compress the vertebral column, causing back problems. A thorough stretching program can prevent difficulties later.

Stretching before exercise has not been shown useful for injury prevention.[2] However, that does not mean stretching should be ignored in the training program. Flexibility has been shown to decrease injury[3] and is even a predictor of who will be injured.[4] Increased flexibility means there is decreased muscular tension, which results in greater range of motion. This factor can result in an increased stride length. Although earlier research on stretching and running economy suggested that flexibility was detrimental to running, recent studies have disproved this theory.[5] For a fixed-position sport such as cycling, where the same arcs are carved out, an increased range of motion may not at first seem important, but it enables the rider to set a slightly higher or further set-back saddle position and thus deliver more power to the pedals. Although flexibility clearly is important in maintaining an injury-free season, the significant factors are the timing, type, and duration of stretching.

Increasing flexibility should be worked on after exercise has been begun and completed. Stretching daily over as little as six to ten weeks will increase muscle flexibility.[6] Although stretching as part of a warm-up will increase flexibility, temperature has a positive effect on the ability to stretch. After a workout, your muscles are warmer and you can make greater gains in flexibility.[7] Once a workout has begun or when there is a break between competition events, stretching has been found to decrease injury.[8]

The benefits of flexibility are clear; how to achieve flexibility is the question. There are several different ways to stretch. The most commonly used method is the static stretch. Assuming a stretching pose and holding that position without further movement is the static stretch. Ballistic stretching, which incorporates bouncing into the pose, is the second most common. This type of stretching is actually dangerous. As the muscles are stretched rapidly, they respond by contracting, resulting in tears to the muscles.

Proprioceptive neuromuscular facilitation (PNF) is a type of stretching that improves flexibility by stimulation of the nerves and muscles internally by using the stretch receptors in the muscles to give an enhanced muscle relaxation. This is accomplished by having the muscle contracted prior to stretching. The muscle is then passively stretched with the assistance of a partner, while the antagonist muscle is contracted. An example of PNF for hamstring stretch would start by having the athlete sit on the ground with the legs extended in front of her. The athlete leans forward until a stretch is felt in the hamstrings, the trainer applies pressure to help the stretch, and the athlete contracts the hamstrings, pushing the legs into the ground for eight seconds. Once the contraction is released, the athlete stretches to a new point of limitation while the partner applies pressure to the back, assisting the stretch (see Photo 7.1).

Several studies involving the PNF stretch produced greater increases in joint range of motion but failed to produce significant flexibility benefits.[9] The simplest method, static stretching, is the recommended method of stretching and the one on which most of the research has focused. Static stretching is the basic "stretch and hold" in which the athlete assumes a position and holds it for a specified time.

7.1 PNF stretch for hamstring

The length of time to hold a stretch is another topic of research that has led to different recommendations. A period as short as ten seconds has been found to increase flexibility in sedentary women.[10] Another study found that thirty seconds was the time needed to increase flexibility. Stretching more than thirty seconds did not provide any increased benefit.[11]

One reason the research has yielded varied results is that different muscles need different times to achieve a stretch. Some muscles in the body are obviously stronger and thicker than others. Muscles respond to stretching not as elastic (which immediately returns to its original length) or plastic (which never returns to its original length) but as a viscoelastic substance. Like the stretch toys we had as children, our muscles will slowly return to their original length. The time component of a stretching muscle is the key to understanding the variable times needed for stretching different muscles. If a muscle is stretched with a continuous force, it will continue to lengthen over time. Similarly, if a muscle is held at a set length, the force needed to keep it at that length eventually would decrease. A stiffer, more contracted muscle will need more force or more time to maintain the stretch.

When stretching, there is an initial pain response that causes tightening of the muscles. With time, the pain response decreases and the stretch can be increased. Being aware of this reflex is the best way to approach stretching. A stretch should be held, maintained, and increased as the muscle relaxes. This should be continued for thirty seconds or until there can be no further increases. The result will be increased stretch tolerance and flexibility.

STRENGTH

The third addition to the training program is the addition of strength (resistance) training. Although the image of endurance athletes is the opposite of power lifters, strength training prepares the body for the rigors of hill training and interval sessions. Working strength training into the training plan for endurance athletes can be tricky, but several months of weight training can take you a long way during the competitive season. Not only will you notice performance benefits, but weight training also can keep you competing longer and without injury.

Frequently, sport-specific training will develop certain muscles preferentially to others. For example, a cyclist might have well-developed quadriceps and gluteus muscles but relatively weaker hamstrings. Strength training will help to bring opposing muscles into uniform strength. Equalizing the muscle strength can decrease the risk of injury.[12]

Sport-specific and general strengthening should be part of the training program. Strength training should be done as a progressive, periodized training plan. Weight training should follow a several-month progression: one or two months of foundation strength of lower weight and high repetitions; a second month of strength building during which the weight is increased and the number of repetitions is decreased; and a third month for power development when the weight and repetitions are decreased but the weight is moved at high speed.

Weight gains should be made before attempting any changes in the primary sport. Before doing hill repeats, you should complete the strength phase; similarly, you should finish the power phase before doing sprint training.

WARM-UP

It is not a coincidence that the majority of track and field records are set late in the afternoon. Human athletic performance differs between morning and evening.[13] One theory is that this difference (which occurs not only in performance but also in perceived exertion) is due to the changes throughout the day in core body temperature. Higher body temperature raises the muscles to a temperature at which they can best function. Additionally, warmer muscles become more flexible as muscle viscosity decreases, which in turn will yield an increased range of motion, the benefits of which were previously discussed.

There are three types of warm-ups. Passive warm-up increases muscle temperature by external means such as heat lamps or blankets. General warm-up increases temperature by nonspecific body movements (an example is the speed skater who runs before competition). Specific warm-up uses activity-specific movements to increase temperature. Unless there is a risk of injury from doing an activity without a warm-up, specific warm-up is probably the best option because it not only increases temperature but also allows the neurons and muscles to rehearse the activity to come, leading to increased speed of nerve impulses.[14]

Numerous studies have shown that a warm-up period will increase maximal aerobic and anaerobic performance. Nevertheless, the research has been contradictory because of the different types of warm-up and the different types of exercise tested.

For muscles to function optimally, they must contain some lactic acid[15] to lower the pH so that oxygen metabolism is improved. A warm-up not only will warm the muscles but should produce a slight decrease in the pH. This slightly acidic environment allows improved oxygen delivery to the muscles by allowing the red blood cells to unload oxygen more freely at the muscles. If the warm-up is too intense, however, the muscles will not contract optimally.

Warm-ups can even prevent complications resulting from exercise-induced asthma. Intense intervals performed during a warm-up will make the lungs resistant to further changes from exercise-induced asthma during that workout.[16]

The type of warm-up to undertake depends upon the type of exercise you are about to perform (Sidebar 7.1). For an aerobic or anaerobic interval lasting two minutes, a fifteen-minute warm-up has been effective halfway between the aerobic and anaerobic thresholds.[17] During a maximal sprint, the body uses the phosphocreatine system for fuel. A mild warm-up has been shown to inhibit the development of further muscle acidosis in a four-minute maximal test; further, there was no decrease in the amount of available phosphate for use as energy.[18] For aerobic performance to exhaustion, there was a significant increase in time to anaerobic fatigue following a fifteen-minute warm-up below the lactate threshold but above the aerobic threshold.[19] In the same study, joint range of motion did not increase with the warm-up, despite the increase in body temperature. This same warm-up can also keep exercise-induced asthma at bay.[20] A warm-up lasting less than twenty-five minutes and at a moderate intensity was also found to increase respiratory function.[21]

Sidebar 7.1

RECOMMENDED WARM-UP FOR DIFFERENT EVENTS

A fifteen-minute warm-up between the aerobic and lactate thresholds will be sufficient for most activities lasting between two minutes and several hours.

A light aerobic warm-up was not different from a high-intensity interval warm-up for high-intensity performance, probably because the intense warm-up was performed until exhaustion.[22] When you warm up at or above the lactate threshold, there is a depletion of muscle glycogen that limits anaerobic performance.[23]

Because even a long event can start fast, the athlete should be properly warmed up before beginning. There is general consensus that a warm-up should be of moderate intensity in the aerobic training zone.[24] This warm-up has resulted in increased muscle oxygen consumption and decreased lactate production in the muscle.[25] Research on the need to warm up has focused only on short, intense exercise, but certainly all training sessions should start with a fifteen-minute period in heart rate zones two and three.

PROTECTIVE GEAR

Endurance sports are velocity sports. When speed is involved, injury from falling is a reality. To decrease the risk of injury, sport-specific protective gear should always be used. This includes eyewear to limit the damage from foreign bodies lodging in the eyes and causing additional falls.

Numerous studies have validated the use of helmets. Also, consider skin protection if you have a habit of crashing on the same side. Soccer shin guards can be useful to protect one particular side of the body if you have a tendency to land on that side, especially with in-line skating or mountain biking.

NOTES

1. G. J. Rietjens, H. A. Keizer, H. Kuipers, W. H. Saris. A reduction in training volume and intensity for 21 days does not impair performance in cyclists. *British Journal of Sports Medicine* December 2001, 35(6): 431–34.

2. R. P. Pope, R. D. Herbert, J. D. Kirwan, B. J. Graham. A randomized trial of preexercise stretching for prevention of lower-limb injury. *Medicine and Science in Sports and Exercise* February 2000, 32(2): 271–77.
I. Shrier. Stretching before exercise does not reduce the risk of local muscle injury: A critical review of the clinical and basic science literature. *Clinical Journal of Sport Medicine* October 1999, 9(4): 221–27.
W. van Mechelen, H. Hlobil, H. C. Kemper, W. J. Voorn, H. R. de Jongh. Prevention of running injuries by warm-up, cool-down, and stretching exercises. *American Journal of Sports Medicine* Sept–Oct 1993, 21(5): 711–19.

3. P. Tabrizi, W. M. McIntyre, M. B. Quesnel, A. W. Howard. Limited dorsiflexion predisposes to injuries of the ankle in children. *Journal of Bone Joint Surgery, British volume* November 2000, 82(8): 1103–6.

4. D. E. Hartig, J. M. Henderson. Increasing hamstring flexibility decreases lower extremity overuse injuries in military basic trainees. *American Journal of Sports Medicine* Mar–Apr 1999, 27(2): 173–76.
S. Jonhagen, G. Nemeth, E. Eriksson. Hamstring injuries in sprinters: The role of concentric and eccentric hamstring muscle strength and flexibility. *American Journal of Sports Medicine* Mar–Apr 1994, 22(2): 262–66.

5. Jonhagen et al. Hamstring injuries in sprinters.

6. W. D. Bandy, J. M. Irion. The effect of time on static stretch on the flexibility of the hamstring muscles. *Physical Therapy* 1994, 74(9): 845–52.
A. G. Nelson, J. Kokkonen, C. Eldredge, A. Cornwell, E. Glickman-Weiss. Chronic stretching and running economy. *Scandinavian Journal of Medicine and Science in Sports* October 2001, 11(5): 260–65.

7. P. J. McNair, S. N. Stanley. Effect of passive stretching and jogging on the series elastic muscle stiffness and range of motion of the ankle joint. *British Journal of Sports Medicine* 1996, 30(4): 313–18.

8. B. Bixler, R. L. Jones. High-school football injuries: Effects of a post-halftime warm-up and stretching routine. *Family Practice Research Journal* June 1992, 12(2): 131–39.

9. I. Shrier, K. Gossal. Myths and truths of stretching: Individualized recommendations for healthy muscles. *Physician and Sportsmedicine* August 2000, 28(8): 57–63.

10. J. Borms, P. Van Roy, J. P. Santens, A. Haentjens. Optimal duration of static stretching exercises for improvement of coxo-femoral flexibility. *Journal of Sports Sciences* Spring 1987, 5(1): 39–47.

11. W. D. Bandy, J. M. Irion, M. Briggler. The effect of time and frequency of static stretching on flexibility of the hamstring muscles. *Physical Therapy* October 1997, 77(10): 1090–96.

12. T. F. Tyler, S. J. Nicholas, R. J. Campbell, M. P. McHugh. The association of hip strength and flexibility with the incidence of adductor muscle strains in professional ice hockey players. *American Journal of Sports Medicine* Mar–Apr 2001, 29(2): 124–28.

13. L. Martin, A. L. Doggart, G. P. Whyte. Comparison of physiological responses to morning and evening submaximal running. *Journal of Sports Sciences* December 2001, 19(12): 969–76.

14. F. G. Shellock, W. E. Prentice. Warming-up and stretching for improved physical performance and prevention of sports-related injuries. *Sports Medicine* July–Aug 1985, 2(4): 267–78.

15. D. Bishop, D. Bonetti, B. Dawson. The effect of three different warm-up intensities on kayak ergometer performance. *Medicine and Science in Sports and Exercise* June 2001, 33(6): 1026–32.

16. C. de Bisschop, H. Guenard, P. Desnot, J. Vergeret. Reduction of exercise-induced asthma in children by short, repeated warm-ups. *British Journal of Sports Medicine* April 1999, 33(2): 100–104.
D. B. Reiff, N. B. Choudry, N. B. Pride, P. W. Ind. The effect of prolonged submaximal warm-up exercise on exercise-induced asthma. *American Review of Respiratory Disorders* February 1989, 139(2): 479–84.

17. D. Bishop, D. Bonetti, B. Dawson. The effect of three different warm-up intensities on kayak ergometer performance. *Medicine and Science in Sports and Exercise* June 2001, 33(6): 1026–32.

18. Y. Kato, T. Ikata, H. Takai, S. Takata, K. Sairyo, K. Iwanaga. Effects of specific warm-up at various intensities on energy metabolism during subsequent exercise. *The Journal of Sports Medicine and Physical Fitness* June 2000, 40(2): 126–30.

19. I. B. Stewart, G. G. Sleivert. The effect of warm-up intensity on range of motion and anaerobic performance. *Journal of Orthopedic and Sports Physical Therapy* February 1998, 27(2): 154–61.

20. D. C. McKenzie, S. L. McLuckie, D. R. Stirling. The protective effects of continuous and interval exercise in athletes with exercise-induced asthma. *Medicine and Science in Sports and Exercise* August 1994, 26(8): 951–56.

21. C. Kesavachandran, S. Shashidhar. Respiratory function during warm-up exercise in athletes. *Indian Journal of Physiological Pharmacology* April 1997, 41(2): 159–63.

22. V. L. Billat, V. Bocquet, J. Slawinski, L. Laffite, A. Demarle, P. Chassaing, J. P. Koralsztein. Effect of a prior intermittent run at VO_2max on oxygen kinetics during an all-out severe run in humans. *Journal of Sports Medicine and Physical Fitness* September 2000, 40(3): 185–94.

23. H. Genovely, B. A. Stamford. Effects of prolonged warm-up exercise above and below anaerobic threshold on maximal performance. *European Journal of Applied Physiology and Occupational Physiology* 1982, 48(3): 323–30.

24. J. A. Houmard, R. A. Johns, L. L. Smith, J. M. Wells, R. W. Kobe, S. A. McGoogan. The effect of warm-up on responses to intense exercise. *International Journal of Sports Medicine* October 1991, 12(5): 480–83.

25. R. A. Robergs, D. D. Pascoe, D. L. Costill, W. J. Fink, J. Chwalbinska-Moneta, J. A. Davis, R. Hickner. Effects of warm-up on muscle glycogenolysis during intense exercise. *Medicine and Science in Sports and Exercise* January 1991, 23(1): 37–43.
B. J. Martin, S. Robinson, D. L. Wiegman, L. H. Aulick. Effect of warm-up on metabolic responses to strenuous exercise. *Medicine and Science in Sports and Exercise* Summer 1975, 7(2): 146–49.

MEDICAL PROBLEMS

II

EXERCISE-INDUCED ASTHMA

Perhaps this situation sounds familiar: You finish a difficult race on a cool, crisp, windy day, and for the next thirty minutes you cough, wheeze, or have chest tightness. If this is a description of your post-exercise activity, you may be one of the 10 percent of cyclists to suffer from exercise-induced asthma (EIA). Even if you don't have symptoms of asthma during daily living, you may still exhibit them during exercise.

EIA can be diagnosed on clinical symptoms. Coughing, wheezing, or chest tightness following exercise are hallmarks, especially if the symptoms resolve within thirty minutes. Only one or any combination of these symptoms need be present for the diagnosis to be made.

According to surveys of the 1984[1] and 1996 U.S. Olympic teams, the cyclists—both road and mountain-bike—showed a higher incidence of EIA than other athletes.[2] By understanding the cause of EIA and its implications, you can seek treatment that is easy, safe, and effective.

PHYSIOLOGY

During a normal breath, air is inhaled through the mouth and moves down the trachea, which splits into bronchi that enter the lungs. The bronchi continue to divide and become smaller in diameter. The bronchi fork four or five times before ending in the alveoli. In the alveoli, the inhaled oxygen is absorbed into the blood for delivery to the muscles, where it is used to create energy for exercise. The symptoms of EIA occur in the smaller bronchi.

PATHOLOGY

When you are at rest, your nose does a good job of filtering the air you breathe as well as providing warmth and moisture. During exercise, however, 90 percent of the inhaled air passes through the mouth and must gain warmth and moisture from the respiratory tract, where it absorbs heat and water vapor. As the ambient air gets colder and drier, successively smaller bronchial tubes lose moisture and heat. In a perfect system, the heat and moisture would be returned to the tubes as the air passed back through the larger bronchi during exhalation. Conservation of heat, however, is not perfect, and the heat and moisture are lost to the inhaled air. This cooling of the bronchi leads to bronchial constriction, the underlying mechanism for exercise-induced asthma.

A study of figure skaters (rink temperature 7–10 degrees centigrade) showed that short efforts (four to ten minutes) in the cold was enough to induce constriction of the bronchi.[3] Imagine the effects of a forty-five-minute race in a cool weather.

It is important to note that the hormones released during exercise keep the bronchi open, but once exercise is stopped, the hormones dissipate and the temperature-induced constriction begins.

TREATMENT

Several medications can be used in the prevention of EIA. Albuterol, cromolyn, and leukotriene inhibitors have all shown utility in preventing respiratory difficulties during exercise. Albuterol is a prescription medication that dilates the bronchi by acting on the bronchial muscle that causes constriction. Many athletes prefer to use a different medication because albuterol increases the heart rate. The effects of albuterol last approximately four hours. If you are exercising for more than four hours, consider adding another medication. Only albuterol in its inhaled form is legal by International Olympic Committee guidelines; oral albuterol syrup is banned. If you plan to participate in any event that requires drug testing, you need written notification from the prescribing physician to use albuterol even in the inhaled form.

Cromolyn is another inhaled medication that works to prevent exercise-induced asthma by a completely different biological mechanism, but the effect is the same. When used up to an hour before exercise, it will prevent constriction of the bronchi. There are no changes in heart rate with use of cromolyn.

The newest inhaled medication in the arsenal against EIA is the family of leukotriene inhibitors. These medications are effective without causing any changes in heart rate. The leukotrienes are inflammatory-mediating chemicals that are a thousand times more potent bronchoconstrictors than histamines.[4] One leukotriene inhibitor in particular, monteleukast, has a beneficial effect on performance in athletes with exercise-induced asthma.[5]

Timing the medication use is important; inhalation should fall within ten minutes and one hour before exercise. These inhalers will prevent EIA only if used before exercise. Their use after exercise will not treat the symptoms. For further information on correct use of an inhaler, see the photo section that follows.

PREVENTION

Exercise that is performed repeatedly within forty minutes of a race will render the bronchi insensitive to further narrowing. A warm-up should include two minutes of race effort within forty minutes of the start time. This will produce desensitization of the airways without causing constriction.

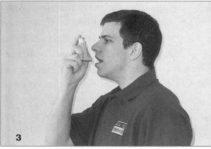

8.1 Using an Inhaler

(1) Inhalers should be used with spacers to deliver the most medication. (2) Using an inhaler with a spacer (3) Using an inhaler without a spacer.

Sidebar 8.1

USING AN INHALER

Shake inhaler as needed. Hold inhaler two inches from your mouth.

Breathe in, exhale.

As you start the next inhalation, squeeze inhaler, releasing the medication.

Inhale medication deeply.

Hold breath for ten seconds.

Repeat according to your doctor's instructions.

During the increased breathing rate that occurs with exercise, the mouth and throat are responsible for 50 percent of total heat and water loss.[6] Keeping the mouth moist with frequent drinks or even a hard candy (lemon drops increase saliva production) may help.

According to some research, exercise releases histamine into the circulation, which causes both hives and bronchoconstriction. There is a strong relation between allergies and EIA.[7] A nonsedating antihistamine such as Zyrtec, Claritin, or Allegra will help offset the effects of histamine on the bronchi. Be sure to avoid the combined antihistamine-decongestant medications, as the decongestant is not only on the IOC banned substance list but can contribute to dehydration and heat-related disorders as well.

Ceasing activity abruptly tends to cause worse EIA than does slow rewarming of the bronchi. Equally as important as the warm-up, the cooldown facilitates recovery of both the muscles and the lungs. I recommend a cooldown of sufficient length for the heart rate and respiratory rate to drop to pre-exercise levels before stopping activity.

Keeping the lungs warm, as well as the blood that circulates through them, is important. Layering clothing over the core with an undershirt, vest, and jersey is necessary and helpful. A muscle rub will bring the blood to the skin, providing warmth to the area that is covered with the cream, but the rub can also alter the sensation of hot and cold, which means the chest can be covered less and kept colder.

Although the symptoms of bronchoconstriction do not occur until exercise is over, there is research suggesting that the level of work achieved while exercising may be lower than optimal with less effective breathing in those that are affected by EIA.

Vitamin C is a factor that may help to prevent the airways from reacting excessively to exercise. Although not useful in all athletes, two grams taken one hour before exercise has been found to be beneficial.[8]

OTHER FACTORS

Although classic exercise-induced asthma is worse in cold and dry climates, many athletes report worsening of their symptoms in hot and humid environments. In these conditions, the heavier barometric pressure keeps ozone and other allergy-causing particles closer to the earth's surface where they are more easily inhaled. The ozone may prime the bronchi for the effects of classic allergy-causing particles.[9] Taking non-sedating anti-histamine allergy medications will help, as will exercising early in the morning or later in the evening when air quality is better.

If you think you have exercise-induced asthma, see your doctor to discuss treatment plans. This condition is easy to overcome. On the 1984 U.S. Olympic team, 67 athletes (11 percent) had EIA and they came away from the games with 41 medals.

NOTES

1. R. O. Voy. The U.S. Olympic Committee experience with exercise-induced bronchospasm, 1984. *Medicine and Science in Sports and Exercise* 1986, 18: 328–30.

2. J. M. Weiler, T. Layton, M. Hunt. Asthma in United States Olympic athletes who participated in the 1996 summer games. *Journal of Allergy and Clinical Immunology* November 1998, 102(5): 722–26.

3. E. T. Mannix, M. O. Farber, P. Palange, P. Galassetti, F. Manfredi. Exercise-induced asthma in figure skaters. *Chest* February 1996, 109(2): 312–15.

4. B. W. Smith, M. LaBotz. Pharmacologic treatment of exercise-induced asthma. *Clinics in Sports Medicine* April 1998, 17(2): 343–63.

5. S. Steinshamn, M. Sandsund, M. Sue-Chu, L. Bjermer. Effects of montelukast on physical performance and exercise exonomy in adult asthmatics with exercise-induced bronchoconstriction. *Scandinavian Journal of Medicine and Science in Sports* August 2002, 12(4): 211–17.

6. E. R. McFadden. Exercise-induced airway obstruction. *Clinics in Chest Medicine* December 1995, 16(4): 671–82.

7. I. J. Helenius, H. O. Tikkanen, T. Haahtela. Occurrence of exercise-induced bronchospasm in elite runners: Dependence on atopy and exposure to cold air and pollen. *British Journal of Sports Medicine* 1998, 32:125–29.

8. H. A. Cohen, I. Neuman, H. Nahum. Blocking effect of Vitamin C in exercise-induced asthma. *Archives of Pediatrics and Adolescent Medicine* April 1997, 151: 367–70.

9. D. B. Peden. Mechanisms of pollution-induced airway disease: In vivo studies. *Allergy* 1997, 52(38 Suppl): 37–44.

ROAD RASH

Most of us participate in endurance sports for the same reason. We love the feeling of translating our physical strength into speed. That love of speed is temporarily suspended, however, when we crash and leave patches of our skin on the ground. We then suffer for several nights with the problem of "bed stick" when we awaken to find our wounds have oozed onto the bed and dried, creating some bizarre physical bond with our once-clean linens. Sound familiar?

Road rash is a condition that afflicts almost every forward-motion athlete at some point in his or her athletic pursuits. Although it is much more common among the pavement athletes than snow athletes, it is important to be familiar with wound care to hasten return to training and competition.

From my work in the hospital's emergency department, I have seen the many painful, harmful regimens people have used at home to treat wounds. Many misconceptions exist about wound care, and these are frequently promoted in the popular press. In this chapter I explain the physiology of wound care, how to care for your wounds, and the recent research and treatment options for treating road rash.

THE SCIENCE OF ROAD RASH

Forward motion requires energy. The faster you go, the more kinetic energy you carry. This is described by the physics equation that states that the amount of kinetic energy an object possesses equals half of the mass times the square of the velocity, or

$$KE = 1/2 \ mv^2$$

where m is the mass (weight) of the object and v is the velocity (speed).

As you can see from the equation, your energy rises exponentially with your speed. Stopping will dissipate this energy. If you are on a bicycle, the energy is dissipated as heat between the brake pads and the rim. If you are running, the energy is dissipated in your joints as you slow down. If you come to a stop by your body sliding across the pavement, the energy is dissipated as heat/friction between the skin and the ground. In short, road rash is a burn that ranks in severity greater than sunburn and less than a skin-destroying third-degree burn.

INFLAMMATION AND HEALING

In road rash, the skin injury is called an abrasion. Abrasions are injuries to the skin that are scrapes of varying thickness. The loss of the most superficial layer of skin, the epidermis, is common to all abrasions. Because the skin is not punctured in a pure abrasion, regeneration of the skin occurs unless complicated by infection or embedded foreign objects.

As a wound begins to heal, there is an immediate migration of healing cells to the injury site. These cells start to lay the groundwork for repair of the skin defect. This is the initial inflammatory response. The hallmark of acute inflammation is a change in the permeability of the blood vessels that allows the necessary cells to leave the bloodstream and deposit themselves at the wound. Along with cells, however, fluid also leaves. This fluid is called edema and is a normal part of wound healing. A combination of immune system cells, called neutrophils and macrophages, appear to clean up the microscopic dirt and contaminants. An early accumulation of fluid and neutrophils is normal and may give the edema a yellow tint. Fluid full of neutrophils is called pus but is normal for the first one to two days. A wound infection would also have pus but would not appear for at least three days. Clotted blood is the first to appear with its mixture of blood cells and the clotting chemical fibrin, which when dehydrated forms the scab. Within the first twenty-four to forty-eight hours, the epithelial layer of skin begins to grow and divide. This is first noticed as a thickening of the skin edges around the abrasion.

By the third day, granulation tissue has begun to invade the wound. This is a pink, bumpy substance made of collagen that begins to cover the wound. The epidermis continues to thicken. Around the fifth day, granulation tissue has covered the wound. New blood vessels are being created in a process called neovascularization that is at maximal activity as the epithelium continues to grow.

The second week brings continued healing and accumulation of collagen fibers. By then, the inflammatory response and the edema, neutrophils, macrophages, and neovascularization have largely disappeared.

After one month, the inflammatory infiltrate is gone, and the wound is covered by an intact epithelium. At this point, the strength of the wound is about 80 percent; it will be several more months before it reaches 100 percent.

CLEANING

Wounds should be cleaned immediately to remove dirt and road contaminants. The best procedure is to use a gentle soap and water. A commercially available soap for wound cleaning (Shur-Clens) is another option but is probably no more effective.

One mistake people frequently make is to use harsh cleaners such as iodine, peroxide, alcohol, and chlorohexidine. These are intended for cleaning intact skin, not open wounds. They are toxic to the exposed tissues and will not help the healing process. (Peroxide is good, however, for removing bloodstains from clothing.)

Gauze and wound sponges are the preferred cleaning modality. They are soft and will not leave particles of lint or other small fibers in the wound.

Sidebar 9.1

ROAD RASH REPAIR KIT

Since you can never plan for crashes or abrasions, you should keep these items on hand and bring them to races.

Saline: *You can make your own saline for cleaning and debriding, or you can buy it by the bottle. The saline sold as contact lens solution comes in a squirt bottle, which is useful for irrigating. If you make your own solution, boil one tablespoon of salt in four cups of water for fifteen minutes. When it cools, it is ready to use.*

Liquid soap: *One brand is Shur-Clens.*

Gauze: *The four-by-four-inch squares are preferable because they give more coverage.*

Colloid dressings: *Some brand names are Tegaderm, Duoderm, and OpSite.*

Tape: *A good adhesive tape is important to keep the dressing in place. Do not wrap tape completely around an arm or leg, as the swelling might cause pressure and cut off circulation.*

Bacitracin: *This ointment is available in small tubes and should be reapplied every twelve hours.*

DEBRIDEMENT

Debridement refers to the removal of all small and large particles that may have become embedded in the wound during the fall. The two main methods of debridement are irrigation and scrubbing.

Irrigation is relatively painless yet effective in removing particles. This method is dependent upon the pressure of the irrigation fluid. Higher-pressure fluid will remove small particles but will also destroy the tissue, whereas lower-pressure irrigation will remove large particles but will not be effective in removing the small particles that will prevent optimal wound healing.

One technique I have found particularly useful is to make a squirt bottle by punching a small hole with a needle in the top of a plastic bottle to create a high-pressure stream of water. This will allow you to irrigate the wound well. Proper irrigation can also be obtained with dental cleaning devices that use water, such as a Water-Pik. A volume of at least 100 ml (3.5 oz) should be used for every square centimeter of abrasion.

The second method of debridement is scrubbing the wound to remove debris. This can be done with a wound cleaning sponge or gauze. Both should be wet when used. Gently rub the wound, taking care not to destroy the tissue beneath; however, a small ooze of blood will assure that you have removed the clot and the pieces of road surface that can contaminate the wound.

DRESSING

This topic has been long debated in the medical community. Whether it is better to leave a wound dry, have it scab over, and heal or to keep it covered with ointment has left road-rash sufferers understandably confused.

Much of the recent research has shown that a moist dressing is beneficial. The different strategies discussed next are all effective. Some are easier, some are cheaper, and some are faster, but they all work and there is no "right" answer. The one definite factor is that the use of ointments and other dressings creates a better healing environment than plain gauze[1] and has a lower incidence of infection.[2]

Silvadene

Silvadene is the brand name of silver sulfadiazine cream, which is available by prescription. It comes in a small tube and can be applied to burns. Silvadene is a favorite of many people because it soothes the wound. As the name implies, one ingredient of Silvadene is silver. Unfortunately, because it is so soothing, a common mistake is to use too much of the cream, and the result is staining

9.1 *Proper application of a thin layer of Silvadene to gauze*

of the skin. If it is used sparingly on gauze, staining is not as common (see Photo 9.1). Properly dressing a wound with Silvadene has yielded superior results over many other modalities.[3] Silvadene has long been considered the standard against which most new products are measured.

Bacitracin

Bacitracin (Neosporin and Polysporin are two brands) is a readily available, cheap, over-the-counter topical ointment that can be applied to burns and lead to good healing. Also available in a spray, bacitracin is a combination of three antibiotics (Bacitracin/Neomycin/Polymixin) that provides good coverage for many of the types of bacteria that infect burns.[4] If clothing doesn't cover the wound and you don't engage in dirty activities, you won't need any gauze covering (open technique), and bacitracin still can be an effective barrier to dirt and debris. The ointment should be applied and changed every twelve hours.

Colloid

Colloid dressings are one of the newest and probably easiest burn treatments. They are sold under the trade names Duoderm Hydroactive, OpSite, Second Skin, and Tegaderm. Colloid dressings are applied to clean, debrided wounds and are left on for one week. When compared with Silvadene in head-to-head trials,[5] they were found to be superior in wound healing, skin color, less pain, fewer and quicker dressing changes (ease of care), and lower overall cost. Also, patients with the Duoderm dressing had less limitation of activity and greater comfort, factors that translate into quicker return to activity. Because of the ease of use, there was better compliance with the therapy and the patients preferred it.

Treated gauze

Gauze impregnated with antibiotics (Xeroform) or petroleum (Petroleum gauze or Vaseline gauze) can be applied and left in place for five days while healing occurs.

The advantages of impregnated gauze are similar to those of colloid dressings in several respects, including ease of use and minimal dressing changes. Still, the gauze covering is needed to keep the medication in place. Healing is faster with colloid dressings.[6]

Lidocaine

Anyone familiar with a dentist's shot of anesthesia has experienced the numbing effects of lidocaine. Lidocaine is also available from your doctor in an ointment that can make wounds more comfortable. Although it can be toxic at high levels, the cream has not been shown to be absorbed through burn wounds as large as 28 percent of the body (your palm is roughly 1 percent of your body surface area). In the same study, greater comfort was achieved by covering wounds in lidocaine cream than in bacitracin. Although not an antibiotic, lidocaine does prevent further growth of bacteria. Because it is available only in a 2 percent concentration (5 percent was used in the study), its effectiveness can't be known definitively, but if your abrasion is small and painful and limits activity, lidocaine should be used preferentially over bacitracin.

PAIN

Let's face it—road rash hurts. The removal of the top layer of skin exposes the nerve fibers and causes pain. A large abrasion can even hurt from light touch and being brushed against clothing and sheets. Because the skin is so sensitive, it is difficult to clean the wound adequately.

Ibuprofen (in Advil and Motrin, for example) has proved helpful in reducing the pain associated from light touch.[7] In fact, due to the anti-inflammatory properties of ibuprofen, it has been used extensively for serious burns, though with variable degrees of success in more severe burns. I recommend that athletes take ibuprofen for the first five days after sustaining an abrasion.

Acetaminophen (for example, Tylenol) has been very successful as a first-line analgesic for minor burns and abrasions.[8] If the pain relievers mentioned here do not adequately control your pain and you are using lidocaine ointment, you should contact your physician.

PREVENTING COMPLICATIONS

You want to create the best possible environment for wound healing. As skin heals, vitamin C and zinc are needed. Both should be taken as supplements all the time if you don't get adequate dietary sources, but you should definitely take both if you have an abrasion.

Antibiotics are not needed to prevent an infection if good wound care is practiced. If infection sets in, however, antibiotics are needed, and the sooner they are started, the better. Signs of infection include increased pain, redness around the wound, red streaks radiating out from the wound, fever, and pus. Remember that a pus-like drainage is part of the normal inflammation process in the first forty-eight hours. After that, pus signals infection.

You should know your tetanus immunization status. After the initial shots children receive, a tetanus booster is needed every ten years provided there has been no injury in the interim. If you have a cut, burn, abrasion or any other violation of skin integrity it is a good practice to receive a tetanus booster every five years. Tetanus is a rare infection caused by a bacterial toxin that can lead to paralysis and death. Tetanus toxoid boosters are quick and effective to prevent tetanus.

SUMMARY

Good wound care is the key to preventing infections. After the wound is cleaned and debrided, it should be kept moist with any of the dressing techniques described in this chapter. The wound will continue to "weep" for several days, so a dry sterile gauze covering should be used. Avoid gauze that you can rip apart, as the small fibers will impair the healing process. Instead, use woven gauze or gauze that is nonadherent (such as Telfa). Even if a colloid dressing is used, gauze covering will prevent leakage from soiling your clothes.

Pain management with acetaminophen or ibuprofen is appropriate. If the pain worsens, you should consider the possibility of infection and be checked by your physician.

NOTES

1. R. S. Berger, A. S. Pappert, P. S. Van Zile, W. E. Cetnarowski. A newly formulated topical triple-antibiotic ointment minimizes scarring. *Cutis* June 2000, 65(6): 401–4.

2. D. J. Dire, M. Coppola, D. A. Dwyer, J. J. Lorette, J. L. Karr. Prospective evaluation of topical antibiotics for preventing infections in uncomplicated soft-tissue wounds repaired in the ED. *Academic Emergency Medicine* January 1995, 2(1): 4–10.

3. O. G. Hadjiiski, M. I. Lesseva. Comparison of four drugs for local treatment of burn wounds. *European Journal of Emergency Medicine* March 1999, 6(1): 41–47.

4. M. A. Walton, E. Carino, D. N. Herndon, J. P. Heggers. The efficacy of Polysporin First Aid Antibiotic Spray (polymixin B sulfate and bacitracin zinc) against clinical burn wound isolates. *Journal of Burn Care and Rehabilitaion* Mar–Apr 1991, 12(2): 116–19.

5. D. Wyatt, D. N. McGowan, M. P. Najarian. Comparison of a hydrocolloid dressing and silver sulfadiazine cream in the outpatient management of second degree burns. *Journal of Trauma: Injury, Infection, and Critical Care* July 1990, 30(7):857–65.
T. O. Stair, J. D'Orta, M. F. Altieri, M. S. Lippe. Polyurethane and silver sulfaziazene dressings in treatment of partial thickness burns and abrasions. *American Journal of Emergency Medicine* May 1986, 4(3): 214–17.

6. J. A. Griswold, T. Cepica, L. Rossi, J. S. Wimmer, H. H. Merrifield, C. Hester, T. Sauter, C. R. Baker. A comparison of Xeroform and SkinTemp dressings in the healing of skin graft donor sites. *Journal of Burn Care and Rehabilitation* Jan–Feb 1996, 17(1): 93–94.

7. K. L. Petersen, J. Brennum, J. B. Dahl. Related Articles. Experimental evaluation of the analgesic effect of ibuprofen on primary and secondary hyperalgesia. *Pain* April 1997, 70(2–3): 167–74.

8. S. K. Pal, J. Cortiella, D. Herndon. Adjunctive methods of pain control in burns. *Burns* August 1997, 23(5): 404–12.

ACID REFLUX:

A HARD PROBLEM TO SWALLOW

A friend once called to cancel a ride due to his upset stomach. "What do you mean you can't ride?" I said with all the bravado that comes from being young. "Haven't you ever puked during a bike race? You just spit it out and keep going."

Although many people have had a race or hard effort cut short by what seems to be a mouth full of stomach contents, it's not vomit. It comes from a problem called acid reflux. This condition can take many forms, but once it is recognized, it can be controlled and overcome to help the athlete achieve harder efforts and more intensity in training and racing.

In a survey of endurance athletes, many were found to have symptoms related to acid reflux: heartburn (11 percent), chest pain (18 percent), and nausea (21 percent).[1] The most severe symptom of acid reflux, however, is regurgitation followed by sudden-onset choking or persistent coughing with each breath, a debilitating but temporary setback that can end competition.

ANATOMY

The intestinal tract (mouth to anus) is a system that does not respond and adapt well to exercise training. As a result, exercise causes more problems, not fewer. This chapter deals with the upper-gastrointestinal (upper-GI) tract and its associated problems. (The lower-GI tract is discussed in Chapter 11.)

The GI tract is essentially a long tube that runs from the mouth to the anus. Following is a brief sequential description of the different upper-GI structures discussed in this chapter:

Mouth: Chews food and initiates swallowing. (Of course, it also aids in shouting at motorists who crowd bicyclists.)

Esophagus: A muscular tube that runs behind the windpipe (trachea) and connects the mouth and the stomach. The muscular wall of the esophagus contracts from the top down, as an aid to squeezing contents to the stomach. This action is known as peristalsis.

Lower esophageal sphincter: The valve that keeps stomach contents in the stomach. It relaxes when you swallow to allow food into the stomach, then tightens to keep the food in.

Stomach: A large muscular bag that holds food until it is broken down and passed along to the small intestine. Digestion of food is accomplished by acid and enzymes secreted by the stomach. The acid in the stomach is caustic and would damage other parts of the GI tract if mechanisms weren't in place to neutralize the acid such as mucus-secreting cells that provide a protective layer over the lining of the stomach.

PHYSIOLOGY

Acid reflux occurs when the lower esophageal sphincter (LES) relaxes and acid escapes into the esophagus. These relaxations occur frequently (several times a day) in everyone, but they are not usually felt because the body is equipped to deal with them. LES relaxations don't always occur spontaneously. They can be caused by foods, a full stomach, or even exercise. Certain types of foods have been implicated in acid reflux (see Table 10.1).

Table 10.1
FOODS COMMONLY ASSOCIATED WITH ACID REFLUX
Chocolate
Caffeine
Alcohol
Peppermint
Fatty or fried foods
Protein
Tomato sauce
Citrus juices

Several studies have been performed to investigate both the type and intensity of exercise most commonly associated with reflux. One study found that reflux was more common during running and rowing than during rest. Not surprisingly, reflux was even worse when the run was performed after a meal.[2] Reflux was also found to continue for up to two hours in the post-exercise period.

In a comparison of different types of exercise,[3] subjects engaged in cycling, weight lifting, and running. In this study, running produced the most reflux, but it was performed after the other activities, so it is unclear if the reflux was a result solely of the running.

The esophagus is protected by two mechanisms. First, reflux contents can usually be cleared from the esophagus through peristalsis. This process is aided by gravity in a seated or standing individual. Second, the acid is usually neutralized by saliva. Saliva, known as the body's antacid, will neutralize most acid that hits the muscular esophageal wall. If the acid load is large, or if there is decreased saliva, the muscular wall will tighten, resulting in chest pain and difficulty swallowing. During exercise, especially intense efforts, most athletes breathe through their mouth. The constant flow of air in and out of the mouth has a drying effect and results in decreased saliva. Dehydration also contributes to decreased saliva. The net effect is a loss of the body's natural defense against stomach acid.[4]

In a study of cyclists, esophageal contractions decreased as the intensity of the effort increased.[5] When contractions decrease, the esophagus loses the ability to remove acid. Another study found that during exercise the force and duration of contractions decreased.[6] The reason for this decrease is unclear but is probably related to the diversion of blood away from the intestines during exercise. Blood must be delivered to the exercising muscles, and this comes at the expense of the GI tract. The result is a 60–70 percent decrease in GI tract blood flow.[7]

This decrease in blood flow is compounded by dehydration. If there is less fluid to carry the blood cells, the blood flow to the gut will be decreased even further. Decrease in blood flow is also responsible for feelings of nausea. This may be felt during hard interval training and may leave the athlete with a decreased appetite following exercise.

The stomach has two sphincters that control emptying: the esophageal sphincter at the top and the pyloric sphincter at the bottom. The stomach can empty from either direction, but the pyloric end is the natural spot. Gastric emptying is greatly affected by exercise. During moderate exercise (70 percent of VO_2max), the stomach operates as it would regardless of effort or the type of exercise. Exercise above 70 percent VO_2max delays gastric emptying.[8] When the stomach is full, pressure is increased and is relieved through the esophageal sphincter, and the result is powerful reflux.

The mouth and the space behind it, called the pharynx, are not usually affected by reflux, because the acid doesn't typically make it up to the mouth. When it does, however, the acid can be swallowed or spit out. A flap called the epiglottis alternately covers the esophagus or the trachea (windpipe) depending upon whether you are swallowing or breathing. The epiglottis prevents food from "going down the wrong tube," or being aspirated.

Aspiration is not a normal occurrence in healthy individuals, but when it happens, it can cause coughing and choking, cutting an exercise session short. If enough acid reaches the vocal cords, they can spasm and prevent adequate air from reaching the lungs.

Reflux has also been described as a mechanism for inducing asthma exacerbations in asthmatics. It has not been shown to be a cause of exercise-induced asthma, however.

TREATMENT

This knowledge of how reflux works and affects performance can help you devise simple strategies to improve the condition.

A full stomach wants to empty. If you stretch the stomach with food, air, and water, it will want to relieve pressure in whatever way possible. One mechanism for this is to relax the esophageal sphincter. The top part of the stomach has stretch receptors that will detect if it is full. When stomach contents bounce around (say, when you're running or leaning forward on a bicycle), the stomach will be fooled into feeling more full than it is, and this will predispose you to reflux. Breathing hard will fill the stomach with air; this cannot be avoided, but what is fed to the stomach can be controlled.

The pre-exercise meal is important. Getting the necessary fuel into the body is useful, but a full stomach will not provide you with more energy. Nutrients are not absorbed by the stomach, but by the intestines, so allow plenty of time for the stomach to empty. Normal emptying times for the stomach (gastric emptying) are between three and six hours. Some factors that affect gastric emptying are composition of the food, amount of food, and exercise.

Sidebar 10.1

REFLUX QUICKSHEET

Recognition
Symptoms: Regurgitation, belching, pain on swallowing, burning, choking, persistent coughing, nausea. Symptoms worsen with increased exertion.

Treatment and Prevention

Pre-event
- Avoid large meals within three hours of event.
- Have smaller meals more frequently and avoid fat and protein.
- Take 150 mg of ranitidine (available over-the-counter as 75 mg pills) one hour before intense exercise.

During event
- Take frequent small sips of cool (not cold), hypotonic liquids.
- Ingest sugar as a complex carbohydrate; avoid sucrose and fructose.
- Decrease exercise intensity if symptoms become severe.
- Avoid feeding on solid foods.

Post-event
- Continue hydration with hypotonic fluids for one hour.

Simple foods do not need to be digested by the stomach. A meal heavy in fat and protein will take longer to digest than a meal of carbohydrates. Carbohydrates such as rice, pasta, and bread will be easily broken down and pass through the stomach faster than the greasy bacon, egg, and cheese sandwich bought at the drive-through on the way to the race. At the race hotels before a professional cycling event, riders can be seen eating cereal, pasta, and bread in the morning. Then they get dressed and ready to race. This strategy is helpful, although difficult to employ for early morning races.

Food particle size is also an important factor. The stomach will retain particles larger than 2 mm until they are broken down.[9] Chewing food well for the pre-race meal and avoiding solid food during exercise entirely are two other strategies to combat reflux.

Osmolality is defined as the concentration of particles in a solution. Solutions with a higher osmolality contain many particles, and lower-osmolality solutions contain fewer. Lower-osmolality substances will empty from the stomach faster. This is an important concept. One particle of sucrose (table sugar) has two glucose molecules. One particle of a glucose polymer has many glucose molecules. Each particle has the same osmolar effect in the stomach, but the glucose polymer contains more usable energy. Therefore, it is more efficient to use glucose polymers to make a lower-osmolar solution than to ingest a commercially prepared energy drink with sucrose and fructose as its energy source. A colder drink will also enhance gastric emptying, so keep your water bottles slightly chilled.

Similarly, one study found that during a run-bike-run test with triathletes, those who drank a 7 percent carbohydrate solution during exercise produced significantly longer and more reflux episodes than those who drank water during exercise. There were more and longer reflux episodes during the run than during cycling.[10] A mixture containing 40 grams of glucose per liter (4 percent solution) leaves the stomach at the same rate as water.[11]

It also makes sense that the less acid there is in the stomach, the less likelihood of acid causing problems. One study examined runners with no history of acid reflux and the effectiveness of medication.[12] The esophageal acid levels (pH) were recorded using a pH monitor. The runners were fed a low-fat breakfast of orange juice (8 oz.), corn flakes (1 cup), milk (4 oz.), and one-half of a banana. The subjects were then given either a sugar pill or the antacid ranitidine (Zantac), one hour before a lactate threshold run of six to ten miles. When the pH in the esophagus was compared with at-rest levels, with ranitidine and without ranitidine, a clear pattern emerged.

Running produced significantly more reflux than the athletes experienced at rest. Fifty percent of the runners had reflux at the lowest pH threshold tested (most acidic). Among runners who took ranitidine, there was significantly less reflux during exercise (nine episodes compared with 57 episodes for placebo.)

It is clear that acid reflux plays a major role in affecting how athletes feel during exercise. Acid reflux symptoms can be manipulated and controlled through dietary modifications and medication. Many of the symptoms of acid reflux do not cause cessation of exercise or competition and are probably overlooked as a condition requiring treatment. By carefully regulating diet, however, you can control these symptoms.

If, despite manipulating diet and pretreating with ranitidine (Zantac), you are still symptomatic, you should follow up with a physician for pH monitoring and a gastrological workup.

NOTES

1. L. J. Worobetz, D. F. Gerrard. Gastrointestinal symptoms during exercise and enduro athletes: Prevalence and speculations of the etiology. *New Zealand Medical Journal* 1985, 98: 644–46.

2. E. Yazaki, A. Shawdon, et al. The effect of different types of exercise on gastro-oesophageal reflux. *Australian Journal of Science and Medicine in Sport* 1996, 28 (4): 93–96.

3. C. S. Clark, B. B. Kraus, J. Sinclair, et al. Gastroesophageal reflux induced by exercise in healthy volunteers. *JAMA* 1989, 261: 3599–601.

4. A. Shawdon. Gastro-oesophageal reflux and exercise. *Sports Medicine* 1995, 20(2): 109–16.

5. E. E. Soffer, R. K. Merchant, G. Duethman, et al. Effect of graded exercise on esophageal motility and gastroesophageal reflux in trained athletes. *Digestive Diseases and Sciences* February 1993, 38(2): 220–24.

6. M. A. Van Nieuwenhoven, F. Brouns, R. J. Brummer. The effect of physical exercise on parameters of gastrointestinal function. *Neurogastroenterology Motility* December 1999, 11(6): 431–39.

7. H. P. Peters, L. M. Akkermans, E. Bol, W. L. Mosterd. Gastrointestinal symptoms during exercise: The effect of fluid supplementation. *Sports Medicine* 1995, 20(2): 65–76.

8. F. Brouns, E. Beckers. Is the gut an athletic organ? *Sports Medicine* 1993, 15(4): 242–57.

9. J. P. Wright. Exercise and the gastro-intestinal tract. *South African Medical Journal* 1993, 83: 50–52.

10. H. P. Peters, J. W. Wiersma, J. Koerselman, L. M. Akkermans, E. Bol, W. L. Mosterd, W. R. de Vries. The effect of a sports drink on gastroesophageal reflux during a run-bike-run test. *International Journal of Sports Medicine* January 2000, 21(1): 65–70.

11. Brouns, Beckers. Is the gut an athletic organ?

12. B. B. Kraus, P. A. Sinclair, D. O. Castell. Gastroesophageal reflux in runners: Characteristics and treatment. *Annals of Internal Medicine* 1990, 112: 429–33.

LOWER-GI SYMPTOMS

T he gastrointestinal (GI) tract is arbitrarily divided into upper and lower parts. The upper-GI tract encompasses the structures discussed in the last chapter. The lower-GI tract starts with the first part of the small intestine and ends with the anus.

The combined length of the small and large intestine is forty feet. These forty feet of intestine have a surface area of several miles and can contribute to the many abdominal problems endurance athletes often experience, such as bloating, cramps, side pain, flatulence, and diarrhea. In fact, one study showed that 80 percent of athletes have experienced GI symptoms.[1] These unpleasant symptoms have been cited as the most common reason to quit exercise.[2]

Fans of the New York City Marathon will remember the winner of the women's race finishing the race with diarrhea dripping down her leg. Most athletes have probably not had such extreme symptoms, but abdominal pain and cramping have probably affected most people at some point in their athletic endeavors.

The lower-GI tract begins with the latter part of the duodenum, the first third of the small intestine. The duodenum continues into the jejunum, the second section of the small intestine. The third part of the small intestine, the ileum, follows and ends with the start of the large intestine. The colon, or large intestine, starts in the lower right part of the abdomen and wraps around the outside of the abdominal cavity, ending with the rectum in the lower left quadrant of the abdomen.

Although usually responsible for absorption of nutrients from the food you eat, the intestines are certainly not designed for exercise. The gut is controlled by the parasympathetic nervous system under conditions that are usually meant for resting. Therefore, the intestines do not adapt well to exercise, and the result can be nausea, side pain, cramps, diarrhea, and bloating (see Table 11.1).

Table 11.1

GASTROINTESTINAL SYMPTOMS OF EXERCISE

Nausea
Vomiting
Sideache
Bloating
Diarrhea
Fecal urgency

BLOOD FLOW

When you exercise, your body will send blood (and the oxygen it carries) where it is needed most. During exercise, the muscles get the majority of the blood flow. This redirecting of blood comes at great expense to the GI tract. At 70 percent of VO_2max, there is a 60–70 percent decrease in blood flow to the intestines. At maximal exercise, when the body temperature rises and dehydration ensues, the blood becomes thicker, and the flow can decrease by up to 80 percent.[3] These numbers can vary widely among athletes, however. One study[4] among cyclists showed an 80 percent decrease after one hour at 70 percent of VO_2max, with two cyclists registering no blood flow to their intestines at all. This variability explains why some athletes are more susceptible to GI symptoms than others.

Another factor that may play a role in decreased blood flow is the conditioning of the athlete. There have been conflicting studies regarding the effect of training on GI blood flow, but a decrease in the relative intensity of exercise can contribute to increased blood flow. In other words, a well-trained athlete will be able to sustain an effort at the lactate threshold more easily than will an untrained person. Athletes who were trained at a given intensity registered decreased heart rate and increased blood circulation to the gut.[5]

When there is inadequate blood flow to the intestines, the lack of oxygen reaching the intestinal tissue comes at the expense of the microscopic fingerlike projections on the surface of the inside of the intestines. This explains the finding of erosions to the stomach lining in five of nine runners who had completed a marathon[6] as well as the overall appearance of damage that is indicative of lack of blood and oxygen, known as ischemia. The lining of the GI tract does not tolerate ischemia well and suffers ulcerlike lesions. Further evidence of ischemia has appeared in traces of blood found in stools of 13 percent of postrace runners. Three-quarters of competitive cyclists studied were found to have at least one sample of stool that showed microscopic amounts of blood.[7]

The pain from intestinal ischemia is most pronounced in the zones where the large intestine bends in the upper right and left parts of the abdomen, known respectively as the hepatic and splenic flexures. Pain results when these ischemic areas come into contact with the diaphragm while inhaling, a plausible explanation for the well-known "side stitch." If you are having persistent side pain during exercise, you should see your doctor about having your stool examined for the presence of microscopic (occult) blood.

Blood flow has many hormonal influences, including vasoactive intestinal peptide (VIP), glucagon, and neurotensin. Although the exercise-induced secretion of these hormones might increase blood flow, they can also contribute to dehydration through fluid secretion into the intestines. Another hormone that increases blood flow to the intestine is prostaglandin. Prostaglandin also plays a role in inflammation and is decreased by taking nonsteroidal anti-inflammatory drugs (NSAIDs), such as ibuprofen. NSAIDs should be avoided if you experience any intestinal symptoms, not only because of the decrease in prostaglandin-induced blood flow but also because of the damage they can do to the stomach lining. If you must take NSAIDs for an inflammatory condition, take them after exercise and with food.

Oral contraceptives have also been found to be responsible for decreased flow to the intestines and colon.[8]

Blood flow to the gut is also compromised during states of dehydration and increased body temperature, but both conditions can be minimized by proper ingestion of water. In a study of runners, a 3–4 percent loss of water weight was associated with an increased incidence of GI symptoms. The same runners had decreased symptoms when they were well hydrated.[9]

Intestinal blood flow will increase after a meal, as this is when the intestines must do their work. If you exercise after a meal, problems likely will arise. Research has shown, however, that if a small amount of carbohydrate (no protein, no fat) is ingested in conjunction with water, the intestinal blood flow will not show the same degree of decrease and can remain above critical levels. This brings us back to the low-osmolality carbohydrate drink discussed in the previous chapter.

MECHANICAL CAUSES

In a study of multisport athletes, more GI symptoms occurred during the running phase than during cycling or swimming. One explanation for this finding is the constant up-and-down motion of the body during running, which causes mechanical irritation of the intestines, especially the end of the intestine, called the sigmoid. This leads to the urge to defecate and can produce diarrhea. Mechanical stimulation also leads to an increase in hormonal secretion that can last for up to two hours after an event. Physical jarring of the intestines is perhaps the best explanation for the higher prevalence of symptoms among runners and has been hypothesized as the result of not only the up-and-down motion but also the relative increase in size of the psoas muscle that lies along the back of the abdominal cavity.[10]

MOTILITY

The intestinal contents (which enter the body as food and leave as stool) move along the GI tract by a series of contractions, called peristalsis. These contractions are controlled by a variety of hormones. The complete process is known as GI motility, and it too, is affected by exercise. The motility of the small intestine is usually fast; food travels from the stomach to the large bowel in four to eight hours. Once food reaches the large bowel, it takes another eighteen to sixty-four hours to be removed from the body. Exercise slows motility of the small intestine, but the entire bowel transit time is largely due to the time spent in the large intestine. This is where the exercise effects on motility are significant.

Contractions can be either absent, irregular, or regular and organized. Regular, organized contractions are the ones that functionally move the intestinal contents along the GI tract. By directly affecting these contractions, exercise can cause acid reflux, vomiting, cramps, diarrhea, and fecal urgency. Exercise intensity affects the contractions. At low intensity, early on in exercise, motility speeds up,[11] but as intensity is increased from 60 percent to 90 percent of VO_2max, the pattern of contractions is interrupted. The net result is a slowing of the intestinal contents and feelings of fullness, bloating, and cramping. In addition, the initial increase in contractions, followed by a relative relaxation in the tone of the intestines, can lead to a strong urge to defecate.[12] It is therefore recommended that the bowels be emptied before competition.

Although never studied during exercise, GI motility is stimulated by the presence of glucose and nutrients. If there is too much glucose, however, the slowed intestines won't be able to absorb it, which can result in bloating and too little energy for endurance. If you are a woman and occasionally have these symptoms, it may be because intestinal transit time is delayed during the luteal phase of the menstrual cycle.

If the intestine is slowed and lacks the necessary oxygen and blood flow, it will be unable to absorb the necessary carbohydrates. As the body attempts to dilute the carbohydrate load, this will cause a shift of fluid into the intestines, leading to dehydration and diarrhea. As the glucose absorption is limited in the small intestine, some of the glucose will end up in the large intestine. Glucose does not belong in the colon, and the bacteria that normally live in the large intestine will start to ferment the glucose; this process can lead to excessive gas production that can cause cramping, bloating, and stretching of the large intestinal wall. Stretching of the wall produces cramps and is another mechanism of side pain.

The weight of a fluid-filled colon will pull on the ligaments that anchor the colon. This stretching is also felt as side pain. The condition was reproduced experimentally in an interval session during which athletes performed five sets of intervals (five minutes of hard effort interspersed with ten minutes of rest). All of the athletes drank the same amount of fluid. Side stitch was equally intense with all different types of fluids ingested during the workout (water, hypertonic carbohydrate-electrolyte solution, hypotonic carbohydrate-electrolyte solution, or flat cola). After the first two intervals, the pain intensity decreased with the hypotonic carbohydrate-electrolyte solution and declined to the intensity experienced without any fluid intake.[13]

The same study found that bending forward while tightening the abdominal muscles, tightening a belt around the waist, or doing deep breathing through pursed lips would alleviate the stitch within a few seconds. Anecdotal treatments (usually based on speculation) for side pain, such as attempting to relax the abdominal muscles or increasing the impact of foot strike, had little effect on the pain.

Malabsorption is a problem worsened by the intake of fluid having an exceedingly high glucose concentration or by consuming too much carbohydrate during exercise. This does not mean you must forgo food or glucose-containing beverages during exercise, but only that you should be judicious in your choices of what and when to eat or drink.

The recommended amounts of carbohydrate- (glucose-) containing drinks are 600–1,000 ml/hr of exercise to keep up with losses. The glucose concentration should be 6–8 percent. The solution should contain some sodium to facilitate the absorption of glucose and water; sodium also increases palatability. One study found that replacing only 17.1 ml/kg/hr (17.1 ml x 70 kg = 1197 ml/hr for a 150-pound athlete) of fluids lost maintained blood volumes and glucose levels and did not result in the feeling of fullness experienced with replacement of 83–94 percent of losses.[14] Although ingesting large quantities of fluid at once leads to increased symptoms of nausea and fullness, frequent ingestion of small amounts of glucose is well tolerated.

No discussion of the GI tract is complete without mention of the liver. Although not part of the intestines, the liver makes bile, an important digestive enzyme. Liver damage has been seen with dehydration or increased body temperature with endurance activity. Blood flow to the liver decreases at the same rates and by the same intensities as flow to the intestines. Perhaps the decrease in liver blood flow causes the transient rise in liver enzymes that is seen with exercise. In the absence of disease, liver enzymes should return to normal levels with abstinence from exercise.

RECOMMENDATIONS

To accommodate the physiological mechanisms just discussed, you can take several steps to avoid experiencing GI symptoms during exercise.

Training must be adequate before you undertake competition in earnest. Maintain training at an intensity sufficiently high to be prepared for race situations. This includes being able to produce sustained power at the lactate threshold. If cramps occur frequently with exertion, decrease training intensity to a level where you have no symptoms, and gradually increase exercise as tolerance permits.

Aside from concentrating on the race, staying well hydrated should be your primary focus during competition. Research has shown that fluid ingestion has no effect on performance in one hour or less of intense cycling.[15] If you are prone to GI symptoms of nausea, reflux, bloating, or cramps and you are competing for less than one hour, you might not need to drink at all, except to keep your mouth moist.

For longer events, ingest at least 500 ml (18 oz) of fluid every hour. You may need more than this in warmer, more humid environments. Hydration drinks should have 6–8 percent glucose (6–8 grams of carbohydrate in 100 ml of fluid) and should contain a pinch of salt.

Table 11.2

DIETARY MODIFICATIONS TO AVOID GI SYMPTOMS

Training
Fluid supplementation with 6–8% glucose solution when training exceeds one hour; drink 500 ml an hour.

Precompetition
Low-residue (low-fiber) diet 24 hours before competition.

Last meal 3 hours before competition: low in protein, fat, fiber, and lactose.

Avoid extra caffeine, vitamin C, bicarbonate.

Ingestion of easily digestible (semisolid or gel) carbohydrate with warm-up.

Ingestion of 500 ml water during warm-up followed by frequent sips of water.

Competition
Fluid replacement with cool, 6–8% glucose and electrolyte solution, 500 ml every hour. Goal: to keep weight loss less than 2%.

If using dense carbohydrate beverages or gels, ingest extra water.

Use complex carbohydrate beverages versus simple sugars (fructose, glucose).

Postcompetition
Fluid supplementation to replace losses.

If nausea and loss of appetite persist, replace glycogen stores with hypotonic solution.

Source: Adapted from H. P. F. Peters, L. Akkermans, E. Bol, W. Mosterd. Gastrointestinal symptoms during exercise. *Sports Medicine* 1995, 20(2): 65–76.

Cooled beverages will help to prevent an increased body temperature and will also leave the stomach faster, preventing upper GI symptoms as well. A cool (not cold) beverage will be absorbed faster and thus help prevent dehydration.

Pay careful attention to your diet before, during, and after competition (see Table 11.2). Avoid a high-fiber meal before a race, as it can cause excessive gas.

The contents of the bowel and bladder should be emptied before competition. Eating can stimulate a bowel movement, which should be attempted after breakfast.

Avoid anti-inflammatory medications before exercise. The inhibition of the prostaglandins can lead to decreased blood flow and damage to the protective lining of the stomach. Prostaglandin stimulants such as misoprostal (for example, Cytotec) have not been studied but might be helpful and should not affect exercise negatively. If NSAIDs are needed to treat sprains or strains, take them after exercise and with plenty of fluids.

Medications known as aluminosilicates (Maalox, Mylanta), which both protect the stomach lining and prevent diarrhea, have been shown to be more effective in alleviating diarrhea, side pain, and abdominal cramping than has loperamide (Imodium).[16] In general, however, medications that can alleviate lower-GI symptoms typically affect athletic performance negatively and should probably be avoided in endurance athletes. If symptoms are severe, however, and do not respond with nonpharmacological interventions, consult your physician about trying an antispasmodic medication (Donnatal).

In all cases, follow up with your physician if lower-GI symptoms persist despite following the suggestions listed here or if symptoms persist in the post-exercise period.

NOTES

1. H. P. F. Peters, L. Akkermans, E. Bol, W. Mosterd. Gastrointestinal symptoms during exercise. *Sports Medicine* 1995, 20(2): 65–76.

2. S. N. Sullivan. Exercise-associated symptoms in triathletes. The *Physician and Sportsmedicine* 1987, 15: 105–8.

3. Peters, et al. Gastrointestinal symptoms during exercise.

4. N. J. Rehrer, A. Smets, E. Reynaert, et al. Direct measurement of splanchnic blood flow during exercise in man (abstract). *Medicine and Science in Sports and Exercise* 1992, 24: S165.

5. J. P. Clausen, K. Klausen, B. Rasmussen, J. Trap-Jensen. Central and peripheral circulatory changes after training of the arms or legs. *American Journal of Phsysiology* 1973, 225: 675–82.

6. O. Oktedalen, O. C. Lunde, P. K. Opstad, et al. Changes in the gastrointestinal mucosa after long-distance running. *Scandinavian Journal of Gastroenterology* 1992, 27: 270–74.

7. T. W. Dobbs, M. Atkins, et al. Gastrointestinal bleeding in competitive cyclists. *Medicine and Science in Sports and Exercise* 1988, 20(Suppl 2): S78.

8. F. J. Tedesco, N. A. Volpicelli, F. S. Moore. Estrogen and progesterone-associated colitis. *Gastrointestinal Endoscopy* 1982, 18: 247–49.

9. Rehrer et al. Direct measurement of splanchnic blood flow during exercise in man (abstract).

10. D. J. Dawson, et al. Psoas muscle hypertrophy: Mechanical cause for "jogger's trots"? *British Medical Journal* 1985, 292: 787–88.

11. J. P. Wright. Exercise and the gastro-intestinal tract. *South African Medical Journal* 1993, 83: 50–52.

12. F. Brouns, E. Beckers. Is the gut an athletic organ? *Sports Medicine* 1993 15(4): 242–57.

13. B. T. Plunkett, W. G. Hopkins. Investigation of the side pain "stitch" induced by running after fluid ingestion. *Medicine and Science in Sports and Exercise* August 1999, 31(8): 1169–75.

14. J. B. Mitchell, K. W. Voss. The influence of volume on gastric emptying and fluid balance during prolonged exercise. *Medicine and Science in Sports and Exercise* March 1991, 23(3): 314–19.

15. G. K. McConell, T. J. Stephens, B. J. Canny. Fluid ingestion does not influence intense 1-h exercise performance in a mild environment. *Medicine and Science in Sports and Exercise* 1999: 386–92.

16. A. A. Lopez, J. P. Preziosi, P. Chateau, P. Auguste, O. Plique. Digestive disorders in triathletes: Comparison of effectiveness between diosmectite and loperamide. *Gastroenterology* 1991, 100: A226.

OVERTRAINING, SLEEP, AND RECOVERY

A ndy is a thirty-one-year-old graduate student who trains very hard. Because his training time is limited, he tends to ride hard every chance he gets. While preparing for the collegiate cycling season, he spent several weeks riding hard for sixty to ninety minutes. When race time arrived, he had no energy. He could not replicate the efforts he had produced in training. The start of a race was not a problem, but he would fall off the pack as racers approached the finish line. Even when he made it to the last kilometer, he could never figure into the finish. In addition, he was having disrupted sleep, was waking feeling tired, and was contracting frequent upper respiratory tract infections. After consulting a coach, he took several weeks off the bike and cut back on the intensity of training. He regained energy, felt better, and returned to racing after the season ended with a higher fitness level than he had experienced before the season.

Decreased performance despite training is a concern to athletes and coaches alike. To experience stagnant fitness or, worse, a decline in fitness despite what is thought to be a well-designed training program is damaging not only to race results but to an athlete's motivation as well.

During training, athletes purposely push themselves in both volume and intensity so that their bodies will adapt to these hard efforts. These efforts are followed by mini-, micro-, and macro-recovery periods. Micro-recoveries are the rest periods in between efforts or sets of exercise, each lasting thirty seconds to five minutes. Mini-recovery periods are the days off in a training program or sometimes even a good night's sleep. Macro-recovery periods are those lasting longer than a day; these represent rest periods of several days or a week or more within a training program or after a season. Each type of rest is essential for proper recovery; without each, overtraining can occur.

An athlete's hard efforts during training are known as overreaching. When overreaching is followed by a mini-, micro-, or macro-recovery, supercompensation occurs, resulting in increased fitness. Without these recovery periods, overreaching can easily become overtraining within seven to ten days. There is a fine line between overreaching and overtraining. Indeed, one maxim holds that the best way to know how to avoid overtraining is to overtrain. Of course, this is extreme, but the point is that overtraining is frequently a hindsight diagnosis. Some signs and symptoms of overtraining are listed in Table 12.1.[1]

Overtraining is a syndrome that consists of an increase in training volume and/or intensity with a resultant decrease in performance lasting for two weeks despite adequate rest. Medical experts have identified two types of overtraining, each relating to a different part of the central nervous system. Both the sympathetic nervous system, which is responsible for stimulating the body, and the parasympathetic nervous system, which controls relaxation of the body, can be affected. The sympathetic syndrome includes increased sympathetic activity while at rest, and the parasympathetic syndrome includes decreased sympathetic activity with an increase in parasympathetic activity at rest and with exercise.

Table 12.1

SIGNS AND SYMPTOMS OF OVERTRAINING

Early fatigue in races

No power at the end of races

Fatigue

Heavy muscles

Depression

Sleep disturbance
  Difficult sleep onset
  Waking during the night
  Nightmares
  Waking unrefreshed

Mood changes
  Anxiety
  Irritability
  Emotional lability

Loss of appetite/weight loss

Decreased competitive drive

Increased resting heart rate

Decreased libido

Frequent upper respiratory infections

Parasympathetic activity is normally responsible for maintaining a low heart rate and becomes operable after meals, producing the sleepiness you may feel after eating. With the parasympathetic syndrome, you will have a low heart rate during rest and exercise alike. After you exercise, the heart rate will quickly return to baseline, and you will find it unusually difficult to maintain a given heart rate for the same perceived exertion as before. In addition, there will be a decrease in circulating catecholamines, the stimulant hormones. Symptoms of the parasympathetic syndrome include fatigue, depression, low blood sugar during exercise, and decreased plasma lactate during exercise.

The sympathetic syndrome usually precedes the parasympathetic syndrome. The activity of the sympathetic nervous system normally increases during exercise and decreases at rest. Sympathetic drive is responsible for increased heart rate, blood pressure, alertness, and anxiety. Adrenalin (epinephrine) is a sympathetic nervous system hormone that falls into the category of catecholamines. The first sign of sympathetic syndrome is an increase in the resting heart rate. This syndrome is also responsible for sleep disturbances, irritability, anxiety, loss of appetite, prolonged recovery after exercise, and excessive sweating.

Overtraining is a continuum, and these two syndromes are often mixed. Therefore, the symptoms of each can be present within the same overtrained individual.

DEVELOPING OVERTRAINED ATHLETES

Attempting to achieve simultaneous increases in both volume and intensity is a sure way to become overtrained. In scientific studies, increased volume has resulted in both decreased performance and unaffected performance. These mixed findings have caused some experts to postulate that there is a threshold of training volume that must be reached before increased volume has a negative effect on performance.[2] Large-volume monotonous training is generally identified as a predisposing factor in overtraining.

Increased intensity has not shown the same effect as increased volume in several studies. These studies have used low volumes and very intense workouts, resulting in increased performance. However, increasing intensity with very difficult intervals, especially as the season begins, without allowing for adequate rest can lead to an overtrained athlete.

Hormonal changes that occur with overtraining reflect the symptoms seen in the overtrained athlete. The effects of overtraining on the natural secretion of testosterone, growth hormone, cortisol, and epinephrine are important factors in preventing and understanding overtraining.

Testosterone, the male sex hormone, confers strength, lean muscle mass, and improved recovery. Chronic aerobic exercise decreases the resting levels of testosterone, and a long session of aerobic exercise will decrease testosterone levels in further sessions. Heavy resistance exercise, in contrast, increases the testosterone response.

Testosterone is an anabolic steroid—that is, it promotes building of muscle. During overtraining, the ratio of testosterone to cortisol is decreased. This represents an imbalance in anabolic (muscle building) to catabolic (muscle breakdown) properties.[3]

Cortisol, unlike testosterone, exerts its influence by creating energy for the body to use. It is also used medically to decrease inflammation. Cortisol falls into the steroid class of glucocorticoids, so named because of the increase in glucose, which is provided from the liver. Although it contributes to muscle glycogen stores, cortisol increases with training stress and is responsible for a decrease in immune system function and muscle breakdown (catabolic properties).

Increases in the ratio of testosterone to cortisol are associated with increased strength, however, an opposite imbalance does not automatically lead to decreased performance or overtraining.[4]

Growth hormone has several positive effects on the body of the endurance athlete. It affects lean muscle mass by increasing the uptake of amino acids and increasing the use of fat as an energy source. It is not surprising that a decline in the hormone is experienced with overtraining.[5]

The hormones of the sympathetic nervous system, epinephrine and norepinephrine, have been shown to decline by up to 50 percent in studies where overtraining was induced.[6] These hormones are responsible for increasing heart rate, blood pressure, and alertness during exercise.

DETECTING OVERTRAINING

Although several blood parameters such as ferritin, ammonia, creatinine kinase, c-reactive protein, interleukin-6, serum urea, and zinc will change with overtraining, it is easier to follow the body's response to training.[7] One sign of overtraining is a decrease in maximal intensity performance. Test for this decline by observing if there is any decrease in power over a short time interval. Perform a one- to two-minute maximum power test using either a bicycle ergometer or a bicycle power meter. Also, an overtrained runner performing a maximal timed run on the track will not achieve the same distance as when the runner was not overtrained. Results in both cases are valid only if the tests have been performed before the athlete became overtrained.

A more reliable method of detecting an overtrained athlete might be to repeat the anaerobic (lactate) threshold test. During overtraining, there is a decrease in the lactic acid produced during exercise.[8] This will shift the heart rate/power curve to the right, resulting in a higher lactate threshold.[9] If this test is performed on an athlete who has been training hard, the rightward shift more likely represents an overtrained athlete than increased fitness. In contrast, if the repeat test is done when the athlete is not exhibiting any symptoms of overtraining, especially a performance decrease, the shift more likely is a fitness improvement.

Fatigue

Overtrained individuals show a decline in performance. However, when stimulated via an external source, muscles can produce efforts similar to those managed before overtraining. These results indicate that the overtraining syndrome does not affect the muscles as much as it does the central nervous system.

The hormonal changes previously mentioned contribute to the general theory of overtraining. Another theory, however, involves a brain transmitter known as serotonin.

Serotonin is the "feel-good neurotransmitter" responsible for giving us that relaxed, happy feeling we get after having a warm glass of milk or Thanksgiving dinner. The reason is that tryptophan, the precursor to serotonin, is found in turkey and warm milk and is converted to serotonin. Serotonin is also implicated in depression, and increasing serotonin availability is the goal of several antidepressants.

The amino acids leucine, isoleucine, and valine, known as branched-chain amino acids (BCAA), also play a role. Together, they account for one-third of the amino acids found in muscle protein. When muscle glycogen is depleted, the BCAAs, in particular leucine, are used for energy. They enter the brain by the same carrier that brings tryptophan to the brain. As the BCAAs are used up for energy, there is less competition for tryptophan to enter the brain. The theory is that as the tryptophan is converted to serotonin, it causes fatigue, early exhaustion during exercise, and disruptions in the secretion of testosterone and cortisol.[10] This theory is controversial,[11] but athletes and trainers should not ignore the role of BCAAs and carbohydrate in fatigue and overtraining.

Prevention

Most athletes fear undertraining, not overtraining, and their exercise sessions reflect this focus. There is no proven way to predict whether a particular program will cause overtraining or benefits. Factors to consider are the different types of fatigue and exhaustion that the endurance athlete feels once the program is underway. There are several different types of fatigue with which you should be familiar. Recognizing which type of fatigue you are feeling can help you to redirect the training plan in a way that will minimize overtraining.

- **Endurance capacity limits.** Also referred to as the "bonk," the limit of endurance capacity is reached when there is no longer any substrate to fuel further exercise. This can be prevented by regular feedings and maximizing glycogen stores.
- **Interval exhaustion.** Usually limited to the muscles, this is the type of exhaustion felt after a hard interval. The athlete often feels better after several minutes rest; the amount of rest needed depends upon the individual's fitness, the level of exertion, and the length of the work interval performed.
- **Workout fatigue.** This is marked by the inability to perform intervals or get the heart rate to the desired zone for the same perceived exertion as previously performed in that workout session. This does not happen on the first interval, but might occur on the second or third interval of a session. The effort is the same as that in previous sessions, but the power and heart rate are less than before. When this occurs, the athlete should end the session, rest, recover, and adjust future interval sessions accordingly.
- **Overreaching.** When the body is so tired that the athlete is unable to get the heart rate or power output to the desired zone for the *first time* in the workout session, fatigue has set in. This is usually due to a few days or a week of hard exercise. Usually a rest week or several days off are needed to recover. Overreaching could occur after a stage race or a difficult training camp. After a several-day rest period, fitness is increased. The benefits of overreaching are limited to a few days of hard training, and fatigue should not last more than three days.[12] Beyond this stage, fatigue is not beneficial.
- **Extended chronic and debilitating fatigue.** This type of fatigue lasts weeks to months and does not respond to a week of rest. This is the step past overreaching and signals an overtrained athlete.

Understanding the preceding principles and adjusting the training program accordingly will prevent reaching the overtrained state. It is important that a training program is progressively increased in either volume or intensity but that the two are not increased together.

Flexibility must be incorporated into programs to allow for proper rest. If a plan has a peak for a certain race, the race should fall within the second week of the peak period. This will allow for ample recovery if needed.

In addition to monitoring the effort needed to get to a specific heart rate or power zone during exercise, monitoring during rest also can help in creating a training plan. Knowing the resting heart rate on a daily basis is useful information. Although it is generally well accepted that an increase in resting heart rate signifies an overtrained state, a sudden decrease in heart rate may also be an indication of overtraining. Watching for a trend or sudden increase or decrease is more important than simply recording numbers.

It is possible to be overtrained without training. A job with heavy physical demands, a stressful personal life, and insufficient sleep can all contribute to an overtrained state with a moderate amount of training and exercise.[13] If possible, when other stressors are present, it is best to limit exercise by decreasing volume while maintaining intensity.

Proper diet and nutrition before, during, and after training sessions is paramount to recovery. Maximizing muscle glycogen will help to fuel exercise and will prevent the serotonin-induced fatigue associated with overtraining. Glutamine depletion (which is discussed in depth on exercise-induced immunosuppression in Chapter 14), is also responsible for some of the symptoms of overtraining. Glutamine is a nutritional supplement in some sports drinks, which can spare the metabolism of glutamine stores during exercise.

Research on the use of branched-chain amino acid supplements for resistance training has produced mixed results. The same is true of their use in prevention of overtraining. Nevertheless, supplementation may help to counteract the effects of serotonin-induced central fatigue.[14]

RETURN FROM OVERTRAINING

One strategy for returning to exercise from a state of overtraining is to start building up slowly. Heart rate should be in heart zones one or two (below the lactate threshold) for five to ten minutes at a time, increased slowly over six weeks. Once you can repeatedly perform at zone two for sixty minutes, you can begin intensity in higher heart rate zones. Expect to allow six to twelve weeks for recovery before undertaking any intensity training. In other words, a periodized training program is needed to return to normal. In this situation, you should consult your previous training diary and decrease the program from there.

To avoid monotony, weekly power/sprint sessions can be done as one set of three efforts, allowing for full recovery between each sprint. It is important that the new training program have at least one day of complete rest each week.

RECOVERY

Because recovery is an important part of athletic performance, one study set out to determine whether passive recovery (complete rest), active recovery (50 percent of VO_2max), massage, or a combined recovery (active and massage) was more effective in removing blood lactate and enhancing subsequent performance. Active recovery, defined as exercise at 50 percent of VO_2max, was the best strategy for removing blood lactate in the immediate post-exercise period. For repeat performance on an exercise test, combined recovery was more effective.[15]

These results are in direct conflict with other studies that have not shown massage to be useful.[16] Massage is associated with a perceived recovery,[17] which gives a psychological advantage. The performance advantage seems to rest with active recovery,[18] and combining it with massage can give the athlete a holistic approach to recovery.

Warm underwater jet massage was found to be useful in improving repeat performance after five days of exhaustive exercise sessions.[19] More available and convenient than a masseuse, underwater jet massage can be helpful when combined with active recovery. This explains why it is necessary to soak in a hot tub after exercise.

SLEEP

An important part of recovery and repair is sleep. There is no set answer to the question of how much sleep is enough. Yet we all seem to feel it when we don't get enough sleep. Sleep is important not only for recovery but also for performing at peak levels. Elite athletes who travel across multiple time zones face the problem of jet lag. Recreational athletes face a similar problem when they must compete at a time different from normal training time or must wake early for a competition.

Sleep is not a single monolithic block of time but has five distinct stages: stages one through four and REM (rapid eye movement) sleep. Differing brain waves, as characterized by electroencephalograph recordings, distinguish one stage from the next. During the awake state, the brain waves are fast, but as we progress through sleep, the brain waves slow down, resulting in what is known as slow-wave sleep. Each successive stage of sleep demonstrates slower waves and deeper sleep, during which arousal is more difficult. After we progress through all four stages in the first thirty to forty-five minutes of sleep, the stages reverse themselves and progress through a similar time span. Once stage one is again reached, after sixty to ninety minutes, a period of sleep begins that is marked by dreams, easy arousal, and gyrating eye movements; this is the REM stage. REM sleep occurs at the end of every cycle and becomes progressively longer throughout the night.

After the first two cycles (stages 1–4, then 3–1, then REM), there is no stage-four sleep. After the third cycle, stage three disappears. The remainder of sleep involves only stages one and two and REM.

The deepest, slowest wave stages, three and four, are responsible for the restorative effects after exercise. Collectively called slow-wave sleep, these stages are when the brain secretes growth hormone and other restorative hormones.

Figure 12.1

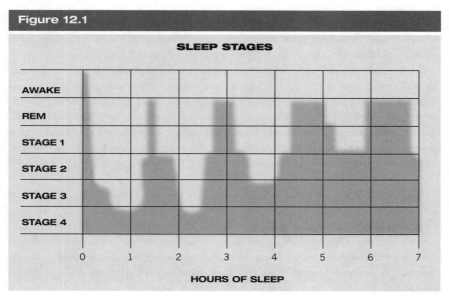

SLEEP STAGES

HOURS OF SLEEP

In one study, slow-wave sleep increased after a marathon.[20] After exercise stress, the sleep requirements increased for four nights, with the longest and best-rated sleep period on the second night after the marathon. During the first night after exercise, runners experienced the most frequent waking, which could be attributed to muscle soreness or other discomfort. Despite this, slow-wave sleep increased as a percentage on the first two nights. The increase came at the expense of REM sleep. This is a trained response to exercise; untrained individuals do not experience this sleep difference. Athletes also fall asleep faster following exercise.

Similarly, a study of national-level cyclists[21] found a decrease in the amount of REM sleep and an increase in the time to the start of REM sleep. The increase in catecholamines (epinephrine and norepinephrine) was correlated with the decrease and delay in onset of REM sleep.

The effects of exercise on sleep appear to be twofold.[22] First, in an overwhelming exercise bout for which the body is not prepared, there is an acute stress response resulting in a delayed decrease in total sleep time and slow-wave sleep. Second, moderate exercise results in a delayed increase in slow-wave sleep. Temperature acclimatization has the same effect: Acute change disrupts, but with adjustment to heat there is an improvement in sleep.

The effects of sleep on exercise, on the other hand, are less well defined. It is true that exercise is performed best when the athlete is well rested, but what about the multisession training day or multievent competition day? In one study, a brief nap improved running economy in the early part of a session but not in the latter part.[23] There was no difference in the athletes who had the extra sleep. Although it may be tempting to nap, there is no clear evidence that the same amount of sleep would not be better if it were added to the nighttime sleep.

Sleep deprivation of up to seventy-two hours does not affect the response to intensity of exercise. Also unaffected are muscle strength and aerobic and anaerobic performance capability. Time to exhaustion, however, is decreased by sleep deprivation.[24]

Several mechanisms are responsible for the occurrence of sleep at particular times. These physiological clocks dictate body temperature, level of arousal, and athletic performance. Among the biological rhythms described in studies are those that are in cycle with the moon (circamensal), the seasons (circannual), or the day (circadian). The circadian rhythms that repeat nearly every twenty-four hours have garnered the most attention, for they are believed to exert the most influence on biological function. Within the day, there are also many environmental factors that help guide the body's clock; these are called *zeitgeibers* (time givers).

World records frequently fall in the late afternoon or early evening. This could correlate with peak in body temperature, which occurs around six o'clock in the evening.[25] Strength follows this rhythm even when an athlete is deprived of sleep for four consecutive nights.

This timing is important for performance of muscles that are not at the temperature peak. A proper warm-up will elevate the muscles to 39 degrees Celsius (102.2 degrees Fahrenheit). For competition or exercise during the earlier part of the day, you should undertake a proper warm-up for exercise to progress well.

In a study that examined partial sleep loss, either through early waking or delayed onset of sleep, the lighter stages of sleep (one and two) were decreased.[26] This loss of sleep did not affect the overall growth hormone and catecholamine concentrations, since the deeper stages of sleep were not affected. Although there were not many hormonal alterations during this sleep deprivation, REM sleep was decreased. The frequently used sleep aid zolpidem (trade name Ambien) did not affect sleep stages and could be considered a good sleep medication for traveling athletes.

Sleep deprivation is similar to air travel in that the sleep-wake cycle is disconnected from circadian rhythms. By examining the effects of air travel and sleep deprivation, we can get a sense of sleep requirements; more important, we can understand what is needed to perform when the time is not optimal for the circadian rhythm. Athletes frequently are required to wake earlier than normal for a competition. The disconnection between the circadian rhythm and the need to perform can be manipulated for athletic competition, but you must do this in a way that will not affect performance.

Without manipulation, it takes approximately four days to recover from the feelings of jet lag.[27] If you know that a race will require you to rise early for travel to the event, plan on getting up at that time for four days prior. This will establish a rhythm that will enable you to perform better. For this strategy to work, you must get to bed earlier for those same four days. If it is difficult to fall asleep, sleep aids may be useful.

Melatonin has been used with varying levels of success. Some studies of it have not shown improved sleep in the general population.[28] Melatonin does not change the quality or time of sleep, but neither does it affect athletic performance the day after it is taken. This lack of negative effects on athletic performance has led to research on melatonin. Of ten melatonin studies reviewed,[29] nine reported that melatonin reduced jet lag when taken in a dose of 0.5 to 5 mg at bedtime. There was no difference in jet-lag symptoms at a dose of either 0.5 or 5 mg, but subjects fell asleep faster with the 5 mg dose. This dosage also produced better sleep. A higher dose was not useful, and neither was 2 mg sustained-release dose.

Melatonin is readily available over the counter, in contrast to the class of drugs known as benzodiazepines also used as sleep aids. One such drug, temazepam (Restoril), did not seem to improve jet lag symptoms in British athletes who flew to the United States. Their athletic performance was worse the first day after arrival but improved in subsequent days. Although the difference was not significant, there was a trend toward improvement in the group who took temazepam.[30]

If you are getting enough sleep, you should feel refreshed when you wake up. If you feel tired, try going to sleep thirty minutes earlier each night and repeat until you wake up refreshed. When that happens, you have found your sleep requirement.

SUMMARY

Overtraining has no early signs except perhaps a change in resting heart rate. It typically is manifested as fatigue that does not improve with a one-week rest period. Another sign of overtraining is frequent upper respiratory infection. Typical precipitators of overtraining are heavy volume or increased volume and intensity, although you can become overtrained even on a normal training schedule because of other life stressors. Prevention of overtraining can be augmented by a well-planned training program, good recovery, and proper nutrition. Sleep can be increased with an incremental training plan so as not to put the body under overwhelming stress. Finally, sleep disturbances can be manipulated to provide the body with adequate rest.

NOTES

1. M. J. Lehmann, W. Lormes, A. Opitz-Gress, J. M. Steinacker, N. Netzer, C. Foster, U. Gastmann. Training and overtraining: An overview and experimental results in endurance sports. *Journal of Sports Medicine and Physical Fitness* March 1997, 37(1): 7–17.

2. A. C. Fry, W. J. Kraemer. Resistance exercise overtraining and overreaching. *Sports Medicine* February 1997, 23(2): 106–129.

3. A. Urhausen, H. Gabriel, W. Kindermann. Blood hormones as markers of training stress and overtraining. *Sports Medicine* October 1995, 20(4): 251–76.

4. A. R. Hoogeveen, M. L. Zonderland. Relationships between testosterone, cortisol and performance in professional cyclists. *International Journal of Sports Medicine* August 1996; 17(6): 423–28.
C. Vervoorn, A. M. Quist, L. J. Vermulst, W. B. Erich, W. R. de Vries, J. H. Thijssen. The behaviour of the plasma free testosterone/cortisol ratio during a season of elite rowing training. *International Journal of Sports Medicine* June 1991, 12(3): 257–63.

5. A. Urhausen, H. H. Gabriel, W. Kindermann. Impaired pituitary hormonal response to exhaustive exercise in overtrained endurance athletes. *Medicine and Science in Sports and Exercise* March 1998, 30(3): 407–14.

6. A. L. Uusitalo, P. Huttunen, Y. Hanin, A. J. Uusitalo, H. K. Rusko. Hormonal responses to endurance training and overtraining in female athletes. *Clinical Journal of Sport Medicine* July 1998, 8(3): 178–86.

7. A. Aissa Benhaddad, D. Bouix, S. Khaled, J. P. Micallef, J. Mercier, J. Bringer, J. F. Brun. Early hemorheologic aspects of overtraining in elite athletes. *Clinical Hemorheology and Microcirculation* 1999, 20(2): 117–25.
U. Gastmann, K. G. Petersen, J. Bocker, M. Lehmann. Monitoring intensive endurance training at moderate energetic demands using resting laboratory markers failed to recognize an early overtraining stage. *Journal of Sports Medicine and Physical Fitness* September 1998, 38(3): 188–93.
U. Hartmann, J. Mester. Training and overtraining markers in selected sport events. *Medicine and Science in Sports and Exercise* January 2000, 32(1): 209–15.
S. J. Thomas, T. E. Cooney, D. J. Thomas. Comparison of exertional indices following moderate training in collegiate athletes. *Journal of Sports Medicine and Physical Fitness* June 2000, 40(2): 156–61.

8. A. Urhausen, H. H. Gabriel, B. Weiler, W. Kindermann. Ergometric and psychological findings during overtraining: A long-term follow-up study in endurance athletes. *International Journal of Sports Medicine* February 1998, 19(2): 114–20.

9. A. Urhausen, W. Kindermann. Diagnosis of overtraining: What tools do we have? *Sports Medicine* 2002, 32(2): 95–102.

10. U. A. Gastmann, M. J. Lehmann. Overtraining and the BCAA hypothesis. *Medicine and Science in Sports and Exercise* July 1998, 30(7): 1173–78.

11. H. Tanaka, K. A. West, G. E. Duncan, D. R. Bassett Jr. Changes in plasma tryptophan/branched chain amino acid ratio in responses to training volume variation. *International Journal of Sports Medicine* May 1997, 18(4): 270–75.

12. G. Kentta, P. Hassmen. Overtraining and recovery: A conceptual model. *Sports Medicine* July 1998, 26(1): 1–16.

13. F. L. Smoll, R. E. Smith. Psychology of the young athlete: Stress-related maladies and remedial approaches. *Pediatric Clinics of North America* October 1990, 37(5): 1021–46.

14. L. M. Castell, T. Yamamoto, J. Phoenix, E. A. Newsholme. The role of tryptophan in fatigue in different conditions of stress. *Advances in Experimental Medicine and Biology* 1999, 467: 697–704.

15. J. Monedero, B. Donne. Effect of recovery interventions on lactate removal and subsequent performance. *International Journal of Sports Medicine* November 2000, 21(8): 593–97.

16. E. Cafarelli, J. Sim, B. Carolan, J. Liebesman. Vibratory massage and short-term recovery from muscular fatigue. *International Journal of Sports Medicine* December 1990, 11(6): 474–78.

17. B. Hemmings, M. Smith, J. Graydon, R. Dyson. Effects of massage on physiological restoration, perceived recovery, and repeated sports performance. *British Journal of Sports Medicine* April 2000, 34(2): 109–14; discussion 115.

18. S. Gupta, A. Goswami, A. K. Sadhukhan, D. N. Mathur. Comparative study of lactate removal in short-term massage of extremities, active recovery and a passive recovery period after supramaximal exercise sessions. *International Journal of Sports Medicine* February 1996, 17(2): 106–10.

19. J. T. Viitasalo, K. Niemela, R. Kaappola, T. Korjus, M. Levola, et al. Warm underwater water-jet massage improves recovery from intense physical exercise. *European Journal of Applied Physiology* 1995, 71(5): 431–38.

20. C. M. Shapiro, R. Bortz, D. Mitchell et al. Slow-wave sleep: A recovery period after exercise. *Science* December 1981, 214(11): 1253–54.

21. N. C. Netzer, D. Kristo, H. Steinle, M. Lehmann, K. P. Strohl. REM sleep and catecholamine excretion: A study in elite athletes. *European Journal of Applied Physiology* June 2001, 84(6): 521–26.

22. A. Buguet, R. Cespuglio, M. W. Radomski. Sleep and stress in man: An approach through exercise and exposure to extreme environments. *Canadian Journal of Physiology and Pharmacology* May 1998, 76(5): 553–61.
H. S. Driver, G. G. Rogers, D. Mitchell, S. J. Borrow, M. Allen, H. G. Luus, C. M. Shapiro. Prolonged endurance exercise and sleep disruption. *Medicine and Science in Sports and Exercise* July 1994, 26(7): 903–7.

23. E. F. Pierce, R.W. McGowan, E. Barkett, R. W. Fry. The effects of an acute bout of sleep on running economy and VO$_2$max. *Journal of Sports Sciences* April 1993, 11(2): 109–12.

24. T. VanHelder, M. W. Radomski. Sleep deprivation and the effect on exercise performance. *Sports Medicine* April 1989, 7(4): 235–47.

25. M. Harries, C. Williams, W. D. Stanish, L. J. Micheli, eds. *Oxford Textbook of Sports Medicine,* 2d ed. Oxford: Oxford University Press, 1998.

26. F. Mougin, H. Bourdin, M. L. Simon-Rigaud, N. U. Nguyen, J. P. Kantelip, D. Davenne. Hormonal responses to exercise after partial sleep deprivation and after a hypnotic drug-induced sleep. *Journal of Sports Sciences* February 2001, 19(2): 89–97.

27 D. W. Hill, C. M. Hill, K. L. Fields, J. C. Smith. Effects of jet lag on factors related to sport performance. *Canadian Journal of Applied Physiology* March 1993, 18(1): 91–103.

28 G. Atkinson, P. Buckley, B. Edwards, T. Reilly, J. Waterhouse. Are there hangover-effects on physical performance when melatonin is ingested by athletes before nocturnal sleep? *International Journal of Sports Medicine* April 2001, 22(3): 232–34.

29 A. Herxheimer, K. J. Petrie. Melatonin for preventing and treating jet lag. *Cochrane Database of Systematic Reviews* 2001, (1): CD001520.

30 T. Reilly, G. Atkinson, R. Budgett. Effect of low-dose temazepam on physiological variables and performance tests following a westerly flight across five time zones. *International Journal of Sports Medicine* April 2001, 22(3): 166–74.

SPORTS
PSYCHOLOGY

An injury that interrupts a carefully planned training season can be devastating. Being sidelined from the activity we enjoy is difficult enough without having our goals and hopes for the season taken away. Dealing with an injury can be enlightening, however, depending upon how attention is focused on goals and expectations of being injured.

Coping with injury and rehabilitation from it have been studied with various psychological models. The broad scope of sports psychology has given rise to several theories and how they apply to the injured athlete.

Both sports medicine specialists and athletic trainers have labeled psychological issues as important to dealing with injury. Psychological distress can decrease the pain threshold, making recovery more prolonged, difficult, and painful. Decreased performance can result when the fear of injury or reinjury is present. Thus, accounting for the emotional and psychological side of injury can provide a faster return to athletic activity.[1]

The psychological profiles of athletes who are likely to be injured reveal many of the same traits: high competition anxiety, poor stress response, and Type A behavior pattern (high achievement motivation, ambition, and competitiveness).[2]

How athletes respond to injury depends largely upon how they view the sport in which they participate. Two concepts help to explain this: motivation and attribution.

MOTIVATION

Athletes compete in a sport for many reasons, including enjoyment, health, and the opportunity to feel competent. None of these three goals is met when an athlete is injured, and this loss can sap much of the person's motivation to return to the sport. Loss of motivation can hamper return from illness or injury. Motivation has been identified by both athletes and therapists as a major component for quick return.[3]

Return to sport and dealing with the injury will be tolerated better if the motivation for participation comes from an internal source. This is called intrinsic motivation, as opposed to motivation that comes from a source outside the athlete, or external motivation. An example of internal motivation is an enjoyment for the activity of the sport itself. External motivation includes such factors as prize money, praise for success, and winning. Distinguishing between intrinsic and extrinsic motivators is not always easy. An external motivator can elicit the internal motivators; for example, individuals who participate in road racing to feel a sense of accomplishment will also enjoy the praise they receive when they are doing well in the sport.

Alternatively, motivation can be viewed as having primary and secondary sources. The primary motivator might be the accomplishment or challenge of competing in the sport itself, whereas the secondary motivator might be the external motivator of receiving praise or winning trophies. Whatever the sources of motivation, there must be the right balance between positive and negative experiences.

An athlete who participates due to internal motivation will be more likely to return to that sport, whereas an externally motivated athlete not only will be less likely to return but may even switch to a different sport that will provide the same motivation (winning, praise from others, and so on).

MOTIVATION FOR REHABILITATION AND SPORTS

The reasons for participation in sports are of primary importance for athletes, but the injured athlete has a secondary motivation of dealing with the injury. There must be motivation to deal with illness by finding the right physician, and physical therapist, for example. The athlete should be able to list the reasons for participation in sport and why these are important. By focusing on these motivators, the road back to full participation should be more rewarding.

Sidebar 13.1   No.2

On a sheet of paper, list the reasons you participate in your primary sport.
Next, make a separate list explaining why the reasons in the first list are important to you.

Reason for participation	*Importance*

A physical problem involving illness or injury can lead to decreased performance in competition and training. The internal motivators, which are usually related to performance, are lost, and the balance between positive and negative can be tipped toward negative primary motivators. When this happens, the focus should shift to motivation for rehabilitation and treatment so that the sport can be resumed quickly, safely, and without further problems.

ATTRIBUTION

Success and failure in life can be attributed to many factors. Attributions are the reasons people point to as the cause of these successes and failures. One theory[4] states that the process of attribution has two separate characteristics: stability and locus of causality.

Stability refers to whether a characteristic is repeatable over time and how much of that trait is due to chance. The locus of causality is either internal (pertaining to oneself) or external (due to environment, other people, and so on). The characteristics of stable-unstable and internal-external characteristics will produce four possible attributions for any outcome (Table 13.1).

How athletes view success and failure on the playing field is related to how they deal with illness. For

Table 13.1

ATTRIBUTION

		Stability	
		Stable	**Unstable**
Locus of causality	**Internal**	Personal	Injury
	External	Treatment	Situation

example, an athlete who has exercise-induced asthma may blame a poor showing on the weather (external and unstable) or may attribute success to the ability to use proper medication (internal and stable).

Athletes tend to use four types of attribution to describe the causes of their injury: personal factors (internal/stable), injury-related factors (internal/unstable), treatment-related factors (external/stable), and situational factors (external/unstable).[5] Successful athletes frequently attribute their successes and failures to stable and internal attributes (strong innate ability), whereas the less successful athletes use unstable and external attribution (luck) to describe their outcomes. When internal attributions are used, the intensity of the outcome tends to be stronger. Future expectations are dependent upon the attribution to stability.

For illness, this reasoning is especially important. Recall the example of the athlete with exercise-induced asthma: If the athlete is unaware of the problem, the cause will be unstable, since the condition frequently changes with the environment. This can become frustrating because the athlete will feel no control over the situation. If the same athlete understands the problem, there can be some stability in use of medication and the locus of causality is internal. By shifting the focus of attribution from unstable and external to stable and internal, the athlete can minimize the problem, and the psychological burden can be lifted. One study found that slower recovery from sports injuries was more commonly associated with unstable attributions and, to a lesser degree, internal attributions.[6]

In competition, however, the internalizing of failure can lead to learned helplessness. Internalizing failure must be addressed so that the attributions in failure are changed to external/unstable characteristics that give the athlete a reason for persistence in seeking improved performance.

STRESS

Training and competing in sports can be very stressful. Adding injury and illness to an already stressful event can place immense stress on the athlete. The accumulated effect of stress both inside and outside the sporting arena can impair both mental and physical function sufficiently to prolong or precipitate injury.[7] There are two ways stress can take its toll on the body and mind. The first is when we are placed in a situation that overloads our physical and psychological reserves. For example, facing strong opponents or a demoralizing illness can overwhelm both the body and the mind. Second, stress also refers to the way we respond to the overwhelming load on a cognitive, emotional, and behavioral level.

In the first sense of the term (the alignment of stress and overloading), a situation that is greater than the resources available to deal with it will be stressful. If an injured athlete makes full use of the resources available (motivation, attributes, family, friends, teammates, coach, trainer, and physician), stress can be avoided and return to competition can be hastened. The specific demands and resources available will contribute to stress in different areas. For instance, the high-school cross-country runner who has multiple external demands (from coach and parents, for example) will have different stress than a masters runner who runs solely for accomplishment of the sport. The second runner can always focus on other parts of the sport (coaching, different distances) for feelings of accomplishment, whereas the stress on the first runner may lead to a dislike of the sport and decreased motivation to return from injury.

Stress can lead to injury by affecting the mind and body. Negative thoughts can interfere with concentration, and this inattentiveness can lead to injury. Stress causes an involuntary contraction of muscles, which can promote decreased flexibility, coordination, and efficiency; these factors can also lead to injury.

Coping with stress can take place on many different levels. The cognitive appraisal uses a person's thought processes to foster an environment in which to respond better to stress. How people perceive the stress will affect their ability to cope with the situation.

Sidebar 13.2

List all of your available resources in the event of injury or disappointing competition.

_____

_____

_____

_____

_____

_____

_____

According to cognitive appraisal theory, the mind gives attention to four elements: demands, resources, consequences, and the meanings of the consequences. The last element is based upon the individual's beliefs and self-worth. Even in two equally talented athletes, the cyclist who defines his self-worth in relation to sport performance will feel differently about a knee injury from the cyclist who would be just as happy if she were a kayaker. In other words, the athlete who sees the injury as devastating will experience a setback as more stressful than one who sees it as a challenge. Athletes who believe their personal worth depends upon their athletic success will more likely attribute increased stress to a setback than will those who have strong feelings of self-worth anchored outside the sport.

Stress has significant consequences for sports. Many studies[8] have demonstrated an increased likelihood that athletes will drop out of a sport in the face of repeated failure. In addition, numerous studies have found a relationship between increased stress and medical and psychological problems. Not only do stressful sports disrupt eating and sleeping patterns, but injury rates are higher in athletes who have experienced increased life stressors. Two athletes may even experience an injury differently depending upon how they are affected by psychological factors.[9] These injuries have increased impact in the face of poor coping skills and low social support.

Smith and Small[10] have proposed a four-part philosophy to help deal with stress:

1. **Winning isn't everything, nor is it the only thing.** Emphasis should be placed on team camaraderie, skill building, fun, and fitness.

2. **Failure is not the same thing as losing.** There is a difference between losing and not winning. The act of losing reflects on the athlete's self-worth. Not winning, even in spite of full effort (internal and stable), should be appreciated and rewarded, especially at the amateur level.

3. **Success does not equal winning.** The outcome is not as important as the race. Good strategy and use of team tactics are constant (and stable), whereas the strength of an opponent is unstable and should not be attributed to success.

4. **Success is found in striving for victory.** Maximum effort, fitness, team bonds, and skill development will last. A victory will last only until the next loss.

Sidebar 13.3

List all of your positive characteristics that are not related to sports.

SPECIALIZED PSYCHOLOGICAL INTERVENTIONS

Reducing the stress of injury and even of competition is accomplished through the use of specialized psychological interventions. Making use of all resources available to you will help you deal with stress. Surround yourself with people who reward effort and share what you value about your sport.

Find a coach who does not focus solely on victory but on your hard effort. There are many sports psychologists who can help deal with stress. The use of relaxation techniques to focus on the stable, internal characteristics, intrinsic motivators, and positive personal attributes can help you to feel grounded in good feelings about your sport.

Goal setting

The field of organizational psychology brings the concept of goal setting to sports. Setting goals helps to provide a focal point for training; fast healers have been shown to practice significantly more goal setting than slow healers. Goals must have certain qualities for the exercise to work. Positive language should describe the goals. What to do, not what to avoid, should guide behavior. This keeps the negative thoughts out and makes the process more effective. Basic guidelines for goal setting are outlined in Table 13.2.

Three types of goals have been described in the literature: outcome-, performance-, and process-oriented goals. Outcome goals describe a performance that is relative to other people, such as a top-ten placing in the state road race championship. Performance-oriented goals establish more concrete criteria, such as beating a personal record for a triathlon course. Process-oriented goals define barometers that the athlete feels are important for success, such as being able to perform slightly above the lactate threshold for forty-five minutes. Because outcome-oriented goals relate directly to competition, there is no control over how others may perform relative to the goal setter; thus these types of goals can often lead to burnout, increased stress, and disappointment. Outcome-oriented goals are also related to increased stress. To maximize performance, concentrate on the process- and performance-oriented approaches.

When you are setting goals for rehabilitation and return to sport, it is important to remain realistic about what can be expected as the level of return. People who have had significant involvement in exercise and sports usually feel they have accomplished less than those with no prior involvement.[11]

Relaxation

There are numerous effective methods to employ for relaxation to counter the negative effects of stress. These techniques can make the muscles more relaxed at rest and more

Table 13.2

GUIDELINES FOR GOAL SETTING

Identify specific targets and measurable outcomes.

Be committed to goals; make them personal and internal.

Athletes should be able to exert control over the targeted goal.

Goals should be realistic yet challenging.

Make goals worthwhile.

Create long- and short-term goals.

Feedback should be available to measure goals.

efficient during exercise. Relaxation is a basic psychological skill to which other skills such as visualization can be added. Although meditation and yoga are two popular practices, the technique of progressive muscle relaxation (PMR) is a more active process that athletes might find useful. PMR employs sequential, systematic, whole-body muscle tensing followed by relaxation of the tensed muscles. The use of PMR among athletes has been shown to increase awareness of muscle tension, reduce injury and pre-competition anxiety,[12] and serve as a platform for other psychological techniques.

To perform PMR, sit in a chair with your elbows bent and your legs uncrossed. The tension/relaxation cycles should proceed in the following order: hands and arms; legs; chest, shoulders, and stomach; back; neck and jaw; face and scalp.[13]

Fully tense the muscles in each group and hold the tension for five seconds, then release the tension halfway and hold for five seconds. Slowly let the tension go and rest comfortably. Focus on the difference between the states of tension and relaxation. Breathe normally and relax the muscles for another ten to fifteen seconds, concentrating on further relaxation with each exhalation. Abdominal breathing is more relaxing than chest breathing. The illustrations on page 116 show the proper way to tense each muscle group.

Thought stoppage

Frequently, negative thoughts can creep into an athlete's mind during competition, training, and rehabilitation. Keeping "I can't" out and replacing it with "I can and will" are the keys to effective thought stoppage. There are many related techniques for preventing negative thoughts from clouding concentration, allowing full attention to be given to the task at hand.

Cue-instructional self-talk evaluates the thoughts that occur during stressful situations and allows the athlete to replace them with useful reminders. For example, as speed increases in the last few laps of a bicycle race, a rider might be afraid of crashing and give up. Using self-instruction, the same rider could repeat to himself, "Follow the fast-moving wheel; move up." Self-instructional cues can help you maintain concentration and keep intrusive negative thoughts out of the consciousness.

In contrast, attention refocusing emphasizes concentrating on external objects to prevent internal negative thoughts. The mountain biker who is having trouble clearing an obstacle might instead be instructed to focus on the top of the tree beyond the obstacle. This places the focus on something other than the stress-inducing element. In addition, this technique has the benefit of keeping the head up and the weight off the front wheel, making it easier to clear the obstacle.

Another example of attention refocusing is the runner who keeps telling herself that she cannot sprint for the finish. By focusing attention on the finish line and noting how it is getting closer, she will have little time to think about how difficult the sprint is.

Similarly, mental rehearsal skills or "visualization" help to focus on the immediate task, whether it is rehabilitation or competition. An athlete who is anticipating reinjury can delay recovery, whereas positive imagery is associated with faster recovery.[14] Imagery, in conjunction with relaxation, has been found to increase confidence and improve performance.

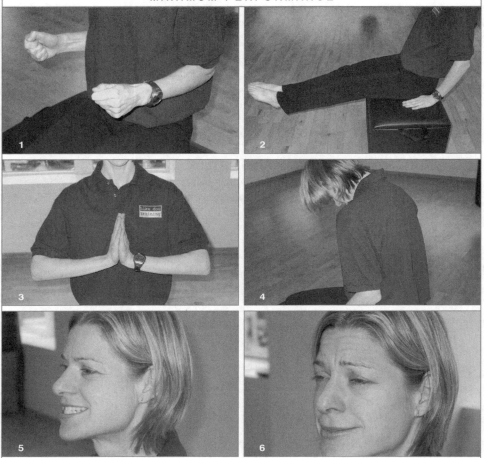

13.1 Progressive Muscle Relaxation *(1) Tensing the hands and arms by making fists. (2) Tensing the thigh and calf muscles by straightening the legs and pointing the toes. (3) Tensing the chest, shoulders, and stomach by pressing the palms together in front of the chest. (4) Tensing the back by arching it and rolling the shoulders. (5) Tensing the neck and jaw by thrusting the jaw forward and drawing the corners of the mouth back. (6) Tensing the face and scalp by wrinkling the forehead and scalp.*

Activation is the readiness to respond, either on a physical or psychological level. Visualization of beneficial content will produce increased alertness, which will lead to increased activation of the body. The type of self-talk and imagery to use to achieve increased activation is dependent upon the task.

There are four types of imagery: affirmation, healing, treatment, and performance. Affirmation imagery is based upon visualization of achieving goals. Healing imagery is directed at envisioning and feeling the repair and recovery taking place. Similarly, treatment imagery emphasizes the efficacy of treatment. Performance imagery is a mental rehearsal of skills used in performance. This type has the most use outside the realm of recovery.

Performance imagery involves mentally rehearsing a task while you are relaxed. An injured athlete will be able to "train" for tasks in which physical participation currently is limited, and the imagery can be continued for success upon return to activity. Imagery can be performed after PMR when the body is relaxed and other thoughts are cleared. Find a separate place and time when you will not be disturbed to work on imagery.

In conclusion, paying attention to the psychological issues in sports will help you use your mind as well as your muscles, and this combined focus can improve performance and make your sport more satisfying.

NOTES

1. A. M. Smith, S. G. Scott, D. M. Wiese. The psychological effects of sports injuries: Coping. *Sports Medicine* June 1990, 9(6): 352–69.

2. I. Ekenman, P. Hassmen, N. Koivula, C. Rolf, L. Fellander-Tsai. Stress fractures of the tibia: Can personality traits help us detect the injury-prone athlete? *Scandinavian Journal of Medicine and Science in Sports* April 2001, 11(2): 87–95.

3. S. R. Francis, M. B. Andersen, P. Maley. Physiotherapists' and male professional athletes' views on psychological skills for rehabilitation. *Journal of Science and Medicine in Sport/Sports Medicine Australia* March 2000, 3(1): 17–29.

4. B. Weiner. *Theories of Motivation: From Mechanism to Cognition.* Chicago: Rand McNally, 1972.

5. J. R. Grove, S. J. Hanrahan, R. M. Stewart. Attributions for rapid or slow recovery from sports injuries. *Canadian Journal of Sport Sciences* June 1990, 15(2): 107–14.

6. Grove et al., Attributions for rapid or slow recovery.

7. M. J. Kelley Jr. Psychological risk factors and sports injuries. *Journal of Sports Medicine and Physical Fitness* June 1990, 30(2): 202–21.

8. F. L. Small, R. E. Smith. Psychology of the young athlete: Stress-related maladies and remedial approaches. *Pediatric Clinics of North America* October 1990, 37(5): 1021–47.

9. R. J. Lysens, M. S. Ostyn, Y. Vanden Auweele, J. Lefevre, M. Vuylsteke, L. Renson. The accident-prone and overuse-prone profiles of the young athlete. *American Journal of Sports Medicine* Sept-Oct 1989, 17(5): 612–19.

10. Small and Smith. Psychology of the young athlete.

11. L. H. Johnston, D. Carroll. The psychological impact of injury: Effects of prior sport and exercise involvement. *British Journal of Sports Medicine* December 2000, 34(6): 436–39.

12. D. K. Ahern, B. A. Lohr. Psychosocial factors in sports injury rehabilitation. *Clinics in Sports Medicine* October 1997, 16(4): 755–68.

13. Small and Smith. Psychology of the young athlete.

14 L. Ievleva, T. Orlick. Mental links to enhanced healing: An exploratory study. *Sport Psychologist* 1991, 5: 25–40.

OTHER REFERENCES

Bull, Stephen J. *Sport Psychology: A Self-help Guide*. Wiltshire: Crowood Press, 1991.

Butler, Richard J. *Sports Psychology in Action*. Oxford: Butterworth-Heinemann, 1996.

EXERCISE IMMUNOLOGY

M aladies ranging from stomach viruses to upper respiratory infections frequently sideline or hamper athletes who could otherwise do well. Several researchers and clinicians have found that athletes are at higher risk of developing upper respiratory infections following heavy training leading up to competition. Staying healthy is especially important, since treatments for common infections impair performance, and some medications appear on the IOC banned-substance list. The field of exercise immunology was started in an effort to find the links among exercise, infection, and health.

Athletes typically want answers to two questions: (1) If I am sick, when can I get back to health and training? (2) If I have an important competition coming up, how can I best prevent illness? The answers to these questions require some basic understanding of the immune system and the way it responds to exercise.

THE IMMUNE SYSTEM
The immune system is the body's defense against infection and foreign microorganisms that can cause disease. Like a country's defenses, the body has a multifaceted system that can fight invaders with different forces. These forces can be divided into three lines of defense: natural barriers, nonspecific cellular responses (innate immunity), and specific immune responses (adaptive immunity).

Natural barriers
The body has barriers to infection that provide the first line of defense. Unless disrupted by burns, abrasions, or cuts, the skin is an impenetrable barrier that will prevent organisms from entering the body. The small hairs lining the inside of the nose act as filters to prevent the entry of organisms. The mucous membrane covering the respiratory tract serves to trap small airborne particles and move them out of the body. The saliva contains an antibody called IgA. This antibody is responsible for preventing many of the

inhaled viruses from gaining a foothold and becoming upper respiratory infections. When protective surfaces fail to prevent microorganisms from entering the body, there are two other mechanisms to ward off infection.

Nonspecific cellular responses

Innate immunity is the arm of the immune system that is always ready to attack foreign microorganisms. Innate immunity relies upon phagocytes, subdivided into macrophages and neutrophils, which are always ready to kill, engulf, and remove foreign microorganisms. These cells are attracted to the invading microbes by chemical signals known as interferon, interleukin, prostaglandin, and complement. After being attracted to the tiny invaders, phagocytes kill the foreign cells by engulfing them and digesting them through release of enzymes.

Specific immune response

Adaptive immunity is specific to a certain virus. With each exposure to that virus, the body adapts by creating specific defenses, which explains why you are more likely to catch a cold when you are younger. With increasing age, the body is exposed to more viruses. As exposure increases, so does immunity to the different viruses. Adaptive immunity is acquired and relies heavily on the lymphocyte (B cell and T cell) response to each exposure.

B cells make the antibodies that attack specific foreign matter. Since each B cell makes only one type of antibody to target a specific cell, there is a large and diverse population of B cells. T cells have several populations to carry out different functions. The functions of T cells are to help the B cells to make antibodies; to recognize and destroy virally infected cells; to activate phagocytes to destroy the cells they have engulfed; and to regulate the overall immune process.

THE EXERCISE EFFECT

A J-shaped curve has been associated with exercise intensity and immune function (see Figure 14.1). In other words, in the absence of exercise, individuals are likely to encounter more infections. As the intensity of exercise increases to a moderate level, so does the immune function. Beyond the level of moderate exercise, however, immune function decreases, and the chance of infection is higher. The J-curve explains why the results of studies

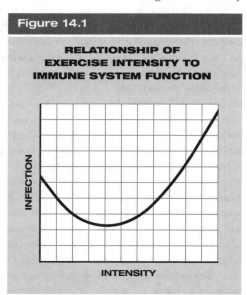

Figure 14.1

RELATIONSHIP OF EXERCISE INTENSITY TO IMMUNE SYSTEM FUNCTION

INFECTION

INTENSITY

can be confusing, with some reporting increased immune function and others report-ing decreased function.

Different cells of the immune system respond differently to various types of exercise. White blood cells, which are a measure of immune function and response to infection, are frequently studied with respect to exercise. For example, several studies have found that one type of white blood cell, the neutrophils, increase during exercise and increase markedly after exercise. This is likely due to the stress response of exercise that mobi-lizes neutrophils into the bloodstream. During heavy training, however, the numbers may increase, but the function of neutrophils is suppressed.[1] Neutrophils play an impor-tant role in the innate immune system, as they are the prominent cell responsible for mopping up bacteria and virally infected cells. In one study of swimmers, intensive training left them with lower neutrophil activity than found in similar people who were not undertaking vigorous exercise.[2] Further vigorous training for national-level compe-tition lowered their function even more.

THE INNATE IMMUNE SYSTEM

The innate immune system, composed of macrophages, neutrophils, and natural killer cells, is thought to be responsible for changes in the immune system after exercise. Exercise stress may exert the strongest influence on innate immune function. Acute bouts of very intense exercise seem to affect these cells more than do moderate bouts of exercise, but moderate exercise still exerts an influence on immune function.

Macrophages

Acute exercise causes an increase in the number of monocytes that circulate in the blood. This does not mean an increase in the total number of cells in the body; instead, there is a shift of these microbe-swallowing cells into the bloodstream where they can be deliv-ered to the site of a potential infection.

Moderate and exhaustive exercise has favorable effects on several of the macrophage functions. Exercise appears to increase the ability of the macrophages to attract, grab, engulf, and kill invading microorganisms.[3] The theory behind this augmentation of function is the secretion of different hormones: corticosteroid or prolactin (to increase attraction) and thyroxine (to increase engulfment).

Exercise has a downside, however. A week of both moderate and exhaustive exer-cise impaired the ability of macrophages to alert the T cells of the virus that has infected an engulfed cell. This prevents the immune system from forming a memory for a par-ticular virus, thus rendering the body susceptible to further infection by the same virus.[4] It has also been shown that stressful exercise may decrease the antiviral function of macrophages.[5]

Chronic exercise has not been studied as extensively as acute, single bouts of exer-cise, but chronic exercise has a decreased immunologic effect on a single exercise ses-sion. It appears that chronic training may cause adaptations in the immune system that decrease the magnitude of response in a single exercise session. There still are changes, however, and they are very different from what is found in a sedentary individual.

Neutrophils

Neutrophils play a central role in the killing of bacteria by engulfing and destroying them. The exercise effect is intensity-dependent. Easy and moderate exercise enhances neutrophil function, but intense exercise suppresses function. These changes could explain the increased susceptibility to infection among endurance athletes.

Acute exercise increases the number of circulating neutrophils, but the function of neutrophils after moderate exercise has been conflicting. Some studies have shown that the neutrophils have a greater ability to kill after exercise; some studies do not demonstrate any difference.

Maximal exercise, on the other hand, globally shows a significant decrease in neutrophil function. There is an initial increase in activity during exercise that is followed by a precipitous decrease in function after exercise. Once a neutrophil is mobilized and its activity is increased during exercise, a cell cannot be reactivated for a while, even if it is needed. This time is known as the "post-exercise refractory period." This refractory period may be partially responsible for the window of opportunity for infections to become established. (This window is discussed in more detail later in this chapter.) One group of researchers has found that a twenty-kilometer running race resulted in double the number of neutrophils in the nose, but these cells lost half their activity for up to twenty-four hours after the race.[6]

Despite the different training regimens studied, the effects of chronic exercise are that moderate training results in an increase in the number of neutrophils at rest, but strenuous training may lead to a reduction in the neutrophil population.

Natural killer cells

The natural killer (NK) cells play the most important role in the killing of invading viruses and also are the cells most responsive to exercise. Following short (less than sixty minutes), intense exercise, the NK cell population increases 150–300 percent. NK cells contain a high concentration of receptors that react to the epinephrine (adrenaline) produced by exercise. The increase is only transient, however, and the cells soon depart the circulation due to the effect of cortisol. Once the NK cells leave, their numbers drop below pre-exercise levels by up to 40 percent.

Longer sessions of exercise do not produce the NK cell increase, but exercise is still followed by a decline, and it lasts longer than the decline with brief exercise. Anti-inflammatory medications[7] and vitamin C[8] do not mitigate the drop in NK cells.

NATURAL BARRIERS

Aside from the cells of the innate immune system, salivary IgA levels are also important in preventing infection. Low salivary IgA levels have been shown to precede upper respiratory infections in squash and hockey players.[9] Salivary IgA levels also decreased before infection in competitive swimmers. Exercise decreases nasal and salivary IgA. As exercise increases, so does the respiratory rate and saliva is dried. With prolonged exercise, there is decreased saliva production due to the dehydrating effects of exercise. Heavy breathing, especially in cold weather, also changes the composition of the mucous lining the respiratory tract. As the mucous dries, it becomes more penetrable by invading microorganisms. Drinking adequate fluids can mitigate these effects.

CLINICAL EFFECTS

Clearly, exercise has a profound effect on the different cells and components of the immune system, as shown by several scientific studies. Nevertheless, does exercise really lead to an increase in the frequency and type of illness? Certainly the connection between exercise and infection was noted in the 1930s when researchers discovered that polio was worse if exercise was undertaken in the early part of the disease.[10]

The most commonly encountered medical condition in athletes and the population in general is the upper respiratory infection (URI). This results in symptoms such as nasal congestion, sore throat, cough, and itchy, watery eyes. The URI is perhaps the easiest infection to study because of its prevalence.

In general, exercise before the URI has no effect or decreases the illness. In contrast, exercise during the early stages of a URI may increase symptoms. The controlled studies performed on URI symptoms have illustrated two principles: Moderate exercise reduced the number of days of URI symptoms. The URI incidence was 8 percent in athletes, 21 percent in walkers, and 50 percent in sedentary people.[11]

Patients with infections frequently ask why they are sidelined from training. The objective is to avoid the possibility of their developing myocarditis, an infection of the heart muscle. In a study of mice, swimming during the early part of a viral infection increased viral replication, inflammation, and death of the heart muscle cells. The exercising mice had a tenfold increase in death, with the majority of heart cells affected that there was a tremendous decrease in function. This compares with only one-quarter to one-half of cells affected in sedentary mice during the same viral infection of the heart.[12]

The spectrum of disease in myocarditis ranges from no symptoms at all to sudden death. However, myocarditis accounts for only 10 percent of sudden death in young, healthy athletes. Symptoms much more likely to be encountered are chest pain, shortness of breath, or irregular heartbeat. In a series of sudden deaths among sixteen Swedish endurance athletes, autopsies revealed myocarditis-like changes in the heart in nine of the cases.

The theory behind these findings is that exercise suppression of the immune system can result in normally harmless organisms, such as the coxsackie B virus and the bacteria *Chlamydia Pneumonia* (not to be confused with the sexually transmitted disease caused by *Chlamydia trachomatis*), invading the athlete, replicating, spreading from the upper respiratory tract to the blood, and rooting in the lungs and heart.[13]

NUTRITIONAL COUNTERMEASURES FOR STRONGER IMMUNITY

Glutamine

Glutamine is the most abundant amino acid in the muscle and plasma. Because the body is capable of synthesizing it, glutamine is considered a nonessential amino acid. The lymphocytes and macrophages have two primary fuels: glucose and glutamine. Glutamine is used both as an energy source and as a building block for DNA synthesis.[14]

Therefore, it is important that the body synthesize the rest for the immune system function. For the cells of the immune system, glutamine is a vital amino acid.

During the course of exercise, however, the body's glutamine supplies, which are located primarily in the muscles, are depleted. The liver synthesizes glucose from glutamine to provide energy for exercising muscles. The use of glutamine for energy comes at the expense of the immune system. Although the body can resynthesize the used glutamine stores, resynthesis does not occur during exercise. Under the stress of intense exercise, the increased need for glutamine from the muscle forces the body into "glutamine debt," thereby starving the lymphocytes and decreasing their function. Glutamine stores may even decrease further after exercise.[15]

The depletion of glutamine during exercise may be cumulative and can be seen in the overtrained athlete or in someone who trains too frequently to allow recovery of plasma glutamine levels. These athletes, as well as others, could benefit from increased recovery, improved diet, and glutamine supplementation.

One study comparing the availability of glutamine at rest with glutamine availability after a marathon supports this hypothesis. Glutamine ingested as part of a drink (0.1 mg/kg) was shown to increase the blood levels within thirty minutes. Glutamine levels returned to normal within two hours. When glutamine was consumed as a 5 g dose immediately after and then two hours after a marathon (timed to keep the levels of glutamine high), the athletes reported a significantly decreased incidence of infection compared with those who drank only glucose.[16]

Dietary protein has also proved to be important. Three weeks of increased protein (20 g/day), eaten as food, increased glutamine levels in 90 percent of athletes in one study.[17] The intake of protein (0.3 g/kg) along with carbohydrate (0.8 g/kg) as a recovery drink after exhaustive cycling prevented the 20 percent drop in glutamine and low recovery levels seen when only glucose was used for recovery.

Protein needs should be watched carefully in those groups of people who might ingest too little: vegetarians and people who are trying to lose weight by restricting calories. One study of strict vegetarians (no animal protein at all), who received protein supplements of 16 percent of overall intake, had no difference in immune cell function compared with lacto-ovo vegetarians who derived dietary protein from dairy and eggs.

Too much protein, however, can decrease plasma glutamine, especially if it comes at the expense of carbohydrate. Ingestion of carbohydrate during exercise with a high-protein, low-carbohydrate diet prevents the decline. It is important not to overlook the role of glucose in the function of the immune system.

Glucose

The recommended dietary intake of carbohydrate is 8–10 g/kg/day for athletes who train two or more hours a day. This is equal to 60–70 percent of overall calorie consumption. This level of carbohydrate will ensure that muscle glycogen stores are full. Glucose is also used by the immune system as a major fuel source. Glucose is used by stimulated lymphocytes and macrophages. In fact, the use of glucose by these cells is almost five times that of glutamine when supplied separately.[18]

Exercise stimulates the production of cortisol, as does a drop in blood sugar. This appears to be the main way that a lack of glucose inhibits immune function. Cortisol inhibits a number of immune functions: NK cell activity, lymphocyte function and IgA secretion.

Drinking a 6 percent glucose beverage during a 2.5 hour run at 70–80 percent of VO_2max prevents these changes in immune function.[19] Consumption of a glucose-containing solution also prevents a drop in saliva flow during exercise.

Lipids

Fats do not play a major role in fueling the immune system, but some fats will suppress it. Of the different types of fats, the important ones for immune function are the n-3 polyunsaturated fatty acids (PUFAs). During stress conditions (exercise), the n-3 PUFAs may reverse the effects of immunosuppression and reduce the incidence of new infections. In a group of animals receiving different oils, those that were fed linseed oil (n-3) did not have a post-exercise immune suppression as did those receiving beef tallow or safflower oil.[20] A diet rich in n-3 PUFAs results in reduced glutamine utilization. The n-3 PUFAs are the primary fat in fish oil.

Antioxidants and vitamins

During hard exercise, the increase in oxygen metabolism can lead to production of destructive free radicals. Athletes may need foods and supplements that contain antioxidants to deactivate the free radicals and prevent the damage they cause. Free radicals inhibit the neutrophils' ability to kill bacteria, reduce lymphocyte proliferation, and decrease the killing ability of NK cells. Athletes should consume nutritional antioxidants such as vitamin C (ascorbic acid), vitamin E (tocopherol), and vitamin A (retinol).

Vitamin A deficiency results in decreased lymphocyte response, decreased IgA production, and a higher incidence of spontaneous infection. Fewer URI symptoms were reported in marathon runners who had taken a daily supplement combining three antioxidants, including 18 mg of beta-carotene (a vitamin A precursor).[21]

Vitamin C increases the T cell response and decreases the cortisol-mediated immune suppression. The clinical effect of vitamin C has been debated and researched with conflicting results. One study, which found a positive result, discovered that vitamin C reduced the URI incidence in the two weeks following a marathon if supplementation began three weeks before the marathon.[22] The dose was 1,000 mg daily. Similarly, another study found the lowest incidence of URI among marathoners who had the highest total mean daily vitamin C intake (1,004 mg).[23] After a twenty-one-kilometer race, vitamin C levels dropped 20 percent below prerace levels and remained low for two days, presumably due to usage and uptake by the lymphocyte population of white blood cells.[24] This demonstrates the need for vitamin C to bolster the immune system. A dose of 1500 mg of vitamin C for one week prior to race day, on race day, and for two days after the race decreased the amount of cortisol, the steroid that weakens the immune system.[25]

Vitamin E may fight the immunosuppressive effects of exercise stress by reducing cortisol levels. In athletes, doses of vitamin E supplements of 300–800 mg (450–1,200 IU) have been given for antioxidant protection following exercise.[26]

Zinc is vital to the development of the immune system, and zinc deficiency causes a decrease in several of its parameters. High zinc concentrations are found in nuts, legumes, and grains but are better absorbed from meat and seafood. During exercise, zinc is lost in sweat and increased urine excretion. An acute bout of high-intensity exercise will increase urinary zinc losses by 34 percent. Furthermore, carbohydrate-rich diets are usually deficient in zinc.

Six days of zinc supplements in male runners had two effects: worsening of lymphocyte proliferation and protecting against the detrimental effects of free radicals. Megadoses of zinc are detrimental; the recommended dose of zinc in athletes is 10 mg daily.[27]

WINDOW OF INFECTION

Athletes have reported an increase in the number of URI symptoms during the period immediately following heavy training or racing. The changes in the immune system due to exercise have led to an explanatory theory: The "Open Window Theory" describes a period shortly after exhaustive (not moderate) exercise that allows infections to gain a foothold due to the athlete's suppressed immune system. According to this theory, the window represents a clinically significant period of time when there is an increased chance of getting sick.

Not only are the cells of the immune system transiently suppressed during exercise, but so too are the immune regulatory molecules. These regulatory elements of immunity, molecules called cytokines, are suppressed for a time after exhaustive bouts of exercise.[28]

The window of infection can last between three and seventy-two hours, depending on the measure of function that is examined. Therefore, the window can be opened by repeated physical stress, and an athlete exposed to new viruses and further weakened by other stressors (travel, lack of sleep, poor nutrition, weight loss) can contract clinically significant infections.

PRESCRIPTION FOR THE RETURN TO EXERCISE

Exercise is generally regarded as a healthy pursuit. The purpose of this chapter is not to prevent you from exercising but to help you to exercise smarter. I am frequently asked when it is safe or even beneficial to return to exercise.

In general, it is important to determine if returning to training will be detrimental to your overall health. Having minor symptoms may not hinder performance, but they can make you feel worse. If you know when to go easy, you will feel better and not exacerbate your condition. Consider these two scenarios:

Steve is a twenty-eight-year-old competitive cyclist who is feeling nasal congestion and a sore throat. He replaces the anaerobic threshold intervals that he planned to do that day with an easy ride. Although his nose has more mucus than usual, he feels good and is able to resume his normal training schedule two days later.

Mark is a twenty-seven-year-old runner who develops a fever, muscle aches, swollen glands, and fatigue the day before a 10K race. He has already preregistered and doesn't want to miss the race. He enters the race, feels horrible, and turns in a mediocre time. His symptoms continue for two more days, and he misses the next week's training due to continued fatigue.

Most physicians will agree that the "neck check" is a safe guideline. According to this rule of thumb, if symptoms are limited to above the neck, it is safe to resume intense training once symptoms have resolved. Steve fits this category. Mild to moderate exercise may even be resumed if above-neck symptoms are present. If you feel worse after twenty minutes of activity, stop and resume activity once you are rested and your symptoms have improved.

The catecholamines that the body makes during exercise (such as epinephrine) may even help to alleviate symptoms of a URI. The catecholamines act as a natural decongestant to help reduce nasal congestion. Naturally, many athletes tend to want to return to their usual training program. Nevertheless, excessive training will not be beneficial at this time, as the exhaustive stress will further hurt immune function. Trying for hard exercise will not be fruitful because you are likely to be tired and may be unable to reach target heart rate and power zones.

Below-neck symptoms are an indication to treat the illness seriously. Mark falls in this category. If you have symptoms such as fever, fatigue, muscle aches, or swollen glands, intense exercise should not be performed until two to four weeks after the symptoms have resolved. Light and moderate exercise can be resumed once the symptoms improve.

FINAL RECOMMENDATIONS

To avoid increased chance of developing a URI, use the following checklist as a guide to your activity:

- Keep other stressors to a minimum: Job, emotional, and physical stressors are related to an increased risk of URI.
- Avoid rapid weight loss.
- Avoid touching your eyes and nose—a prime way of exposing yourself to viruses.
- Avoid contact with sick people before major events or in a hard training phase.
- Get a flu shot if you compete during the winter months.
- Replace chicken and beef with fish as a primary animal protein source.
- Follow the "neck check" for returning to training.
- During exercise, rehydrate with a 6–8 percent carbohydrate solution.
- Use a recovery drink that contains 5 g of glutamine immediately after and two hours after exhaustive exercise.
- Use a recovery drink with 1 g/kg carbohydrate and 0.3 g/kg protein. Supplement with the following:
  Beta-carotene 18 mg daily.
  Vitamin C 1,500 mg daily.
  Vitamin E 300–800 mg IU daily.
  Zinc 10 mg daily.

NOTES

1. D. C. Nieman, K. S. Buckley, D. A. Henson, et al. Immune function in marathon runners versus sedentary controls. *Medicine and Science in Sports and Exercise* 1995, 27: 986–92.

2. D. B. Pyne, M. S. Baker, P. A. Fricker, et al. Effects of an intensive 12-week training program by elite swimmers on neutrophil oxidative activity. *Medicine and Science in Sports and Exercise* 1995, 27: 536–42.

3. J. A. Woods, J. M. Davis, J. A. Smith, D. C. Nieman. Exercise and cellular innate immune function. *Medicine and Science in Sports and Exercise* January 1999, 31(1): 57–66.

4. J. A. Woods, M. A. Ceddia, C. Kozak, B. Wolters. Effects of exercise on the macrophage MHC II response to inflammation. *International Journal of Sports Medicine* 1997, 18: 483–88.

5. J. M. Davis, M. L. Kohut, L. M. Hertler-Colbert, D. A. Jackson, A. Ghaffar and E. P. Mayer. Exercise, alveolar macrophage function, and susceptibility to respiratory infection. *Journal of Applied Physiology* 1998, 274: R1454–59.
M. L. Kohut, J. M. Davis, D. A. Jackson, et al. Exercise effects on IFN-Beta expression and viral replication in lung macrophages following HSV-1 infection. *American Journal of Physiology* 1998, 27: L1089–94.

6. G. Muns. Effect of long-distance running on polymorphonuclear neutrophil phagocytic function of the upper airways. *International Journal of Sports Medicine* 1993, 15: 96–99.

7. D. C. Nieman, J. C. Ahle, D. A. Henson, et al. Indomethacin does not alter natural killer cell response to 2.5 hours of running. *Journal of Applied Physiology* 1995, 79: 748–55.

8. D. C. Nieman, D. A. Henson, D. E. Butterworth, et al. Vitamin C supplementation does not alter the immune response to 2.5 hours of running. *International Journal of Sports Nutrition* 1997, 7: 173–84.

9. L. T. Mackinnon, E. M. Ginn, G. J. Seymour. Temporal relationship between decreased salivary IgA and upper respiratory tract infection in elite athletes. *Australian Journal of Science and Medicine in Sport* 1993, 25: 94–99.

10. B. K. Pedersen, L. Hoffman-Goetz. Exercise and the immune system: Regulation, integration, adaptation. *Physiological Reviews* July 2000, 80(3): 1055–81.

11. D. C. Neiman, B. K. Pedersen. Exercise and immune function: Recent developments. *Sports Medicine* February 1999, 27(2): 73-80.

12. B. G. Gatmaitan, J. L. Chanson, A. M. Lerner. Augmentation of the virulence of murine coxsackie virus B-3 myocardiopathy by exercise. *Journal of Experimental Medicine* 1970, 131: 1121–36.

13. Gatmaitan, et al. Augmentation of the virulence of murine coxsackie virus B-3 myocardiopathy by exercise.

14. M. J. O'Leary, J. H. Coakley. Nutrition and immunonutrition. *British Journal of Anaesthesia* 1996, 77(1): 118–27.

15. N. C. Bishop, A. K. Blannin, N. P. Walsh, et al. Nutritional aspects of immunosuppression in athletes. *Sports Medicine* September 1999, 28(3): 151–76.

16. L. M. Castell, E. A. Newsholme. The effects of oral glutamine supplementation on athletes after prolonged, exhaustive exercise. *Nutrition* 1997, 13(7/8): 738–42.

17. K. J. Kingsbury, L. Kay, M. Hjelm. Contrasting plasma free amino acid patterns in elite athletes: Association with fatigue and infection. *British Journal of Sports Medicine* 1998, 28: 285–90.

18. P. Newsholme, E. A. Newsholme. Rates of utilization of glucose, glutamine, and oleate and formation of end products. *The Biochemical Journal* 1989, 261: 211–18.

19. Bishop et al. Nutritional aspects of immunosuppression in athletes.

20. Pederson and Hoffman-Goetz. Exercise and the immune system.

21. Bishop et al. Nutritional aspects of immunosuppression in athletes.

22. E. M. Peters, J. M. Goetzsche, B. Grobbelaar, T. D. Noakes. Vitamin C supplementation reduces the incidence of postrace symptoms of upper-respiratory tract infection in ultramarathon runners. *American Journal of Clinical Nutrition* 1993, 57: 170–74.

23. Bishop et al. Nutritional aspects of immunosuppression in athletes.

24. M. Gleeson, J. D. Robertson, R. J. Maughan. Influence of exercise on ascorbic acid status in man. *Clinical Science* (London, Eng.) November 1987, 73(5): 501–5.

25. D. C. Nieman, E. M. Peters, D. A. Henson, E. I. Nevines, M. M. Thompson. Influence of vitamin C supplementation on cytokine changes following an ultramarathon. *Journal of Interferon and Cytokine Research* (the official journal of the International Society for Interferon and Cytokine Research) November 2000, 20(11): 1029–35.

26. Bishop et al. Nutritional aspects of immunosuppression in athletes.

27. Bishop et al. Nutritional aspects of immunosuppression in athletes.

28. C. Weinstock, D. Konig, R. Harnischmacher et al. Effect of exhaustive exercise stress on the cytokine response. *Medicine and Science in Sports and Exercise* March 1997, 29(3): 345–54.

OTHER REFERENCES

Gleeson, M. Overview: Exercise immunology. *Immunology and Cell Biology* October 2000, 78(5): 483–84.

Schuler, P. B., L. K. Lloyd, P. A. LeBlanc, et al. The effect of physical activity and fitness on specific antibody production in college students. *Journal of Sports Medicine and Physical Fitness* September 1999, 39(3): 233–39.

Shephard, R. J. Overview of the epidemiology of exercise immunology. *Immunology and Cell Biology* October 2000, 78(5): 485–95.

RHINITIS, SINUSITIS, AND THE **COMMON** COLD: **IT'S ALL IN YOUR HEAD**

In my first four years as the race doctor for the USPro cycling championships, the majority of athletes I treated were suffering from either allergies or the common cold, also known as the upper respiratory tract infection. These two conditions are not dangerous or life-threatening, but they are irritating if peak performance is a goal. Nasal congestion, irritated eyes, and sore throat can be due to either an upper respiratory tract infection (URI) or allergic rhinitis. Knowing the specific symptoms, treatments, and prevention will help keep you exercising longer.

The URI is responsible for 429 million illnesses each year.[1] The family of viruses known as rhinoviruses causes the majority of URIs. Clinically, most people know when they are getting a URI. The illness may start with a mild sore throat, malaise, nasal stuffiness, nasal discharge, nonproductive cough, and an occasional low-grade fever.

Postnasal drip is the phenomenon of nasal discharge dripping backward down the throat. As the mucus hits the vocal cords, it will be coughed up. This is the only reason you should have a productive cough with a URI. The cough may be worse in the morning but should clear shortly after you awake. If you have a continued productive cough, consult a physician, as pneumonia or bronchitis may have developed.

Other signs that a more serious infection may be present include continued nasal drainage of green or yellow discharge, high fever (more than 101 degrees), difficulty breathing, voice changes, or difficulty (not just pain) swallowing.

Because there are hundreds of rhinoviruses that can infect the upper respiratory tract, a specific vaccine cannot easily be made. Antibiotics target only bacterial infections; they are useless against virus-caused illnesses.

Treatment of URI targets the symptoms. Decongestants, cough suppressants, and analgesics can curb most of them. Athletes must be judicious in the use of medication because the International Olympic Committee has banned several substances, and some medications can predispose an athlete to dehydration and heat illness.

There are numerous categories of decongestants, each with its own mechanism of action. Alpha agonists (pseudoephedrine, phenylpropanolamine) are responsible for constricting the small blood vessels in the mucous membranes, ameliorating congestion. Alpha agonists are banned by the International Olympic Committee but have recently been shown to have no significant effect on athletic performance.[2] Side effects of alpha agonists include increased heart rate, anxiety, dizziness, and increased blood pressure.

Another class of decongestants is the anticholinergics. These medications can be used topically (ipratropium) or orally (methscopalamine). Anticholinergics dry congested nasal passages. Side effects of anticholinergics are excessive drying, which can cause nosebleeds, dry mouth, and constipation. However, the most significant side effect is the dysfunction of heat regulation. Oral anticholinergics can cause the body to overheat during exercise, a response that can lead to heat exhaustion and heatstroke. For this reason, anticholinergics in the oral form should be avoided.

Topical decongestants such as oxymetalazone are useful for athletes with congestion. This class of medications acts directly on the mucous membranes to cause vasoconstriction. Although use for longer than two or three days can lead to dependence, short-term use is effective to clear a congested nose.

Guiafenasin is an ingredient found in many combination cold medications, which acting alone will thin secretions, making them easier for the body to clear. To achieve the maximum effect of guiafenasin, it is important to be well hydrated.

Cough suppressants can improve comfort during a URI. Codeine, dextromethorphan, albuterol, and benzonatate are widely used, but athletes should be aware of possible side effects. Codeine and dextromethorphan can cause drowsiness and are not particularly effective for cough during a URI.[3] Benzonatate is an anesthetic that can numb the throat, which is useful for preventing the cough from postnasal drip; the only side effect is mouth numbness if the capsule is chewed.

Also used for exercise-induced asthma, the bronchodilator albuterol is effective in reducing the cough associated with viral-induced bronchospasm. Albuterol can increase the heart rate and cause anxiety and jitters. For elite athletes, a doctor's note must accompany use along with a U.S. Anti-doping Agency Restricted Substance Notification form.

Preventing URI is a better strategy than treating it. The viruses that cause the condition are spread by contact of them with mucous membranes either directly or from airborne exposure. Airborne spread occurs when an infected person sneezes or coughs and virus droplets are aerosolized. Other people can contract the illness when a droplet hits their eyes, nose, or throat. Enclosed environments, such as buses or airplanes, can exacerbate this. One professional racer's strategy has been never to use the central air conditioning in a hotel but instead to keep the window open. This seems to be a good tactic, although there is no supporting evidence for it.

Not using towels and water bottles of infected people will help to prevent URIs.[4] Frequent hand washing will keep your hands virus-free and help to prevent transmission.[5]

Exercising in the cold has long been felt to cause illness. Research has shown that this may not be true. In fact, exercising in cold environments may even stimulate the immune system.[6] However, if the cold is extreme, or the exercise is exhausting, or both, there can be an immunosuppressive effect leading to an increased susceptibility to viral infections.[7]

The best defense may be smart training to prevent a decline in immune function that can be seen with overtraining.

The most frequently asked question from athletes I coach who contract illness is when to return to exercise. The simple rule is to perform the "neck check"[8] described in the last chapter. With above-neck symptoms only (sore throat, runny nose, dry cough, nasal congestion), it is safe to return to exercise. Start slowly and assess how you feel after ten minutes. If you are feeling better, continue; if you are feeling worse, stop. If there is improvement, it is probably due to the effects of the circulating catecholamines during exercise that act as alpha agonists to aid in decongestion.

One issue is whether exercising if you have a mild infection will be beneficial. Exercising with certain URIs may leave you too tired for competition. You might not perform hard workouts as well as when you are healthy, which prompts the question of whether rest would be better for you.[9] If you are suffering from decreased endurance, strength, or speed, rest is probably the better option.

Return to exercise gradually. If you have been off for several days, consult your coach for guidance, or return to your pre-illness level.

SINUSITIS

Among the several conditions that mimic URI is sinusitis. People with nasal congestion frequently refer to their problem as "sinus infection." The sinuses are air spaces in the forehead and cheekbones. With increased nasal congestion, the openings to these spaces can become blocked, leading to a bacterial infection. The symptoms of sinusitis are facial pain and headache, fever, and purulent drainage. Treatment of sinusitis is with antibiotics and decongestants. Typically, the person with sinusitis is significantly sicker than the person with a URI.

ALLERGIC RHINITIS

Another condition that can be difficult to differentiate from URI is allergic rhinitis, which causes clear nasal discharge, sneezing, sore throat, and itchy eyes. Although these symptoms are similar to those of URI, allergies can be differentiated by seasonal flare-up or history of exposure to allergy-causing factors (pollen, for example). Fever is not a part of allergic rhinitis.

The outdoor athlete is more likely to be affected by environmental allergies. Many airborne allergens can cause the symptoms of allergic rhinitis. Exercise by itself does not precipitate allergies but can worsen allergies in people who are already susceptible. For example, if someone is allergic to a particular food and eats that food before exercise, the allergy can lead to a life-threatening condition called anaphylaxis.[10]

Another environmental factor is outdoor temperature. Exposure to cold during exercise can mimic symptoms of allergies, such as by causing nasal discharge. Cold exposure also can worsen the symptoms of hay fever.[11]

The effects of allergies on exercise rarely cause decreased performance. Nasal congestion can alter breathing in such a way that the athlete may feel short of breath during high-intensity exercise. During intense exercise, most air intake to the lungs is through the mouth, not the nose. However, if you generally breathe through the nose, decongestants, antihistamines, and inhaled nasal steroids may be helpful. Anecdotal evidence indicates that use of external nasal spring dilator strips has some merit.

The first order of treatment for allergy sufferers is to remove themselves from the environment causing the allergies. Obviously, this is not possible during a race or a favorite outdoor sport, but set your goals with allergies in mind. Workouts can be scheduled for midday when pollen concentration is lowest. Training routes should be noted so that particular allergens can be avoided; for instance, during allergy season, avoid a stretch of road that has a high concentration of allergy-stimulating grass.

Allergies can be treated with antihistamines. Older antihistamines, such as diphenhydramine (Benadryl) and hydralazine (Atarax), are sedating and can also lead to problems of heat illness. Newer antihistamines have been developed that don't have sedating properties. Medications such as cetirizine (Zyrtec), fexofenadine (Allegra), and desloratadine (Clarinex). Adequate hydration and the use of other decongestants can also help. When you have identified the season for allergies, you might want to take daily antihistamines until the environmental concentrations of the particular allergen have decreased.

Other medications that have been found useful are inhaled steroids that act on the mucous membranes and have minimal systemic effects. Cromolyn sodium inhalers have less potency than steroids and are also useful. Both steroids and cromolyn must be used daily for their antiallergy properties to work.

Allergic rhinitis and exercise-induced asthma frequently coexist in the same athletes. Controlling rhinitis will decrease the severity and frequency of exercise-induced asthma symptoms.[12]

EXERCISE-INDUCED URTICARIA AND ANAPHYLAXIS

Along the spectrum of allergies and asthma lies the condition of exercise-induced urticaria. Urticaria, or hives, are small, round, red skin spots that are raised and may coalesce to form larger hives.

This condition, which affects females twice as frequently as males,[13] often is accompanied by intense itching, skin flushing, and swelling of the lips. Attacks typically occur within five minutes of beginning exercise and usually resolve spontaneously within thirty minutes to four hours after exercise. Environmental conditions affect the severity of exercise-induced urticaria.

Exercise-induced anaphylaxis is a condition along the same spectrum that can have dangerous consequences. Anaphylaxis is a life-threatening infection that can occur during exercise. It can happen at any time and can be made worse when you exercise after eating a particular food to which you are allergic. Check labels of energy foods carefully to ensure that they do not contain any food items to which you may be allergic. Symptoms of exercise-induced anaphylaxis are tightness in the throat, difficulty breathing, cough, dizziness, and low blood pressure. If these symptoms appear, stop exercise immediately. After an episode of exercise-induced anaphylaxis, ask your doctor to prescribe epinephrine, which comes in an auto-injector to deliver a fast and automatic injection of epinephrine, which may be lifesaving should the condition recur.

In summary, prevention of exercise-induced allergies is achieved with nonsedating antihistamines taken before exercise.[14] If you are on this treatment, you will need to drink more fluid to prevent heat-related illness.

NOTES

1. R. A. Swain, B. Kaplan. Upper respiratory infections: Treatment selection for active patients. *The Physician and Sportsmedicine* February 1998, 26(2): 85–95.

2. R. Swain, D. Harsha, J. Baenziger, et al. Do pseudoephedrine or phenylpropanolamine improve maximum oxygen uptake and time to exhaustion? *Clinical Journal of Sport Medicine* 1997, 7(3): 168–73.

3. M. B. H. Smith, W. Feldman. Over-the-counter cold medications. *JAMA* 1993, 269(17): 2258–63.

4. W. A. Primos, J. R. Wappes. Exercising—or not—when you are sick. *The Physician and Sportsmedicine* January 1996, 24(1): 55.

5. L. L. Gibson, J. B. Rose, C. N. Haas, C. P. Gerba, P. A. Rusin. Quantitative assessment of risk reduction from hand washing with antibacterial soaps. *Symposium series* (Society for Applied Microbiology) 2002, (31): 136S–43S.

6. I. K. Brenner, J. W. Castellani, C. Gabaree, A. J. Young, J. Zamecnik, R. J. Shephard, P. N. Shek. Immune changes in humans during cold exposure: Effects of prior heating and exercise. *Journal of Applied Physiology* August 1999, 87(2): 699–710.

7. R. J. Shephard. Immune changes induced by exercise in an adverse environment. *Canadian Journal of Physiology and Pharmacology* May 1998, 76(5): 539–46.

8. E. R. Eichner. Infection, immunity, and exercise. *The Physician and Sportsmedicine* 1993, 21(1): 125–35.

9. W. A. Primos. Sports and exercise during acute illness: Recommending the right course for patients. *The Physician and Sportsmedicine* January 1996, 24(1): 44.

10. S. U. Chong, M. Worm, T. Zuberbier. Role of adverse reactions to food in urticaria and exercise-induced anaphylaxis. *International Archives of Allergy and Immunology* September 2002, 129(1): 19–26.

11. M. N. Blumenthal, C. Sherman. Managing allergies in active people. *The Physician and Sportsmedicine* August 1997, 25(8): 29–34.

12. J. Corren. The relationship between allergic rhinitis and bronchial asthma. *Current Opinion in Pulmonary Medicine* January 1999, 5(1): 35–37.

13. A. W. Nichols. Exercise-induced anaphylaxis and urticaria. *Clinics in Sports Medicine* April 1992, 11(2): 303–12.

14. R. G. Hosey, P. J. Carek, A. Goo. Exercise-induced anaphylaxis and urticaria. *American Family Physician* October 15, 2001, 64(8): 1367–72.

EATING
DISORDERS

AND THE FEMALE ATHLETE TRIAD

his chapter does not contain any information that will directly enhance your athletic performance, but it could save the health, athletic career, and even the life of you or your teammates. Disordered eating has become a pervasive problem in society, especially among endurance athletes who associate being lean with athletic success.

When we watch the Ironman® triathlon or the Tour de France, we see athletes who are at their performance peak and have been training so hard that they must give special attention to maintaining weight. Because these athletes are performing well in their events, it is not surprising that other people try to emulate their successes by putting abnormal emphasis on losing weight.

The repercussions of dieting, weight loss, and negative energy balance reach beyond performance issues and have impacts on the athletes' health long after they stop competing. Most athletes with disordered eating do not necessarily have a definitive eating disorder, but fall somewhere on the spectrum that ranges from calorie restriction to outright eating disorders. The preoccupation with weight among endurance athletes has led to a description of disordered eating known as "anorexia athletica."

Among women, the "female athlete triad" is a combination of disordered eating, loss of menses, and osteoporosis (bone loss) that can lead to debilitating stress fractures. These three components are related in physiological and psychological etiologies and are interwoven in the diagnosis and treatment.

DISORDERED EATING

Eating disorders are diagnosed by standards set forth in the American Psychiatric Association's *Diagnostic and Statistical Manual,* or the DSM-IV. These criteria appear in Table 16.1.[1] They all have in common an individual's abnormal notion of appropriate body weight and a fear of weight gain.

Table 16.1

DIAGNOSTIC CRITERIA FOR EATING DISORDERS

Refusal to maintain body weight at or above a minimally normal weight for age and height

Intense fear of gaining weight or becoming fat, even though underweight

Disturbed by body image, undue influence of body weight on self-evaluation

Absence of at least three consecutive menstrual cycles without hormones

Source: American Psychiatric Association. *Diagnostic and Statistical Manual,* 2000.

Anorexia nervosa is defined as a fear of getting fat, amenorrhea (loss of three consecutive menstrual periods), distorted body image, and inability to maintain 85 percent of expected body weight. Bulimia nervosa is a disorder characterized by binge eating with behavior that compensates for the binge, either through purging by vomiting or laxative use or through starvation. There is also an unhealthy concern about body image.

The prevalence of disordered eating among women is approximately ten times that in men. Estimations of eating disorders in female athletes range from 1 to 62 percent.[2] The prevalence is higher in those sports where leanness or weight is valued. In men, bodybuilders and wrestlers have higher tendencies toward disordered eating from trying to make weight. Other weight-class athletes are also predisposed to eating problems.

The prevalence of the female athlete triad is difficult to assess because of the vague definition of "disordered eating," but data support a frequency of amenorrhea between 3.4 percent and 66 percent and prevalence of disordered eating in female athletes between 15 percent and 62 percent.

RISK FACTORS

A number of factors have been identified that can lead to the development of eating disorders. Whether in combination or alone, these elements can be a start to identifying and treating the eating disorder.

Athletes who tend toward disordered eating gravitate toward sports in which leanness is a preferred trait. This orientation not only provides an atmosphere that is more supportive of the disorder, but it also hides the unnaturally thin body type that might otherwise draw attention as being the result of disordered eating.

Even exercise may be the stimulus for disordered eating. During exercise, the appetite is suppressed, making food less appealing and decreasing the importance of eating. The athlete continues training, probably loses weight, and a pattern ensues, especially as the emphasis on the weight loss is reinforced.

Natural body type will preselect those individuals who are good at a particular sport. Tall athletes will gravitate toward basketball, while leaner athletes might be drawn to running or cycling. Athletes who feel they deviate from the standard body type are more likely to develop disordered eating to match the body type of their peers. This can be exacerbated if other family members are overweight.

Similarly, people who start a sport before puberty but undergo a change in body type during puberty might seek a return to their original weight and body type through disordered eating, especially if their new body type is not as compatible with the sport.

Athletes involved in weight-class sports and aesthetic sports (gymnasts, divers, figure skaters) are prone to diets and binges involving cyclical weight gain and loss, the so-called yo-yo diet. However, endurance and "leanness" athletes are still susceptible to falling into this pattern with the start of every season. Although the health risks of yo-yo dieting have not played out as much as was once thought, this pattern of dieting is a risk for developing disordered eating.

Periods of injury or illness can leave an athlete sidelined. During downtime, there is a feeling that weight gain will occur if diet is not monitored closely. This can result in abnormal calorie restriction and fear of weight gain, and these characteristics can continue even after the athlete returns to activity.

Coaches have a major influence on the start of unhealthy eating patterns in athletes. If coaches and trainers recommend weight loss without providing proper diet and nutrition advice, this further exacerbates the tendency toward pathological eating habits.

Athletes who excel in sports have personality traits that take them beyond being good athletes and make them victors. These traits are responsible for drive, determination, control, and commitment. This "pressure to win" mentality can turn any of the risk factors into a disordered eating pattern (see Table 16.2). Such fixation occurs especially when the inner feelings of "win at any cost" and desire for leanness are affirmed by professional athletes who crow about how much faster they can go since losing "several kilos," or by a coach who claims that weight is hindering a rider's success.

MEDICAL PROBLEMS

The medical problems that arise from anorexia nervosa and bulima nervosa stem from the methods used for weight loss, namely laxatives, diuretics, diet pills, and even starvation. The abuse of these medications can lead to dependence and life-threatening dehydration and electrolyte abnormalities (Table 16.3). The risks of starvation have long-term consequences.

As starvation continues in females, the menstrual cycle becomes irregular. The exact reason is unknown, but the long-held belief

Table 16.2

PERSONALITY CHARACTERISTICS OF DISORDERED EATERS

Perfectionist
Highly self-motivated
Regards others opinions highly
Self-critical behavior
Need for control; feels out of control
Need to win
Low self-esteem
Symptoms of depression

Table 16.3

HAZARDS OF DISORDERED EATING

Amenorrhea
Osteoporosis
Stress fractures
Depleted glycogen stores
Dehydration
Fatigue
Decreased endurance
Electrolyte abnormalities
Decreased muscle mass

that loss of body fat causes an athlete to lose her period has come into question. Athletic amenorrhea (no menstrual cycle or up to only three cycles per year) is due to the effects of exercise on the body. The ovarian cycles of ovulation are controlled by hormones secreted from the brain and pituitary gland. Exercise suppresses the release of these hormones. Exercise, in the absence of proper diet, also leads to a negative energy balance. This so-called energy drain resets the brain's trigger for hormonal secretion. When these women take rest time without a change in the percentage of body fat or weight gain, their periods will return. This result counters the theory that a critical percentage of body fat is necessary for amenorrhea.

Another theory is that the chain of hormone secretion from the brain to the ovaries is disrupted by exercise. Adrenaline secreted during exercise inhibits the hypothalamic secretion of hormones ultimately responsible for the functioning of the ovaries. This disruption has been found to occur only in low-energy states.

Amenorrhea, which is defined as primary if the athlete never starts menstruating or as secondary if the athlete loses her period, is not the only menstrual irregularity that can occur. Menstrual dysfunction is a continuum of disorders that ends with amenorrhea. Menarche, or onset of menstruation, is delayed in athletes who undertake an excessive training load before puberty. This condition can have effects on the athlete's growth and development and should prompt a decrease in training during puberty.

The normal menstrual period lasts about twenty-eight days (range of twenty-five to thirty-eight days) and is divided into two distinct phases: follicular and luteal. In the follicular phase, estrogen is the main hormone secreted; in the luteal phase, progesterone joins estrogen to exert hormonal influence. A short luteal phase is one of the earliest effects of exercise and can lead to a menstrual period of only twenty-one days due to decreased hormones. Oligomenorrhea, defined as three to six periods in a year or cycles at thirty-nine to ninety days apart, is also seen.

There are several reasons an athlete might prefer missed cycles, including convenience, no premenstrual symptoms, and a perception that training is effective. The loss of menstrual cycles, however, has undesirable long-term health effects, including the following:

1. Decrease in bone density (osteopenia) from 1.0 standard deviation above the mean to 0.6 standard deviation below the mean (age-matched so that older women weren't included in standard group), predisposing athletes to stress fractures (overuse injury) and other fractures (due to acute trauma)
2. Lower peak bone mass and an increased risk for postmenopausal osteoporosis
3. Infertility
4. Increase in basal cortisol levels and thus weakening of the immune system.

Osteoporosis results from osteopenia and is defined as low bone density and microscopic bone loss that puts the bones at increased risk of trauma. Bone density comes from calcification of a microscopic bone scaffold, called trabeculae. Several factors control the dietary absorption of calcium and the mineralization of this bony infrastructure. Weight, estrogen, progesterone, weight-bearing activity, and calcium intake are the main factors promoting bone health.

In the absence of estrogen, decreased bone mineral density and irreversible bone loss occur. Disordered eating will also decrease calcium intake, further affecting mineral density in the bony scaffolding. Vitamin D promotes calcium absorption, but in starvation or calorie restriction, the amount of dietary fat in which vitamin D can be absorbed is decreased, leading to deficiency. Since nearly 70 percent of lifetime bone mass is stored during adolescence, these problems can lead to early osteoporosis later in life.

It should be noted that not all athletes with amenorrhea have decreased bone mass; some athletes have increased bone density in areas that support the most stress. For example, the hips of figure skaters have been shown to contain increased bone density. Bone is formed as a reaction to stress, so bearing weight on a bone will strengthen that particular bone. This is the rationale for the elderly to do weight-bearing exercise to increase bone strength. One study of bone density in some aesthetic athletes (figure skaters) prone to disordered eating found that certain bones that bore the most weight were stronger than the same bones in nonskaters.

Table 16.4
RECOGNIZING THE DISORDERED EATER IN THE ENDURANCE ATHLETE
Calorie restriction with small, infrequent meals
Amenorrhea
Frequent trips to the bathroom
Dry, brittle hair
Binge eating
Recurrent stress fractures
Rapid weight loss or weight cycling
Lanugo (soft, fine hair all over body)
Distorted self-perception
Eating alone
Compulsive exercise

PERFORMANCE PROBLEMS

Endurance athletes with disordered eating will have noticeable decreases in endurance capacity. By eating reduced amounts of food, especially in relation to exercise, they create an imbalance between the number of calories and the need for energy. They have limited ability to fuel prolonged performance. Other characteristics of disordered eating are listed in Table 16.4.

Dehydration from decreased intake can lead to decreased performance and decreased ability to regulate body temperature. Those with eating disorders are also prone to depression, which can lead to lack of energy and motivation. At the starvation stage, muscle is lost as well as fat.

Although these athletes will increase their maximal oxygen uptake, lack of glycogen stores will not allow them to maintain high performance levels. However, estrogen seems to have positive effects on performance: Estrogen decreases glycogen depletion and enhances fat burning.

Finally, a skeleton that is weakened from decreased bone mass is more susceptible to stress fractures and other injuries. Since the psychological drive of some athletes with eating disorders is strong, even at times bordering on pathological, small injuries may be overlooked until they become large injuries.

PSYCHOLOGICAL SPIRAL

Despite the multiple factors in disordered eating and the female athlete triad, one factor leads the rest: the athlete's mind-set. The ramifications of the condition are medical and psychological, but the psychological factors are responsible for most of the problems. These factors are self-compounding and can get the athlete caught up in a downward spiral of worsening performance, worsening health, and decreased satisfaction with sport.

At some point in the training macrocycle, athletes may have a bad day or slow race or simply *feel* that way. They look to the individuals leading the race or to those on magazine covers and attribute success to thinness. This is the beginning of the trouble: They focus their attention on appearances rather than on training principles of stress, recovery, and periodization.

Such athletes then become concerned with losing weight and working harder and do not allow adequate time for recovery and repair. This preoccupation can be worsened by the risk factors inherent in their personalities and by comments or advice from outside influences, such as coaches and teammates.

Pathological eating habits can produce a substantial initial weight loss, resulting in a pleased athlete. The pleasure is short-lived, however, as performance wanes due to poor nutritional intake and recovery. The athlete's response is to train harder and lose more weight through starvation. Along with starvation comes decreased calcium and vitamin D intake, which results in weak bones. As the female athlete becomes amenorrheic, bone loss ensues and the risk of injury increases.

Table 16.5
ATHLETES AT RISK FOR DEVELOPING EATING DISORDERS
Participation in aesthetic or sports emphasizing leanness
Early participation in sport-specific training
Training before puberty
Family history of eating disorders
Unsuccessful attempts at weight loss
History of sexual abuse in childhood
Family history of depression

If an athlete is injured, the fear of gaining weight and not being allowed to compete skyrockets, and the athlete frequently tries to hide an injury, going to great lengths to participate. This aggravates the injury, resulting in prolonged time out of practice and increasingly extreme dietary measures to compensate for the fear of weight gain and time off from activity. The troubled athlete now feels isolated from the sport and can feel the effects of fatigue and poor nutrition. Again, the response is to undertake even more training in the belief that it is necessary to return to competition. And so the cycle continues.

Breaking the cycle through support and a shift in focus to performance, not weight-based performance, is the key to overcoming the downward spiral.

TREATMENT

The treatment of anorexia athletica revolves around nutritional and psychological counseling but requires support from doctors, coaches, friends, and family. Nutritional counseling is aimed at making wise food choices along with energy and caloric needs and goals to help the athlete understand how imbalance is a problem. The objective of this dual counseling is to make the athlete aware of the performance and health problems related to disordered eating and to redirect the focus toward athletic ability and away from body image. Related issues, including participation in the sport, must also be addressed.

Opinions differ about whether an athlete with a suspected eating disorder should be banned from competition. One side holds that the athlete's health comes first. However, others realize that being sidelined is a risk factor for developing or perpetuating disordered eating. Athletes who display excessive exercise tendencies but are sidelined may feel forced to exercise on their own in an unsupervised atmosphere. Instead, such an athlete should be allowed to continue to increase strength and fitness in a program planned in consultation with the physician, sports nutritionist, and exercise physiologist.

All amenorrheic athletes should receive calcium supplementation of 1,500 mg a day. If dietary calcium is low, supplements should be used to obtain a daily intake of 800 IU/day.

Due to the unpredictable nature of ovulation, oral contraceptives are recommended for birth control. The hormones from contraceptives also protect the bones, although the use of these pills to treat patients with menstrual irregularities is debatable and should not be considered a cure. The underlying nature of the dysfunction should be sought out and corrected.

PREVENTION

An athlete with disordered eating must learn proper weight-loss techniques if losing weight is a medically recommended goal. Weight and body composition should be monitored, and nutritional recommendations should be maintained. Monitoring menstrual regularity during the competitive season is important to determine if there is a change. Coaches and teammates should remain constantly alert and keep close watch on friends and teammates who begin to display disordered eating. These individuals should be referred to professional therapists to address their specific issues.

Finally, it is advisable to enlist an expert who can deal adequately with questions and comments about this topic. This person should provide pertinent education of the entire sporting network (coaches, athletes, trainers).

NOTES

1. American Psychiatric Association. *Diagnostic and Statistical Manual of Mental Disorders: DSM-IV*, 4th ed. Washington, DC: American Psychiatric Association, 2000.

2. M. Harries, C. Williams, W. D. Stanish, L. J. Micheli, eds. *Oxford Textbook of Sports Medicine*, 2d ed. Oxford: Oxford University Press, 1998.

OTHER REFERENCES

Clark, N. Food fight: Calling a truce with disordered eating. *The Physician and Sportsmedicine* July 1996, 24(7): 13.

International Federation of Sports Medicine. The female athlete triad: A statement for health professionals from the scientific commission.

Joy, E., N. Clark, M. L. Ireland, J. Martire, A. Aurelia Nattiv, S. Varechok. Team management of the female athlete triad. Part 1: What to look for, what to ask. *The Physician and Sportsmedicine* March 1997, 25(3): 94–110.

Joy, E., N. Clark, M. L. Ireland, J. Martire, A. Aurelia Nattiv, S. Varechok. Team management of the female athlete triad. Part 2: Optimal treatment and prevention tactics. *The Physician and Sportsmedicine* April 1997, 25(4): 55–69.

Martin, D. Appearances are deceiving: The female athlete triad. *Track Technique* 1995, 130: 4144–47.

Nelson, M. A., P. G. Dyment, B. Goldberg, S. B. Haefele, et al. Committee on Sports Medicine: Amenorrhea in adolescent athletes. *Pediatrics* August 1989, 84 (2): 394–95.

Otis, C. L., B. Drinkwater, M. Johnson, A. Loucks, J. Wilmore. ACSM position stand: The female athlete triad. *Medicine and Science in Sports and Exercise* 1997, 29(5): i–ix.

Smith, A. D. The female athlete triad: Causes, diagnosis, and treatment. *The Physician and Sportsmedicine* July 1996, 24(7): 67.

ENVIRONMENTAL INJURY AND ILLNESS

In 1996, a colleague and I undertook a research project to examine the types of injuries that cyclists had encountered. The environment was the one area that nearly all of the cyclists cited as causing injury. The study was done in the desert climate of Tucson, Arizona, where many respondents reported injuries from the effects of the heat and the sun. (Had the study been done at the same time in the colder climates of New England, I'm certain the cyclists would have reported cold-induced injuries.)

As primarily outdoor athletes, participants in endurance sports must deal with the climates where events are held. Injuries from heat and cold can be life-threatening but are easily preventable. If athletes understand the warning signs, endurance sports are safer and can be injury-free.

THERMOREGULATION

Environmental injuries from exercise in both hot and cold temperatures are due to disorders of thermoregulation. Thermoregulation is the body's ability to balance heat gain with heat loss. The body generates heat through several different mechanisms, the most basic of which is the basal metabolic rate (BMR). The BMR is the amount of heat generated during rest from the normal chemical reactions that occur in the body. The BMR is affected by environmental factors, muscular activity, hormones, and the thermic effect of certain foods, which is the amount of heat produced by the metabolism of foods.

The body's thermostat is located in the hypothalamus section of the brain. The hypothalamus maintains the body temperature within one degree Celsius of the normal temperature. The hypothalamus cannot turn off heat production but can increase the mechanisms of heat loss when stimulated by the heat receptors located in the skin.

There are four mechanisms through which the body can lose heat: conduction, radiation, convection, and evaporation. Conduction refers to the direct transfer of heat from one molecule to another, or on a larger scale, from the body to another substance (liquid, solid, or gas) that is in contact with the body. The amount of conductive heat loss depends upon the difference in temperature between the skin and the surrounding substances. That is, if body temperature is significantly greater than air temperature, more heat will be lost from the body. The second factor affecting conductive heat loss is the ability of a particular substance to absorb heat. For instance, heat loss to water is thirty-two times greater than heat loss to air. An example of the importance of thermal qualities is a hand placed in sixty-degree water will get significantly colder than a hand held in sixty-degree still air. In short, water has more ability to absorb heat than air does.

Radiant heat loss is the emission of heat from a warm body to cooler objects. In a cold environment, the body will absorb heat from the sun, reflected snow, or the ground. Likewise, the body will emit heat to the cooler objects in an environment. Unlike conduction, no contact is required to transfer heat. As with conduction, a heat difference (also called a gradient) is required for heat to be transferred.

Movement of air adjacent to the body is responsible for convective heat loss. The speed of air movement influences heat loss. If the air moves slowly, the air next to the skin provides a "zone of insulation" that minimizes heat loss. When air moves quickly, the zone of insulation is blown away. The speed of air movement is the basis for determining the wind-chill factor.

To maximize these mechanisms, the body redirects blood flow to the skin, maximizing the potential for conductive, radiant, and convective heat transfer to the environment. The skin is also responsible for the most important factor in heat loss but in an entirely different way. Evaporation is the paramount mechanism for losing heat and the primary mechanism for prevention of overheating. As water evaporates from the skin and the lungs, the body is cooled from the transfer of heat to the environment. The cooling of skin from sweat evaporation also cools the blood that travels close to the skin. As this blood returns to the central circulation, the entire body gets colder. In hot environments, the body is unable to lose heat to the environment through convection, conduction, and radiation. If the ambient temperature is greater than body temperature, the body actually gains heat from the three other mechanisms; in this case, evaporation through sweat is the only cooling mechanism available.

HEAT STRESS

Temperature alone does not account for the sensation of how hot it feels. The wet bulb-globe thermometer (WBGT) does measure air temperature, but it also takes humidity and radiant heat into account to create a heat index. If no WBGT index is available, you can use air temperature and relative humidity to derive the heat sensation (see Table 17.1).

The American College of Sports Medicine has made recommendations for endurance exercise in the heat based upon the WBGT index (see Table 17.2). Heat-sensitive individuals should take extra precautions when exercising in hot weather. A heat-sensitive individual is defined as someone who is obese or has a low level of physical fitness. Others at increased risk for heat illness include those who are not acclimatized, are dehydrated, or have a history of heat injury.

Table 17.1

SCALE OF HEAT SENSATION

Air Temperature (degrees Fahrenheit)

Humidity (percent)	70	75	80	85	90	95	100	105	110	115	120
Heat Sensation (degrees Fahrenheit)											
0	64	69	73	78	83	87	91	95	99	103	107
10	65	70	75	80	85	90	95	100	105	111	116
20	66	72	77	82	87	93	99	105	112	120	130
30	67	73	78	84	90	96	104	113	123	135	148
40	68	74	79	86	93	101	110	123	137	151	
50	69	75	81	88	96	107	120	135	150		
60	70	76	82	90	100	114	132	149			
70	70	77	85	93	106	124	144				
80	71	78	86	97	113	136					
90	71	79	88	102	122						
100	72	80	91	108							

The zone to the left of the shaded area represents safe exercising conditions.

At 90–105 there is a possibility of heat cramps.

At 105–130 heat cramps or heat exhaustion is likely.

At 130+ heat stroke is a definite risk.

Table 17.2

RISKS AND RECOMMENDATIONS ASSOCIATED WITH WET BULB-GLOBE THERMOMETER TEMPERATURE

WBGT Temperature	Risk	Recommendation
> 82°F	Very high	Postpone training/racing
73–82°F	High	Heat sensitive should not compete
65–73°F	Moderate	Stay well hydrated
< 65°F	Low	No limitations

HEAT ILLNESS

Like most of the environmental-induced injuries, heat illness covers a broad spectrum in terms of severity. Heat injury results from dehydration, electrolyte imbalance, and the sun's ultraviolet rays.

Heat tetany

At the start of the heat-induced injury spectrum is heat-induced tetany. To aid evaporative heat loss through the respiratory tract, the hypothalamus automatically increases the respiratory rate. The increased breathing rate, called hyperventilation, leads to rapid changes in the exhaled carbon dioxide, resulting in calcium changes on a cellular level.

These rapid changes in CO_2 and calcium flux cause shortness of breath, tingling in the hands and feet, and spasms of the hands and feet.

Preventing heat tetany is accomplished by maintaining a lower temperature when you exercise to spare the respiratory tract from contributing to cooling. This means staying well hydrated and avoiding extreme temperatures. If spasms and tingling have occurred, the treatment is rest, cooling, and increasing carbon dioxide levels by breathing into a paper bag.

Heat cramps

Short, severe muscle cramps frequently occur in endurance athletes who nevertheless are well conditioned. The cramps are very painful and occur in muscles experiencing intense activity and fatigue. The cramps usually affect a few bundles of muscle fibers within a given muscle at a time. After the cramps subside in these first bundles, adjacent muscles usually cramp for approximately one to three minutes. This pattern gives the sensation and appearance that the cramps are moving in a wave across the muscle.

Heat does not cause the cramps; depletion of sodium is the culprit. In fact, I have seen athletes have cramps in relatively cool weather during hard races. Other factors include heavy exercise, muscle cooling, and excessive ingestion of plain water. Occasionally, cramps can occur following exercise or in the shower.

Ingesting a diet with sufficient sodium is the key to prevention of heat cramps. It is important that dietary salt comes from food and not from salt tablets, which can irritate the stomach. Acclimatization is also important to prevent heat cramps.

Some football teams have used pickle juice as an adjunct to prevent heat cramps. The high salt concentration may be helpful, but the vinegar can create gastrointestinal upset.

Once cramps have begun, they respond well to an ingested salt solution (one-half teaspoon of salt in one liter of water). Chilled and flavored salt solutions are more palatable.

Heat exhaustion

When the body's efforts to maintain a normal temperature become too difficult, the strain shows itself as heat exhaustion. Symptoms include headache, dizziness, fatigue, anxiety, chills, nausea, and vomiting. At the extremes of heat exhaustion, low blood pressure and fainting may occur.

Treatment of heat exhaustion is to return the body's fluid status to normal, but prevention is more important. To keep heat exhaustion and other heat illness at bay, the paramount strategy is to maintain hydration (discussed in detail in Chapter 5). To prevent further injury in the case of heat exhaustion, move to a cooler environment as soon as possible. If subjected to further heat stress, the brain may experience changes as heat exhaustion progresses to heat stroke and death.

STRATEGIES FOR THE HEAT

Clothing choices should maximize the four methods of heat loss. Wearing light-colored, absorbent, ventilated clothing is the key to dressing for the heat. The military has created an index for the thermal properties of clothing; six factors affect this index: wind speed, body movement, the chimney effect, the bellows effect, water vapor transfer, and permeation efficiency factor.

As wind speed or athlete velocity increases, the zone of insulation next to the skin is lost. Body movements also disturb the zone of insulation. Loose clothing vents and releases the trapped air away from the body, also disturbing the zone of insulation, in a process known as the chimney effect. In the bellows effect, body motion allows for increased ventilation of air layers for conserving body heat. Water vapor transfer is decreased with some clothing, preventing evaporation and decreasing evaporative cooling. The permeation efficiency factor describes the ability of clothing to wick moisture from the skin, decreasing evaporative cooling from the skin. Sweat evaporating from the surface of clothing will cool the clothing, not the skin.

Dry clothing slows cooling by decreasing heat loss through evaporation and conduction. Wetting clothing with cool water will aid in the cooling. To maximize convective cooling, clothing should be loose enough to allow for air circulation around the body that will cool by convection and evaporation. Fabrics that absorb water, such as cotton, will cool an athlete better than a fabric with a high permeation efficiency factor. In high humidity, however, an absorptive garment may not dry and there will be no cooling from evaporation.

Clothing color is also important in remaining cool. Darker colors absorb the sun's rays more than light colors do and therefore have more radiant heat gain.

Heat is a limiting factor in exercise if you are not adequately prepared.[1] Strategies to mitigate the rise in temperature that accompanies exercise will enhance performance.[2] Some of these strategies, such as hydration before and during exercise, have been discussed elsewhere in the book. Two others that are helpful are precooling and acclimatization.

Precooling the body with thirty minutes of immersion in cold water keeps the athlete cooler, allowing for increased power output in a hot, humid environment.[3] Precooling can reduce skin temperature by 5.9 degrees Celsius (10 degrees Fahrenheit).[4] Cooling the skin will decrease blood flow to the skin because the blood is not needed for conductive or radiant heat loss; instead the blood is redirected to the muscles. In addition, precooling prevents a rise in body temperature. These changes result in greater exercise endurance with enhanced heat storage, less dehydration through sweat loss, and decreased stress on metabolic and cardiovascular systems.[5] Although whole-body immersion in cold water is not as practical as cold compresses, it is significantly more effective. Precooling has its drawbacks, however. If the environment is not warm enough to reverse the effects of precooling, there is an increased energy expenditure during exercise.[6]

If a pool or bathtub of cold water could be available before a training session in the heat, it would be worthwhile to soak in it. Precooling in this manner would allow for a more effective and safer workout. Unfortunately, the more practical use of ice packs and cold, wet towels probably does not cool the body sufficiently for precooling to be beneficial. Although studies have shown that body temperature is a limiting factor during performance, precooling is probably effective only for single-event endurance exercise lasting up to forty minutes.[7]

The process by which the body adjusts to optimize heat tolerance is acclimatization. The majority of these adjustments happen in the first week of heat exposure (see Table 17.3). To achieve the best acclimatization, the athlete needs two to four hours of daily heat exposure. The amount and intensity of exercise should increase progressively throughout the week. Acclimatization can also be achieved with thirty-five minutes of exercise at 75 percent of VO_2max for just eight days.[8]

Training alone will force the body to deal with increased heat stress. The adaptations that the body makes during exercise will contribute to heat acclimatization, but full acclimatization cannot be achieved without exposure to environmental heat stress. To induce heat stress, the athlete must train in either a hot climate or an artificially humid and hot environment.

Table 17.3
PHYSIOLOGICAL CHANGES IN HEAT ACCLIMATIZATION
Increased cardiac output
Lowered sweating threshold
Increased sweat volume
More dilute sweat
Decreased sodium loss in urine
Lower core temperature

I have heard about people exercising on a stationary trainer at the side of a warmed indoor pool. The exposure to the heat and humidity helped them adapt to the heat. Another way to induce a more humid environment is to wear a water-impermeable outer layer. Although this "sweat clothing" will create a more humid microclimate next to the skin, mimicking a hot, humid environment, it is not as beneficial as training in a hot environment.[9]

SUN EXPOSURE
Ultraviolet rays
The spectrum of electromagnetic radiation from the sun that reaches the earth can be divided into several subsets, depending upon the wavelength of the radiation. Part of that spectrum is harmless, such as the visible (light) and infrared (heat) segments. Shorter wavelength light is known as ultraviolet radiation (UVR). The UVR that reaches the earth is further divided into UVA and UVB. The effects of UVR on the skin depend upon wavelength (UVA or UVB), duration of exposure, and intensity of exposure.

UVB has a shorter wavelength than UVA, and although 95 percent of UVB is reflected or absorbed by the epidermis, overexposure is responsible for sunburn. The redness of sunburn is a thousand times more likely to come from UVB than UVA. The onset of sunburn redness starts two to six hours after exposure, is at its worst within thirty-six hours, and resolves within about five days. Sunburned cells have damaged DNA from UVR and cannot repair themselves. They also have an increase in histamine and prostaglandins.

Approximately 50 percent of UVA penetrates the epidermis and affects the deeper layer of skin, the dermis. The redness from UVA exposure fades within forty-eight hours, but is associated with more damage on the cellular level.

The sun can also have negative effects on the eyes, leading to macular degeneration, eye irritation, and cataracts.[10]

Sunburn prevention

Sunburn is completely preventable. The best method to prevent the harmful effects of UVR is to block the rays from the skin. The sun protection factor (SPF) is a measure of the protective quality of sunscreen and is the ratio of the UVR needed to burn protected skin (Minimal Erythema or MED) to that needed to burn unprotected skin. Sunscreen with an SPF of 15 (100:6.7) will block 93.3 percent of UVR. An SPF of 30 (100:3.3) will block 96.7 percent of UV radiation. A higher SPF will block more UVR. However, to achieve the protection the SPF number indicates, the sunscreen must be applied at a concentration of 2 mg/cm². Few people apply this concentration, and applying only a light layer of sunscreen reduces the SPF by 50 percent. Another reason to use higher SPF formulations is the decreased cellular changes that cause some types of skin cancer. SPF 15 was once considered the standard, but higher SPF can be used for increased protection, especially since sunscreen is usually under-applied.

Vitamin C acts as an antioxidant to offer protection by scavenging free radicals that are produced by UVR. The vitamin should be taken at a dose of 2,000 mg/day to ensure adequate levels.

To prevent eye damage from UVR, you should wear adequate eye protection. Choose UVR-blocking lenses that provide full coverage from the sun. If lenses are not UVA- and UVB-resistant, the darkened light hitting the eyes will cause the pupils to dilate and allow more UVR to reach the retina where macular degeneration occurs.

Eyewear should be sport-specific. Some general recommendations are rimless and fog-proof lenses to allow for drainage of sweat and condensation, snug fit, and wraparound coverage for maximum protection from UVR (Photo 17.1).

17.1 *Protective Eyewear*

Sunburn treatment

Because sunburn resolves spontaneously, treatment is aimed at controlling the symptoms of pain, itching, and dryness. Topical treatments such as cool compresses are effective, but sometimes a topical anesthetic such as Sarna lotion is needed. This lotion contains camphor and menthol that exert a cooling effect on the skin. Refrigeration of any topical lotions adds to the cooling effect.

Pain can also be controlled with nonsteroidal anti-inflammatory medications. Ibuprofen in a dose of 600 mg every six to eight hours or the prescription medication indomethacin will work to decrease pain.

Of course, ultraviolet rays from the sun are present in cold weather as well, but their effects on the skin increase in hot environments due to the prevalence of exposed skin. Protecting the skin with ultraviolet-blocking sunscreen can decrease the risk of sunburn and UVR-induced skin cancers.

EXPOSURE TO COLD
Heat loss

Like heat injury, cold injury is largely preventable. Prevention requires understanding the science of cold.

Cold exerts great stress on the exercising athlete. During exercise in the cold, the body attempts to minimize heat loss occurring through evaporation, radiation, convection, and conduction. Radiant heat loss is greatest in the body parts with the most blood supply. During exposure to cold, blood flow to the highly vascular hands, feet, ears, nose, and skin is decreased. The body does this automatically by constricting the blood vessels that supply these parts of the body with warm blood from the central circulation. Appendages that are usually well supplied by blood suddenly have little circulation, resulting in their greater susceptibility to cold injury. Maximal vasoconstriction occurs at 59 degrees Fahrenheit (15 degrees Celsius). If cooling continues for another 9 degrees Fahrenheit, the constriction is interspersed with periods of vasodilatation to allow blood flow to the extremity.

The shunting of blood away from body areas exposed to cold reduces heat loss not only from radiation but also from convection and conduction. Heat loss from evaporation plays a major role in staying cool but is also important in staying warm. Heat loss to water by conduction is twenty-five to thirty times greater than heat loss to air. Staying dry is the primary goal in staying warm.

Wind chill

Convective heat loss from circulating air is a major component in determining how cold you feel. Windy conditions feel colder than still air because the air movement continuously disrupts the warm zone of insulation surrounding the body. Convection is the basis for determining the wind-chill index.

Table 17.4 can be used to determine the danger of wind-chill-induced cold injury based upon ambient air temperature and wind speed. In endurance events, the forward velocity adds to the wind speed if there is a headwind, and a tailwind decreases the effective wind speed. Since your direction of travel may not always be the same, however, expect a wind chill based upon actual wind speed plus your average speed. Understand that you will feel colder when going faster.

The combination of cold, wind, and wet will quickly drain any heat that the body generates during exercise. Thus it is helpful to understand the spectrum of cold-induced injury.

The spectrum of cold injury
Frostnip

As increasing cold stress outweighs the body's ability to generate heat, intense vasoconstriction leads to decreased blood flow to the extremities and skin. Numbness of the body parts comes with decreased blood flow, and ice crystals form. Frostnip (also called chilblain) results from high humidity and temperatures that are usually above freezing, although frostnip can occur during subfreezing temperatures as well.

Symptoms of frostnip are pain and discomfort in the affected parts. Once you leave the offending environment, the pain and discomfort usually resolve spontaneously with no

Table 17.4

WIND CHILL INDEX

Ambient Temperature (Fahrenheit)

Wind Speed	40	35	30	25	20	15	10	5	0	–5	–10	–15	–20	–25
	Equivalent Temperature (Fahrenheit)													
Calm	40	35	30	25	20	15	10	5	0	–5	–10	–15	–20	–25
5	37	33	27	21	16	12	6	1	–5	–11	–15	–20	–26	–31
10	28	21	16	9	4	–2	–9	–15	–21	–27	–33	–38	–46	–52
15	22	6	11	1	–5	–11	–18	–25	–36	–40	–45	–51	–58	–65
20	18	12	3	–4	–10	–17	–25	–32	–39	–46	–53	–60	–67	–76
25	16	7	0	–7	–15	–22	–29	–37	–44	–52	–59	–67	–74	–83
30	13	5	–2	–11	–18	–26	–33	–41	–48	–56	–63	–70	–79	–87
35	11	3	–4	–13	–20	–27	–35	–43	–49	–60	–67	–72	–82	–90
40	10	1	–6	–15	–21	–29	–37	–45	–53	–62	–69	–76	–85	–94

Danger of cold-related illness:

☐ little danger　　■ danger　　■ great danger

damage caused. The standard treatment is to warm the affected part, which can be accomplished through immersion in water heated to 104–108 degrees Fahrenheit (40–42 degrees Celsius).

Frostbite

As cooling progresses to 50 degrees Fahrenheit (10 degrees Celsius), skin sensation is diminished and is frequently absent. At this point, it is easy for damage to progress without your feeling it. Once vasoconstriction has occurred, skin temperature may plummet at the rate of 0.9 degrees Fahrenheit per minute. Ice crystals form in the skin, leading to ice crystallization around and within cells and causing cell death.

Frostbite can progress through three different degrees. First-degree frostbite is marked by numbness and redness of the skin with a white or yellow firm zone at the primary injury site. Second-degree frostbite is marked by the appearance of blisters that contain a clear or white fluid and are surrounded by redness. Third-degree frostbite has blood-filled blisters. With all degrees of frostbite, there is considerable numbness of the affected anatomy with an associated feeling of absence or heaviness of that body part.

Warming the affected part is the mainstay of treatment. However, avoid rewarming if there is a possibility of refreezing. Rapid rewarming in a typical hospital emergency room takes place in water that is heated to 104–108 degrees Fahrenheit (40–42 degrees Celsius). Rewarming a body part affected by frostnip or frostbite is usually painful, but water warmer than this range exacerbates the pain. Most frostbite cases should be admitted to the hospital; do not attempt to rewarm a frostbitten extremity at home.

Prevention of frostnip and frostbite should be a primary concern when exercising in the cold. Producing heat as well as conserving heat are the two ways to best avoid frostbite.

Although frostbite is rarely seen in healthy, adequately clothed people, an individual who is frostbitten once has an increased likelihood of becoming frostbitten again.

Hypothermia

Hypothermia occurs when the body's ability to protect itself from heat loss is overwhelmed by the environment. Hypothermia can happen at any temperature and is not limited to subfreezing temperatures. In fact, it is most common between 30 and 50 degrees Fahrenheit. To prevent hypothermia, maintain a diet sufficiently high in calories to keep the body fueled, wear proper clothing, and avoid situations that will result in rapid temperature loss.

The immediate post-exercise period is of particular concern for an endurance athlete because the body is trying to regulate temperature adequately. During this time, the body is trying to lose excess heat that exercise has generated. This is accomplished through vasodilation of the skin and extremities and increased sweat rate. When exercise stops or is ended abruptly, these mechanisms are still active, leaving an open window for heat loss. Hypothermia can quickly occur during this time. It is important to change into dry clothes and add a few extra layers immediately following exercise.

Dressing for Cold

Keeping warm involves minimizing convective, radiant and conductive heat loss by properly insulating the vascular parts of the body: the head, neck, hands and feet. Insulating the head and neck with hats, balaclavas and gators can go a long way toward preventing heat loss.

Hands and feet should be covered with warm, insulating materials that are comfortable, as tight-fitting gloves can further reduce circulation and lead to stasis and cold-induced injury. Socks should be worn wrinkle-free and should be made of synthetic materials. Cotton should be especially avoided for the feet since cotton will keep skin moist and soft and susceptible to frostbite.

Application of heat to the torso during cold exposure is protective against the effects of cold environmental conditions. One study during military operations showed that the body could stay warmer for up to three hours at −15 degrees Celsius[11] when participants wore vests, both insulating and windproof.

Clothing should be chosen to minimize heat loss through convection, evaporation, conduction, and radiation. A base layer of insulation, such as an undershirt with wicking properties, will create a small zone of insulation next to the skin and at the same time remove perspiration from the skin to prevent evaporative heat loss. This layer is probably the most important, as it will also keep the torso warm.

Adding a second layer will increase the zone of insulation next to the body. When you exercise in the cold, clothing should be loose enough to allow for movement but not so loose as to allow for the escape of warm air.

The outer layer of clothing will decrease convective loss by blocking the wind. This layer should be windproof yet allow for moisture loss so that the clothing does not remain wet, which will cause heat transfer to the wet clothes.

Because cold air affects several organ systems, clothing can be used to counteract these effects. Inhalation of cold air causes constriction of the bronchi in the lungs.[12] This results in the coughing, wheezing, and shortness of breath associated with exercise-induced asthma. Keeping the wind off of the chest helps keep the lungs warm and can decrease the occurrence of exercise-induced asthma.

To work effectively and maintain flexibility, the muscles, tendons, and ligaments must be warmed to 102 degrees Fahrenheit. This temperature is harder to attain and maintain during cold-weather exercise. Garments such as knickers or knee warmers can help maintain flexibility of ligaments that would otherwise be stiffened by the cold.

Using ointments as barriers to the cold can also prevent heat loss to convection. Petroleum jelly creates an effective (albeit sloppy) barrier. Combination salicylate and menthol muscle rubs also are effective in staying warm. These rubs act as skin irritants to increase blood flow, which keeps joints warmer, more flexible, and less susceptible to injury. Rubs can increase warmth, but you can also have increased heat loss if you do not dress properly. These rubs also interfere with the skin's ability to sense cold, giving the skin a tingling feeling.

Hands should be covered with mittens unless fine motor coordination is needed. Insulation from cold handlebars or ski poles is needed to prevent conductive heat loss. Use thick tape and gloves or mittens.

NOTES

1. M. A. Febbraio. Does muscle function and metabolism affect exercise performance in the heat? *Exercise and Sport Sciences Reviews* October 2000, 28(4): 171–76.

2. M. Hargreaves, M. Febbraio. Limits to exercise performance in the heat. *International Journal of Sports Medicine* June 1998, 19 Suppl 2: S115–16.

3. D. Marsh, G. Sleivert. Effect of precooling on high-intensity cycling performance. *British Journal of Sports Medicine* December 1999, 33(6): 393–97.

4. J. Booth, F. Marino, J. J. Ward. Improved running performance in hot humid conditions following whole body precooling. *Medicine and Science in Sports and Exercise* July 1997, 29(7): 943–49.

5. D. T. Lee, E. M. Haymes. Exercise duration and thermoregulatory responses after whole body precooling. *Journal of Applied Physiology* December 1995, 79(6): 1971–76.

6. A. Sjodin, A. Forslund, P. Webb, L. Hambraeus. Mild overcooling increases energy expenditure during endurance exercise. *Scandinavian Journal of Medicine and Science in Sports* February 1996, 6(1): 22–25.

7. F. E. Marino. Methods, advantages, and limitations of body cooling for exercise performance. *British Journal of Sports Medicine* April 2002, 36(2): 89–94.

8. J. A. Houmard, D. L. Costill, J. A. Davis, J. B. Mitchell, D. D. Pascoe, R. A. Roberts. The influence of exercise intensity on heat acclimation in trained subjects. *Medicine and Science in Sports and Exercise* October 1990, 22(5): 615–20.

9. B. Dawson. Exercise training in sweat clothing in cool conditions to improve heat tolerance. *Sports Medicine* April 1994, 17(4): 233–44.

10. H. R. Taylor. The biological effects of UV-B on the eye. *Photochemistry and Photobiology* October 1989, 50(4): 489–92.

H. R. Taylor. Ultraviolet radiation and the eye: An epidemiologic study. *Transactions of the American Ophthalmological Society* 1989, 87: 802–53.

K. U. Loeffler, S. M. Sastry, I. W. McLean. Is age-related macular degeneration associated with pinguecula or scleral plaque formation? *Current Eye Research* July 2001, 23(1): 33–37.

11. D. Brajkovic et al. Influence of localized auxiliary heating on hand comfort during cold exposure. *Journal of Applied Physiology* 1998, 85: 2054.

12. I. Helenius, H. O. Tikkanen, M. Helenius, A. Lumme, V. Remes, T. Haahtela. Exercise-induced changes in pulmonary function of healthy, elite long-distance runners in cold air and pollen season exercise challenge tests. *International Journal of Sports Medicine* May 2002, 23(4): 252–61.

OVERUSE INJURIES

III

OVERUSE INJURIES
OF THE KNEE

T he average racing cyclist who pedals at a cadence of 100 revolutions per minute will perform the same repetitive movement 12,000 times in a two-hour ride. If there are slight biomechanical, strength, or flexibility imbalances, these problems can be magnified and lead to pain and injury. The damage from repeated movements without an increase in resistance is referred to as overuse injury. This is in contrast to the increase in resistance that can lead to overload injuries: riding in big gears, doing too much hill work, or undertaking a large increase in mileage. Overuse injuries are three times more common in endurance sports than in power sports. These injuries are associated with the repetitive stress applied to the body during the sport. An average runner will absorb 2.5 times the body weight at ground contact. At a pace of seven minutes per mile, this adds up to 5,100 strikes of the foot, or a total of almost a million kilograms of pressure applied to the body.

The causes of overuse injuries can be divided into extrinsic and intrinsic factors. Intrinsic factors refer to the anatomic and biomechanical aspects of an athlete, whereas extrinsic factors relate to training changes, new surfaces, different equipment, and environmental changes. Common intrinsic factors include flat feet, high arches, bowlegs, pigeon-toed feet, leg-length discrepancy, muscle weakness and imbalance, decreased flexibility, and joint instability. Extrinsic training changes frequently leading to overuse injuries are increases in distance, intensity, repetitions, or progression of workouts. Although overuse injuries occur primarily in the tendons, which attach bone to muscle, overuse can affect muscles, the bursae that cushion the tendons (bursitis), nerves (neuromas), and bones (stress fractures).

All exercise causes microscopic tissue damage. Tendonitis occurs when repeated overload of the tendon causes microscopic damage that exceeds the body's ability to repair it. Examples of muscle overuse injuries include muscle strain and muscle soreness that represent tears in the microscopic structure of the muscle.

The bursae are fluid-filled sacs that rest between tendons and bone. They allow the tendons to glide over the bones, enabling the muscles to move the joints. A bursa can become irritated due to direct trauma or friction from the overlying tendons.

Overuse injuries to the nerves are not common. However, a nerve may become trapped between the bones and the surrounding ligaments if they should become swollen and inflamed. An example of this is Morton's neuroma (discussed in Chapter 19).

Overuse injuries in the bones are called stress fractures. These may develop from repeated loading to a bone, either because the bone is weak or the loading is excessive. The most common injury sites are the bones of the lower leg and the bones of the foot.

This chapter first provides general information about changes from overuse injuries and basic treatment, then goes into more specific detail. This information should be used only as a guideline for improving performance and training and should not replace a medical evaluation.

TREATMENT

The treatment of overuse injuries should begin early. Continuing to exercise with an overuse injury will only worsen the damage and prolong recovery. It is important to resolve the underlying causes, both intrinsic and extrinsic. The training diary should be reviewed, and changes in training should be noted. Return to the pre-injury training level if you have no pain. If you moved to a change in surface, camber, or terrain, return to the previous level. If there is any pain with exercise, stop. It is time to rest.

Malalignments should be corrected, with the use of a combination of orthotics, position changes, and proper athletic footwear. Tight muscles and joints should be stretched, and muscular imbalances should be resolved with strength training.

GENERAL PRINCIPLES

Treatment of overuse injuries is dependent upon the type of damage, but several principles are common to most such injuries. The treatment depends upon the different phases of the healing process.

In the first forty-eight to seventy-two hours after the onset of injury, the initial goal is to decrease pain, prevent further injury, and minimize swelling. Pain can inhibit the muscles, and the body will tend to not use them, which can lead to atrophy and weakness. This is the initial inflammatory phase and can last up to four or five days. During this period, the mnemonic RICE is used as a guideline for treatment: RICE stands for rest, ice, compression, and elevation. Treatment should begin as soon as possible to prevent an overuse injury from becoming chronic.

Rest does not have to be total inactivity. Rest is relative and can still include exercise, though it should be easier than what had been previously undertaken. The amount and intensity of exercise are dictated by the presence of pain. Relative rest should be pain-free.

Ice, also known as cryotherapy, has several advantages. For acute injuries, ice is used in the immediate post-injury period and immediately after exercise for chronic injuries. Cryotherapy is useful for controlling pain and reducing swelling by causing a constriction of the capillaries, reducing the leaking of blood that leads to swelling. Cold raises the threshold at which you feel pain, and it also decreases performance of muscle by reducing the speed at which it contracts (increased viscosity).[1]

Ice can be applied in many forms: for example, gel packs, crushed ice in a plastic bag, or a package of frozen peas. The smaller and more pliable the packaging, the easier it is to apply to a joint surface. Ice packs should never be placed directly on the skin; a towel or a layer of clothing should separate the skin from the ice. Ice massage done with a Popsicle stick frozen in a paper cup can be used for tendonitis. At the twenty-minute point after icing, there is a reflex dilatation of the blood vessels. Therefore, application should be limited to less than twenty minutes, and frequent episodes of ten minutes are preferable.[2]

Adverse effects of ice include nerve damage, especially in endurance athletes with low body fat.[3] Also, there can be an increased risk of injury in the thirty minutes after icing due to decreased muscle performance and slowed reflex time.[4]

Compression is more frequently used with acute injuries to reduce swelling and provide support for the injured part, but it can be used with exacerbated chronic injuries as well. An elastic compression bandage may help decrease pain and provide extra support in an athlete who walks on a knee that has tendonitis. Photo 18.1 illustrates the preferred method of applying a compression dressing to the knee.

Keeping an injured part elevated ensures that the part is rested. The main goal of elevation is to decrease swelling. This use of gravity to reduce blood flow to the tissue minimizes leakage from the capillaries. Note that elevation and compression do not equal immobilization. Early mobilization will help reestablish function faster by restoring the functional tissue.

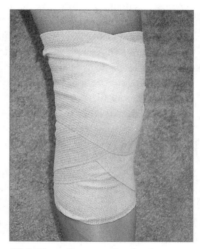

18.1 *Figure-8 compression dressing*

Although not included in the RICE mnemonic, the use of anti-inflammatory medications may be helpful. Because they might mask pain symptoms, however, their use should be limited to the post-exercise period to aid in pain management. Because the inflammation promotes healing, the use of nonsteroidal anti-inflammatory drugs (NSAIDs) will not help the injury heal any faster. Ibuprofen is readily available as an over-the-counter medication and comes in 200 mg pills. A normal-sized adult can take 800 mg every eight hours. Be sure to take it with food, as it can cause stomach upset.

Phase two of the treatment plan is designed to restore strength and flexibility. Even if there is mild pain and swelling, strength and flexibility exercises can be started within forty-eight to seventy-two hours after injury. However, during this time the athlete who wishes to return to sports quickly can push too hard and exacerbate the injury. Such a setback can be psychologically difficult, so slow and consistent progress is the goal. It is difficult to know when to rest and when to pursue rehabilitation of an injury.

Early strength training is important to prevent muscle wasting but should be started slowly and carefully. The strength of a tendon comes from the number of collagen fibers that make up the infrastructure of the tendon. These fibers will increase in response to strength training.

Initially the exercises should be done without any weight; the weight of the limb is sufficient at this point. Weight load then can be increased slowly. As weight load is increased and can be performed without pain, sport-specific exercise can begin.

Strength and flexibility training should go hand-in-hand. Flexibility exercises should be slow and controlled (see stretching guidelines in Chapter 7). Stretches should be held for thirty seconds, but may be broken into two fifteen-second stretches if pain limits a single stretch.

If pain from the injury prevents further rehabilitation exercises, consult a physician. When strength and motion have returned and pain has disappeared, the athlete is ready to return to the sport.

Phase three of the rehabilitation and healing process is the return to sport-specific exercise. This will require careful planning to avoid recurrence of the injury. Consult the training diary to analyze what might have caused injury. A return to training should occur at the level of intensity being used before the injury happened, and progression should be slower than when the injury occurred.

THE KNEE

The knee joint is composed of four bones, several stabilizing ligaments, and multiple muscles that stabilize, flex (bend), and extend (straighten) the knee. Additional components are cartilage that cushions the joint, a lubricating fluid that fills the joint, and small fluid-filled sacs that facilitate the movement of the muscles and tendons over the joint.

The bones of the knee are the femur (thigh bone), the tibia (shin), the fibula, and the patella (knee cap). The fibula is a thin bone that runs parallel to the tibia. The femur meets the tibia with two protuberances called the femoral condyles. The condyles sit in receptacles on the end of the tibia, called the tibial plateau. Surrounding the articular surface of the tibial plateau are C-shaped collars of cartilage known as the meniscus. The femur has a groove between the condyles in which the patella runs. The patella is embedded in the quadriceps tendon (tendons connect muscle to bone, ligaments connect bone to bone). The bones and muscles of the knee are illustrated in Photos 18.2 and 18.3.

The knee is a hinge joint and moves in one plane. The knee can either flex or extend but does not normally move from side to side. As the knee extends, the quadriceps muscle contracts,

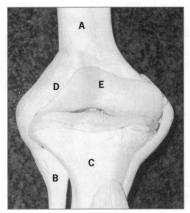

18.2 *Bones of the right knee, frontal view: (a) femur, (b) fibula, (c) tibia, (d) lateral femoral condyle, (e) patellar groove*

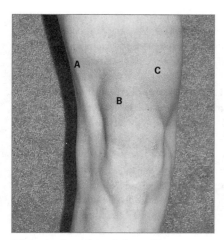

18.3 Muscles of the right knee: (a) vastus lateralis, (b) rectus femoris, (c) vastus medialis

pulling the tibia in line with the femur. The patella tracks in between the femoral condyles, acting as a pulley for the quadriceps tendon. The hamstrings, which run along the back of the thigh, are responsible for knee flexion. Four main ligaments stabilize the knee: the anterior cruciate, posterior cruciate, medial collateral, and lateral collateral. The iliotibial band (ITB) is a thick fibrous band that runs along the outside (lateral aspect) of the thigh, extending from the hip to the tibia. Embedded in the iliotibial band is a muscle that pulls the leg to the side, away from the body (abduction).

To keep the patella from moving from side to side as the knee bends and straightens, different structures provide stabilization. The ITB and vastus lateralis stabilize the patella laterally. The vastus medialis stabilizes it medially.

Overuse injuries are sustained when a repetitive force is applied to the ligaments, tendons, or bursae. The microtrauma caused by each repetition adds up to cause an injury. Tension, compression, and friction are all sources of microtrauma. The nature of the forces across the joint and the misalignments that cause the microtrauma will impact different parts of the anatomy and result in the varied injuries.

Patellofemoral syndrome

There are several names for pain in the front (anterior) part of the knee. All have now been grouped under one diagnosis known as patellofemoral syndrome, a convenient grouping since all of the overuse injuries involved have the same cause. The underlying etiology is poor tracking of the patella through the femoral grooves due to muscle dysfunction, biomechanical problems, or overuse.

Although anterior knee pain is common and treatable with conservative management, the outcome can be worse than for other types of knee pain.[5] The typical symptoms are pain in or behind the patella. This pain worsens with and after activity and is exacerbated by loading the knee with weight, such as when walking up and down hills or stairs or when squatting. The pain can also worsen when sitting for prolonged periods with the knee bent.[6]

Muscle dysfunction

The quadriceps muscle in the front of the thigh is composed of four different muscles that join together to meet at the patellar tendon. Each of the four muscles pulls the patella in a slightly different direction. The most medial muscle, the vastus medialus oblicans (VMO), is frequently the weakest muscle of the four. The VMO is responsible for the last thirty degrees of knee extension and one of the few structures that anchors the patella on the medial side of the knee. The vastus lateralis, the lateral retinaculum, and the iliotibial band pull the patella laterally.[7] The vastus lateralis is the most lateral muscle of the quadriceps.

Due to the relative weakness of the VMO or to overall quadriceps weakness, the patella can be pulled laterally during flexion and extension of the knee. As a result, the patella does not run in the femoral groove and "jumps track," causing pain in and behind the patella.

Other forces that contribute to patellofemoral pain are due to tightness of certain muscles. Tight, inflexible muscles exert more force on a joint than do muscles that are flexible. As the tight muscles pull on the knee, they can also pull the patella in different directions. A tight iliotibial band, which exerts a lateral force on the knee, will contribute to excessive lateral movement of the patella during knee movement. In addition, tightness in the iliotibial band can cause the tibia to rotate slightly to the outside (external rotation), upsetting the balance of the knee mechanism.

The muscles in the back of the knee will pull the patella back into the femoral groove, causing increased pressure between the patella and the femur. Both tight hamstrings and calf muscles are responsible for this increased force.

Biomechanical problems

Three biomechanical issues can lead to patellofemoral pain: pes planus, pes cavus, and an increased Q-angle. The first two refer to poor alignment of bones in the foot and ankle.

In pes planus (overpronation or flat foot), the arch is not adequately supported, and the foot rolls medially. This causes the tibia to compensate by twisting medially. With the anchor for the patella tendon in a more medial location, the net effect is a lateral tracking of the patella during knee movement.

Pes cavus (oversupination or high arches) results in decreased use of the ligaments to provide cushioning for the foot. With repeated weight loading of the foot, especially during running, excessive stress is placed on the knee and especially on the patellofemoral mechanism.

The use of the Q-angle in managing patellofemoral pain has been controver-

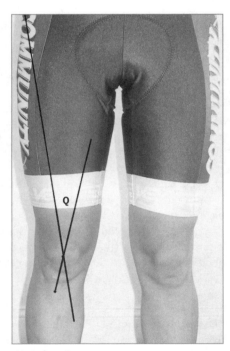

18.4 *Q-angle*

sial. The Q-angle is defined as the angle that is made between the intersection of two lines. The first line is drawn from the anterior superior iliac spine in the front of the hip to the patella; the second line is drawn from the tibial tuberosity through the patella. The second line approximates the path of the patellar tendon (see Photo 18.4). Reliability of the Q-angle has been questioned, however, due to the large variation in its measurement and physiology. It is important to consider the Q-angle, however, if it is increased during a sport such as cycling where the body is set into a fixed position that is not optimal for the anatomy and physiology of the athlete.

Overuse

As the poorly aligned knee flexes and extends, the patella hits the femoral condyles. With repeated use, the injury will worsen, which is why patellofemoral pain is defined as an overuse injury. There is also a component of overload; with increased weight bearing across the knee (such as when running hills excessively, running on uneven surfaces, using large weights or cycling with increased gears), the increased pressure on the knee will worsen the pain. Once the syndrome has developed, even the increased pressure from prolonged sitting will exacerbate the pain (the "moviegoers sign").

Treatment

The treatment of patellofemoral pain in the acute phase should be treated the same as other overuse injuries: rest, ice, compression and elevation. The specific treatment of patellofemoral syndrome should be aimed at correcting the individual causes: muscular weakness, biomechanical problems, and overload. With conservative treatment, there is 60–80 percent recovery.[8] Specific treatments include strength training, flexibility exercises, and postural and biomechanical correction.

Strength training

Strengthening muscles around an affected joint is advisable for almost all overuse injuries. Knowing which muscles to strengthen is important, as is how to build that strength. For patellofemoral syndrome, the quadriceps muscle responsible for knee extension is the primary area of focus.[9]

Quadriceps strength, especially in the last thirty degrees of extension, can be increased through leg extensions. Progressive increase in weight twice a day until the pain is gone and then three times a week while participating in sports has been recommended.[10] This plan does not leave much time for the primary sport, but it can be incorporated into a weight program to develop strength for all joints used in a sport. Ultimately, twenty minutes a day is a reasonable expectation for rehabilitation. It may take several weeks to become pain-free, so do not expect overnight success. If pain worsens, consult a physician.

Knee extension is performed while sitting in the knee extension machine and straightening the knee. You may want to start in a chair without any weight if the pain is severe. To improve the strength of the affected leg (which is probably weaker), exercise one leg at a time. Start with a weight that you can lift fifteen times, and perform

18.5 *VMO strengthening*

18.6 *Hip adductor strengthening without weight*

three sets of fifteen repetitions. Increase weight progressively as outlined in Chapter 7.

To isolate the VMO, knee extensions should be performed in the last thirty degrees of extension (see Photo 18.5). The VMO will be strengthened if the leg is extended fully (without locking the knee), so there is probably no need to isolate the VMO, especially since the entire quadriceps is used during sports.

Other muscles to address for improving patellofemoral syndrome include the adductors of the hip (adductors bring the limb towards the body, abductors move the limb away from the body.) These muscles bring the legs together. The VMO starts on the tendon of the hip adductors, so stronger hip adductors will indirectly increase VMO strength.[11] Hip adductor strength can be increased without weight as shown in Photo 18.6 or with the use of a weight machine or a strong elastic band.

Finally, it is advisable to follow a comprehensive strength-training program in the off-season as a possible way to prevent problems due to muscle weakness.

Flexibility

Just as weak muscles affect the knee, so do tight muscles. Flexibility is lost if it is not maintained, and tight, strong leg muscles can be harmful to the knee. Flexibility must be maintained in four different muscle groups: hamstrings, calf muscles, hip external rotators, and hip abductors (the iliotibial band, or ITB).

The hamstring muscles at the back of the thigh are the strongest muscles for their size in the human body. For many people, they also lack flexibility. Many stretches have been developed to improve flexibility of the hamstrings. Stretching them is a cornerstone of improving patellofemoral syndrome.[12]

For stretching by yourself, try the sitting toe touch. Sit on the floor with your feet together and bend at the waist until you feel tension in the lower back. Keep your knees slightly bent the entire time.

If you can do the sitting toe touch (see Photo 18.7), try another hamstring stretch that gives the back a little more support. Lie on your back with the leg that you want to stretch in the air, bent 90 degrees at the hip. Clasp your hands around the thigh just above the

18.7 *Sitting toe touch*

knee and pull it toward your head (see Photo 18.8). Straightening the knee will increase the stretch. For an increased stretch, grasp the top of the calf. Hold for fifteen seconds, then repeat.

If you have a partner with whom you can stretch, try this PNF stretch. Lie on your back with your ankle on your partner's shoulder. Your partner will place gentle pressure on your patella and slowly move forward until you feel tightness. Once in this position, contract your hamstrings and push against your partner's shoulder (see Photo 18.9). Hold until the hamstrings tire and relax. Have your partner increase the stretch and repeat.[13]

The calf muscles are the gastrocnemius and the deeper soleus. To stretch them, face a wall with your arms on the wall for support. Place the leg to be stretched behind you, keeping it straight, and the other leg in front

18.8 *Solo hamstring stretch*

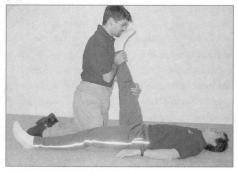

18.9 *Partner hamstring stretch*

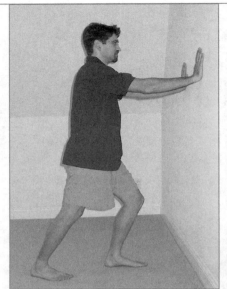 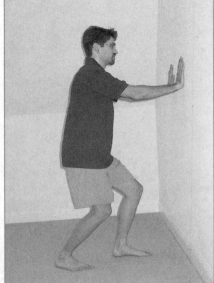

18.10 *Straight-leg stretch for gastrocnemius*   **18.11** *Bent-knee calf stretch for soleus*

with knee bent. Keep the torso straight. Keeping the back leg straight, move it back until you feel the stretch in the calf (see Photo 18.10). Hold for fifteen seconds, release, and repeat. To stretch the soleus, bend the knees while in the same position (see Photo 18.11). Hold for fifteen seconds, release, and repeat.

Decreased flexibility of the external rotators of the hip can lead to biomechanical problems such as foot pronation. Flexibility of the external rotators can improve muscle efficiency.[14] The figure-4 stretch (see Photo 18.12) can improve flexibility of the piriformis,

18.12 *Figure-4 stretch*

18.13 *External rotator stretch*

one of the muscles in the buttock that rotates the hip externally. This stretch also improves flexibility of the gluteus maximus, a prime mover of the hip. To perform the figure-4 stretch, lie on your back and cross your legs so that one ankle is on top of the other knee. Wrap your hands under the bottom leg and pull toward you. You will feel the stretch in the buttock of the crossed leg in front.

Another stretch for the external hip rotators is to lie on your back and bend one knee up to your chest. Use the opposite hand to pull the knee across to the other side of the chest (see Photo 18.13).

The tensor fasciae latae (TFL) is the muscle that is embedded within the iliotibial band (ITB). Flexibility of both structures is important not only for patellofemoral syndrome but for ITB syndrome as well. To stretch the TFL and ITB, stand with your side to the wall and lean against the wall with your arm for

18.14 *ITB stretch*

support. Cross the outside leg in front of the inside leg, and be sure to keep the foot of the outside leg flat on the floor. Move the hips toward the wall and use the outside hand to apply pressure to the hips (see Photo 18.14). This will stretch the TFL and ITB of the inside (back) leg.

Biomechanics

The biomechanical problems of the feet (discussed in greater detail in the next chapter) must be resolved before any other biomechanical problems can be addressed. The use of over-the-counter or custom orthotic arch supports can help to restore ankle and foot alignment for the pronator (pes planus). For the supinator (pes cavus), extra cushion in the shoes can help to compensate for the lack of cushioning in the foot. An arch support may also be useful because it provides a larger base of support over which to spread the impact. Over-the-counter arch supports are less expensive and should be tried before custom orthotics, since one has not been shown to be more beneficial than the other. In running especially, the choice of footwear is critical because it must provide extra arch support or cushioning. For the pronated foot, the shoes should be board-lasted and straight-lasted and have a stable heel counter, extra medial support, and a wider flare. For the supinated foot, a slip-lasted, curve-lasted shoe with softer ethylene vinyl acetate (EVA) and a narrow flare is appropriate.[15] Inserts should be placed in new shoes, not in shoes that have already been worn down.

For sports that involve less impact than running does, such as cycling or in-line skating, arch supports can still be useful to correct biomechanical abnormalities.

The Q-angle is of special importance in cycling. The focus on bicycle fit has traditionally been on the up-down and front-back fit. Little attention has been given to the side-to-side fit. A wide-hipped person on a bicycle that has a relatively narrow distance between the pedals will have an increased Q-angle (see Photo 18.15).

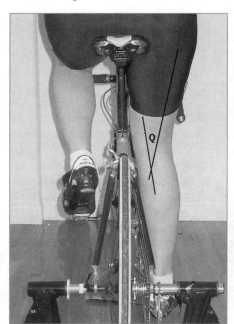

18.16 Decreasing the Q-angle by moving the cleats to the inside of the shoe

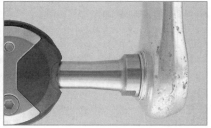

18.17 Decreasing the Q-angle by inserting spacers between the pedal and crank

18.15 Increase in the Q-angle on a bicycle

18.18 *Raising the saddle to 25 degrees of knee extension to strengthen the VMO*

To normalize the Q-angle in this example, a wider stance must be set. This can be done by moving the cleats to the inside of the shoe (see Photo 18.16), choosing a pedal with a longer spindle, or placing spacers between the pedals and the cranks (see Photo 18.17). Conversely, a narrow-waisted rider should have the stance narrowed with shorter pedal spindles.

Raising the bicycle seat is another position change that will strengthen the VMO (see Photo 18.18). This will cause the leg to extend fully, which involves using the VMO. The seat should be set as high as possible without causing the pelvis to tilt from side to side while pedaling. The knee angle will be close to 25 degrees.

The weakness and tightness of muscles cause the patella to shift laterally during leg straightening. One way to prevent this shift is to tape the knee. A technique known as the McConnell method has been shown to provide increased knee stability and decreased mechanical stress.[16]

ILIOTIBIAL BAND FRICTION SYNDROME
Incidence, anatomy, and biomechanics
The iliotibial band friction syndrome (ITBFS) is the second most common overuse injury of the knee,[17] accounting for 12 percent of knee injuries among runners.[18] Research about ITBFS is lacking in other sports, but the overall incidence is up to 52 percent, depending upon the population studied.[19] Although initially described almost exclusively in runners, it is now seen with increasing frequency in other athletes, especially cyclists.[20]

The iliotibial band is a long fibrous tendon that starts at the hip and runs along the outside (lateral aspect) of the thigh and crosses the knee before ending on the bony prominence of the tibia (shin bone) known as Gerdy's tubercle. The muscles of the ITB

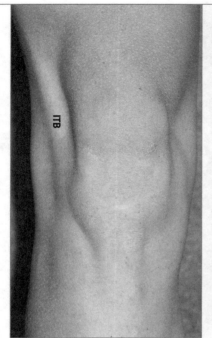

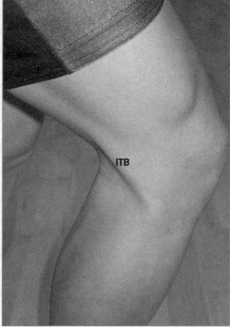

18.19 *The iliotibial band in the right knee*

18.20 *The ITB moves posterior to the lateral femoral condyle during knee flexion*

are the tensor fasciae latae and the gluteus maximus. The tensor fasciae latae is a lateral thigh muscle imbedded in the ITB; the gluteus maximus is the largest of the muscles in the buttock.

When the knee is fully straightened, the ITB lies anterior to the lateral femoral condyle (see Photo 18.19). As the knee is flexed beyond 30 degrees, the ITB slides past the condyle and ends up posterior to it (see Photo 18.20). Since there is no anchor for the ITB, it will slide over the femoral condyle from anterior to posterior each time the knee is bent. The constant friction of the ITB moving this way can lead to irritation and inflammation.

The pain from ITBFS is located on the outer aspect of the knee, near the lateral femoral condyle. Pain is worse during flexion-extension movements of the knee,[21] especially when the injured athlete is running downhill or walking up and down stairs. Once the area is inflamed, any activity that pinches the ITB against the lateral femoral condyle will cause pain. Examples include lateral stretching of the leg, running on an uneven or cambered road, increasing stride length, changing your bicycle position, and skating on your inside edge. Although there may be some creaking of the joint (crepitus) with ITBFS, the syndrome is not associated with swelling or limitation of motion of the knee.

ITBFS is associated with some common alignment issues of the leg: pes cavus, pes planus, bowlegs (genu varum), and pigeon toes (hindfoot valgus).[22] One study of athletes with ITBFS found that injured runners had a significant leg-length difference (greater than 0.64 cm).[23]

Athletes with ITBFS report an increase in mileage and increased hill work. Running downhill predisposes the athlete to ITBFS because the knee is in increased extension (straighter) as the foot hits the ground, which makes flexion with ITB irritation more likely.[24] Similarly, a crowned road will cause the leg toward the curb to be extended more than the leg farther up the crown. Running in worn-out shoes is another predisposing factor.[25] Bicycle positions with a saddle too high or too far back will also worsen the syndrome.

Although ITBFS is usually felt in the knee, the effects of a tight ITB can also cause hip pain. As the ITB moves back and forth across the prominent part of the hip, called the greater trochanter, this movement can irritate the underlying structures. The trochanteric bursa that cushions the ITB from the greater trochanter can become irritated and inflamed. The treatment for both knee and hip pain from a tight ITB is the same regardless of which joint is involved.

Treatment

The treatment of ITBFS primarily involves decreasing the overuse of the knee. Avoiding the extrinsic factors of downhill running and cambered surfaces, correcting biomechanical problems, increasing flexibility, and using NSAIDs judiciously are also useful in getting back to sports without pain.

Reducing stress on the knee is achieved by cushioning the feet when you are participating in impact sports. Orthotics and cushioned insoles can be used for pes cavus feet that lose their natural shock absorption.

If the athlete has internally rotated toes (pigeon toes), the lateral femoral condyle is placed in a more prominent position, allowing increased friction between it and the ITB. This can be adjusted by having the front of the cleat point more toward the inside of the foot (see Photo 18.21). Pedals that offer float will allow for the rider's natural foot angle to be maintained throughout the entire pedaling cycle. Rotation should be adjusted to prevent excessive internal rotation.

Genu varum (bowlegs) can be corrected with custom orthotics or by using a pedal with longer spindles (see Photo 18.22).

18.21 *Float adjustment to prevent internal rotation at the bottom of the pedal stroke*

18.22 *Pedals with longer spindles can correct bowlegs (genu varum)*

18.23 *Adding a cleat shim to compensate for leg-length discrepancy*

18.24 *Seat height should be adjusted to achieve 30–35 degrees of knee flexion*

18.25 *Quadriceps stretch*

Leg-length discrepancies should be adjusted if they exceed 6.4 mm (0.25 in). This can be done by adding a shim to the pedal cleat or by using customized footwear (see Photo 18.23).

The saddle should be lowered to prevent excessive snapping of the ITB over the condyle, which occurs at 30 degrees of knee flexion. Therefore, the knee should not be straightened past 30–35 degrees (see Photo 18.24).[26] Staying seated while cycling will prevent full extension of the leg, as will avoiding hills and running downhill. Adjust saddle set-back so that the tibial tuberosity is just behind the pedal spindle.

Build flexibility of the ITB with the ITB stretch (discussed in the section on patellofemoral pain). Also, do exercises to decrease the tightness of the quadriceps and calf muscles. To stretch the quadriceps, stand on one foot and grab the other foot with the same-side hand. Pull the foot up toward the buttocks. Try to keep the pelvis level. To increase the stretch, pull the foot farther back (see Photo 18.25).

Strength exercises should be aimed at hip abductors. In a study of cross-country runners with ITBFS, these muscles were found to be relatively weak.[27] The gluteus medius was targeted for increased strength.

Initially, strength training should be undertaken without weights. Use lateral leg raises before moving on to increased resistance. To strengthen the gluteus medius, lie on the opposite side of the leg that is being strengthened. The pelvis and shoulders should be perpendicular to the floor. While keeping the leg in line with the trunk, raise the leg toward the ceiling. Avoid any rotation of the leg to prevent other muscles from helping (see Photo 18.26). Resistance can be added later with ankle weights or by using an elastic band stretched between the ankles.

After you can do three sets of fifteen repetitions of leg raises, try pelvic drops.[28] Stand on a stool or a step with the involved leg and hang the uninvolved leg off the stool. Keeping the legs straight, lower the uninvolved side of the pelvis by shifting the body weight to the inside of the involved foot. The pelvis will tilt toward the floor, and the uninvolved foot will drop by a few inches. Return to the starting position by contracting the gluteus medius (see Photos 18.27 and 18.28).

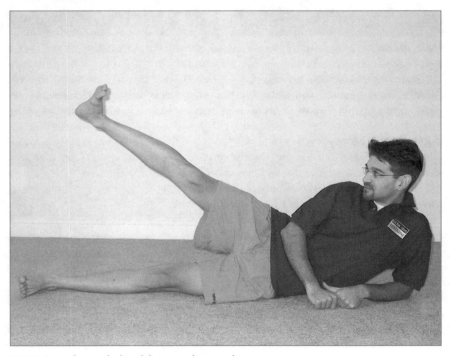

18.26 *Strengthening the hip abductors without weight*

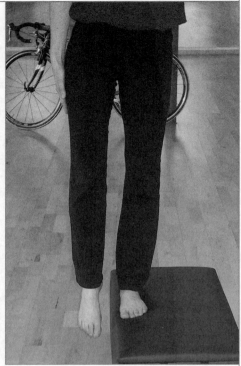

18.27, 18.28 *Dropping and raising the pelvis to strengthen the gluteus medius.*

Studies have shown that massage does not help ITBFS.[29] However, stretching, ice, rest, NSAIDs, training modification, and biomechanical correction have proved 94 percent effective in treating ITBFS.[30] Full recovery for most cases can be accomplished within six weeks.

PATELLAR TENDONOPATHY

The patellar tendon connects the powerful quadriceps muscle to the bone in the shin, the tibia (see Photo 18.29). The tendon arises from the four muscles of the quadriceps and ends on the bony spot called the tibia tubercle. The patella lies within the tendon, and damage occurs to the section of tendon between the patella and the attachment to the tibia tubercle. As the quadriceps contracts, it applies tension across the patellar tendon and causes the knee to straighten. During use of the knee in sports, forces applied to the tendon cause microscopic breakdown of it. The individual collagen fibers that make up the tendon are slightly torn, but with normal rest, they are restored.

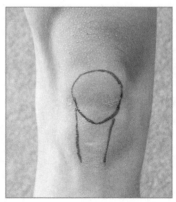

18.29 *Anatomy and location of the right patellar tendon*

Pathophysiology of injury

Increased stress across the patellar tendon causes increased damage, and the body is unable to heal. The result is a breakdown of the tendon, known as tendonosis. Examination of the tendon under a microscope reveals a loss of collagen and an increase in cells called fibroblasts, which make more collagen.

There is limited inflammation involved, which makes the term "tendonitis" a misnomer because the suffix "-itis" refers to a process of inflammation. In truth, patellar tendonitis (the inflammatory process) is rare, and tendonosis (the process of collagen breakdown) is more common. Because of the difficulty in distinguishing the two conditions, the term "tendonopathy" (describes abnormal process in the tendon) is used.[31]

Patellar tendonopathy is most commonly seen in athletes who participate in jumping sports, but it also appears when there are repeated stresses to the tendon. This can occur with weight lifting, running, cycling, increased hill work, and decreased cadence.

Symptoms of patellar tendonitis are pain in the knee just distal (farther down the leg) to the patella. Pain is usually gradual in onset but can be precipitated by a specific workout or, less commonly, a specific jump. Compared with patellofemoral syndrome, the pain is more localized.

In the early course of tendonopathy, the pain may actually improve with exercise. In this case, exercise is usually continued until the damage becomes more than the body can repair. At this point, there is pain at rest or with normal activities. Recognizing and treating the symptoms early can save pain and frustration later.

Stage one is early in the course of the disease, and pain is present only after activity. Stage two is slightly more severe, with pain interfering with performance. Pain before, during, and after exercise is the hallmark of the third stage. Complete tendon rupture occurs in stage four and needs surgical correction.

Treatment

The treatment of patellar tendonopathy depends on the stage of disease. In stages one and two, rest and ice massage will usually relieve the symptoms. Although there is little inflammation, some experts advocate anti-inflammatory medications.[32] NSAIDs should be taken with food to prevent stomach irritation. A prescription-strength dose of ibuprofen is 600 or 800 mg every eight hours. NSAIDs should not be taken before exercise as they may mask the pain that should be used as a signal to rest or lighten the training load.

Early in tendonopathy, the goal is to halt progression of the collagen destruction while the return to sports can be made easily. Once stage three is reached, returning to the activity can take up to six months.

Since tendonopathy is largely due to tendon breakdown from overload, the first step in correcting the problem is to remove the stress from the tendon. This can be done through a reduction in both volume and intensity of training. Extrinsic training factors such as running down hills and heavy weight training must be avoided.

Strain on the patellar tendon increases with knee flexion.[33] As the knee bends and moves ahead of the ball of the foot, there is increased tension across the patellar tendon. With increased knee bending, different parts of the tendon are strained differently, leading to collagen breakdown. This occurs when running downhill, with poor bicycle adjustment, or when using poor weight-training techniques. Lunges and squats are two exercises that expose the patellar tendon to increased forces when poor technique is used, such as letting the bent knee move forward beyond the ball of the foot (see Photo 18.30). This also occurs when running down hills.

Landing on the foot increases stress in the knee. Especially in mountain biking, landings must be well cushioned by landing on the front of the foot (toes down) with shock absorption coming from bending of the knee and hip.

If you have tendonopathy, you should engage only in pain-free exercise. If your chosen sport causes pain, try jogging in water or swimming, two exercises that do not place strain on the tendon. If those hurt, then rest is advised.

Other techniques to remove the load from the patellar tendon include altering bicycle position and fixing alignment problems. Because knee flexion increases tension and strain, bicycle saddle height should be raised to give a knee-flexion angle of 25 degrees. In addition, to prevent the knee from absorbing stress, the knee must be in line with or slightly behind the ball of the foot. To accomplish this, you can make several changes.

First, the bicycle seat perhaps can be moved back; if not, you might need a new seatpost or saddle. Position pedal cleats so that the ball of the foot is resting over the pedal spindle (see Photo 18.31). The cleats may need to be moved farther back on the shoe to bring the foot farther forward on the pedal (see Photo 18.32).

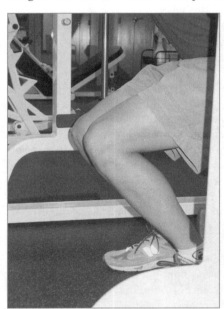

18.31 The ball of the foot should be lined up with the pedal spindle

18.30 Poor squat/lunge technique lets the knee move forward beyond the ball of the foot and places increased tension on the patellar tendon

18.32 Move the foot farther forward on the pedal by moving the cleat back

When the cyclist is in a forward-set time-trial position (see Photo 18.33), the knee is at increased risk of moving beyond the ball of the foot. It is important to have the position set so that a plumb line dropped from the tibial tuberosity will bisect the pedal spindle (see Photo 18.34). If you cannot achieve this position, consider shorter aero bars and keep the saddle set back (see Photo 18.35). This position has been used with a reported increase in power. Although the aerodynamic benefit might be less, a position that keeps you pain-free will produce benefits in the long run.

Orthotic foot inserts that control pronation can help to decrease the load on the patellar tendon. Taping and bracing may also mitigate the load, but no studies have established definite effectiveness.

Since the problem of patellar tendonopathy is not due to inflammation but rather collagen destruction, NSAIDs are not particularly helpful.[34] Ice, however, has been found to be useful. The cold causes vasoconstriction, which helps reverse some of the pathology found in tendonosis.[35]

Strengthening exercises help to prevent and reverse the collagen breakdown. Exercises known as eccentric lifting help to organize collagen fibers.[36] These are exercises in which there is resistance during muscle lengthening. Normally, muscles contract as the load is moved (concentric). In eccentric exercise, the load is lowered slowly after it is lifted.

18.33 *The traditional time trial position offers a more aerodynamic profile, but it can increase tension on the patellar tendon.*

18.34 *A plumb line from the tibial tuberosity should bisect or be slightly behind the pedal spindle*

Strength also must be increased in the quadriceps, calf, gluteal, and lower abdominal muscles. This will help to relieve stress on the patellar tendon by producing increased shock absorption and decreased fatigue. Lack of strength in these muscles leads to abnormal movement in the knee, causing tendon strain.

The athlete with severe patellar tendonopathy can do calf exercises, since they don't involve movement of the knee. Isometric exercise (muscle contraction without movement) to strengthen the quadriceps can be performed while facing downhill on a 30-degree inclined plane. Stand on the affected leg and bend the knee to the limit of pain.

Tightness of the quadriceps, hamstrings, iliotibial band, and calf muscles can restrict the range of motion in the knee, contributing to an increased load on the patellar tendon. Stretches for these muscle groups are given in the sections on patellofemoral syndrome and iliotibial band friction syndrome. Finally, deep-tissue friction massage increases tendon healing in animal studies and has long been accepted as useful in athletes.[37]

18.35 *The set-back "big slam" position keeps the rider's knee bent behind the pedal spindle, reducing strain on the patellar tendon.*

NOTES

1. C. Swenson, L. Sward, J. Karlsson. Cryotherapy in sports medicine. *Scandinavian Journal of Medicine and Science in Sports* August 1996, 6(4): 193–200.

2. D. C. MacAuley. Ice therapy: How good is the evidence? *International Journal of Sports Medicine* July 2001, 22(5): 379–84.

3. J. L. Moeller, J. Monroe, D. B. McKeag. Cryotherapy-induced common peroneal nerve palsy. *Clinical Journal of Sport Medicine: Official Journal of the Canadian Academy of Sport Medicine* July 1997, 7(3): 212–16.
F. H. Bassett 3d, J. S. Kirkpatrick, D. L. Engelhardt, T. R. Malone. Cryotherapy-induced nerve injury. *American Journal of Sports Medicine* Sept–Oct 1992, 20(5): 516–18.

4. R. Meeusen, P. Lievens. The use of cryotherapy in sports injuries. *Sports Medicine* Nov–Dec 1986, 3(6): 398–414.
D.C. MacAuley. Ice therapy.

5. L. C. Almekinders, S. V. Almekinders. Outcome in the treatment of chronic overuse sports injuries: A retrospective study. *Journal of Orthopedic and Sports Physical Therapy* March 1994, 19(3): 157–61.

6. R. Thomee, J. Augustsson, J. Karlsson. Patellofemoral pain syndrome: A review of current issues. *Sports Medicine* October 1999, 28(4): 245–62.

7. M. S. Puniello. Iliotibial band tightness and medial patellar glide in patients with patellofemoral dysfunction. *Journal of Orthopedic and Sports Physical Therapy* March 1993, 17(3): 144–48.

8. K. LaBrier, D. B. O'Neill. Patellofemoral stress syndrome: Current concepts. *Sports Medicine* December 1993, 16(6): 449–59.

9. D. B. O'Neill, L. J. Micheli, J. P. Warner. Patellofemoral stress: A prospective analysis of exercise treatment in adolescents and adults. *American Journal of Sports Medicine* Mar–Apr 1992, 20(2): 151–56.

10. K. LaBrier, D. B. O'Neill. Patellofemoral stress syndrome: Current concepts. *Sports Medicine* December 1993, 16(6): 449–59.

11. F. G. Zappala, C. B. Taffel, G. R. Scuderi. Rehabilitation of patellofemoral joint disorders. *Orthopedic Clinics of North America* 1992, 23: 555–66.

12. J. H. Henry. Conservative treatment of patellofemoral subluxation. *Clinics in Sports Medicine* April 1989, 8(2): 261–78.

13. J. G. Aronen. Team up for thigh stretches. *The Physician and Sportsmedicine* October 1997, 25(10): 129–30.

14. M. S. Juhn. Patellofemoral pain syndrome: A review and guidelines for treatment. *American Family Physician* 1999, 60: 2012–22.

15. D. C. McKenzie, D. B. Clement, J. E. Taunton. Running shoes, orthotics, and injuries. *Sports Medicine* Sept–Oct 1985, 2(5): 334–47.

16. G. L. Shelton. Conservative management of patellofemoral dysfunction. *Primary Care* June 1992, 19(2): 331–50.

C. M. Powers, R. Landel, T. Sosnick, J. Kirby, K. Mengel, A. Cheney, J. Perry. The effects of patellar taping on stride characteristics and joint motion in subjects with patellofemoral pain. *The Journal of Orthopedic and Sports Physical Therapy* December 1997, 26(6): 286–91.

17. J. E. Taunton, D. B. Clement, G. W. Smart, K. L. McNicol. Non-surgical management of overuse knee injuries in runners. *Canadian Journal of Sport Sciences* March 1987, 12(1): 11–18.

18. R. Pinshaw, V. Atlas, T. D. Noakes. The nature and response to therapy of 196 consecutive injuries seen at a runners' clinic. *South African Medical Journal* February 25, 1984, 65(8): 291–98.

19. K. L. Kirk, T. Kuklo, W. Klemme. Iliotibial band friction syndrome. *Orthopedics* November 2000, 23(11): 1209–14.

20. J. C. Holmes, A. L. Pruitt, N. J. Whalen. Iliotibial band syndrome in cyclists. *American Journal of Sports Medicine* May–June 1993, 21(3): 419–24.

21. K. McNicol, J. E. Taunton, D. B. Clement. Iliotibial tract friction syndrome in athletes. *Canadian Journal of Applied Sport Sciences* June 1981, 6(2): 76–80.

22. L. S. Krivickas. Anatomical factors associated with overuse sports injuries. *Sports Medicine* August 1997, 24(2): 132–46.

23. S. P. Messier, K. A. Pittala. Etiologic factors associated with selected running injuries. *Medicine and Science in Sports and Exercise* October 1988, 20(5): 501–5.

24. J. W. Orchard, P. A. Fricker, A. T. Abud, B. R. Mason. Biomechanics of iliotibial band friction syndrome in runners. *American Journal of Sports Medicine* May–June 1996, 24(3): 375–79.

25. F. A. Barber, A. N. Sutker. Iliotibial band syndrome. *Sports Medicine* August 1992, 14(2): 144–48.

26. J. C. Holmes, A. L. Pruitt, N. J. Whalen. Lower extremity overuse in bicycling. *Clinics in Sports Medicine* January 1994, 13(1): 187–203.

27. M. Fredericson, C. L. Cookingham, A. M. Chaudhari, B. C. Dowdell, N. Oestreicher, S. A. Sahrmann. Hip abductor weakness in distance runners with iliotibial band syndrome. *Clinical Journal of Sport Medicine* July 2000, 10(3): 169–75.

28. M. Fredericson, M. Guillet, L. DeBenedictis. Quick solutions for iliotibial band syndrome. *The Physician and Sportsmedicine* February 2000, 28(2): 52–68.

29. L. Brosseau, L. Casimiro, S. Milne, V. Robinson, B. Shea, P. Tugwell, G. Wells. Deep transverse friction massage for treating tendinitis (Cochrane Review). *Cochrane Database of Systematic Reviews* 2002, 1: CD003528.

30. McNicol et al. Iliotibial tract friction syndrome in athletes.

31. K. M. Khan, J. L. Cook, J. E. Taunton, F. Bonar. Overuse tendinosis, not tendinitis. Part 1: A new paradigm for a difficult clinical problem. *The Physician and Sportsmedicine* May 2000, 28(5): 38–48.

32. M. Harries, C. Williams, W. D. Stanish, L. J. Micheli. *Oxford Textbook of Sports Medicine,* 2d ed. New York: Oxford Medical Publications, 1998.

33. L. C. Almekinders, J. H. Vellema, P. S. Weinhold. Strain patterns in the patellar tendon and the implications for patellar tendinopathy. *Knee Surgery, Sports Traumatology, Arthroscopy: Official Journal of the ESSKA* January 2002, 10(1): 2–5.

34. L. C. Almekinders, J. D. Temple: Etiology, diagnosis, and treatment of tendonitis: An analysis of the literature. *Medicine and Science in Sports and Exercise* 1998, 30(8): 1183–90.
L. C. Almekinders, G. Deol. The effects of aging, antiinflammatory drugs, and ultrasound on the in vitro response of tendon tissue. *American Journal of Sports Medicine* July–Aug 1999, 27(4): 417–21.

35. Khan et al. Overuse tendinosis, not tendinitis.

36. K. Jensen, R. P. DiFabio. Evaluation of eccentric exercise in treatment of patellar tendinitis. *Physical Therapy* March 1989, 69(3): 211–16.

37. C. J. Davidson, L. R. Ganion, G. M. Gehlsen, B. Verhoestra, J. E. Roepke, T. L. Sevier. Rat tendon morphologic and functional changes resulting from soft tissue mobilization. *Medicine and Science in Sports and Exercise* March 1997, 29(3): 313–19.
G. M. Gehlsen, L. R. Ganion, R. Helfst. Fibroblast responses to variation in soft tissue mobilization pressure. *Medicine and Science in Sports and Exercise* April 1999, 31(4): 531–35.

OVERUSE INJURIES
OF THE FOOT
AND ANKLE

STRESS FRACTURES

Stress fractures are the result of repetitive trauma to a bone that is too weak to handle the load. The result is a partial bone collapse. During normal bone development, an increase in weight-bearing activity will lead to an increase in bone density and an improved ability to distribute stress.

In stress fractures, the normal resistance to applied loads is altered, resulting in decreased ability to distribute loads. There are two theories behind the etiology of stress fractures. The overload theory states that repetitive contraction of muscles will pull at the insertion points on the bone, reducing the bone's ability to withstand mechanical stress. The theory of muscle fatigue emphasizes the decreased shock-absorbing ability of bone as fatigue progresses. As the muscle's ability to absorb shock decreases, there is increased loading of the bone.

Training errors, playing surface, body type, female gender, age, and footwear selection also predispose the athlete to developing stress fractures (see Table 19.1). Anatomical malalignments such as leg-length discrepancy, low arches, excessive pronation, and high arches are also contributing factors.

Table 19.1	
FACTORS ASSOCIATED WITH STRESS FRACTURES	
Body type	Increased incidence in large people
Female gender	3.5–10 times more common in women
Age	Highest incidence between 18 and 28 years old
Fitness	More common after prolonged activity
Training	Sudden increase in volume
Footwear	Too small; worn or inappropriate cushioning
Playing surface	Hard surfaces increase load
Nutrition	Inadequate calcium intake, anorexia nervosa
Hormonal	Decreased estrogen in women

Athletes will frequently notice a dull aching pain that is localized to the fracture site. Pain starts gradually and worsens with activity. Review of the training diary implicates increased volume or new footwear.

Frequently the physician's exam does not reveal a specific abnormality, especially if there is a lot of muscle or fat around the bone. If the bone is easily felt, swelling and tenderness may be present. X-rays taken early in the course of the injury are usually normal and might remain normal up to twelve weeks after the injury. Your physician may obtain a CT, MRI, or bone scan if suspicion of a stress fracture is high.

Conservative (nonsurgical) treatment of stress fractures is usually successful. Treatment involves decreasing the volume of training and halting any painful weight-bearing activity. The athlete must stop the sport that caused the fracture. Low-impact activity (cycling, swimming) may be done if there is no pain.

Nonsteroidal anti-inflammatory medication can control pain, but analgesics should not be used to mask pain during activity. Ice massage has proved helpful.

After a three-week period without pain, when full weight bearing is normal and x-rays show healing, the athlete can begin the return to the primary sport. Pain should be used to monitor the level of activity.

Any risk factors mentioned in Table 19.1 should be corrected. The easiest to correct are foot and equipment problems, training errors, and playing surfaces.

Tibia

The tibial shaft is the most common site of stress fractures in athletes. An externally rotated hip and foot pronation can predispose an individual to developing tibial stress fractures.

Usually it is the runner who develops pain at the junction of the middle and distal third (far end) of the tibia (see Photo 19.1). Pain is on the inside and the front

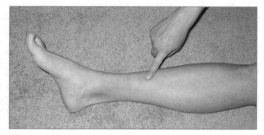

19.1 Stress fractures usually occur at the junction of the middle and distal third of the tibia

of the tibia and follows an increase in training volume or intensity. During recovery, a brace (aircast) can be used if there is pain with walking.

Navicular

Stress fractures of the navicular bone are usually seen in jumpers and sprinters, but distance runners can sustain such injury if there is considerable involvement of the front of the foot when the foot hits the ground.

Diagnosis is often delayed due to the insidious onset. Pain is vague on the inside of the foot along the arch. Activity worsens pain; rest relieves it. Pain returns when the activity is resumed. Because diagnosis is difficult and frequently delayed, the stress fracture can develop into a complete fracture, so do not delay seeking medical care if you feel pain along the medial arch.

Calcaneus

Gradual onset of vague heel pain after increased activity should raise suspicion of a stress fracture of the calcaneus (the major heel bone). Pain is worse when weight is increased on the heel and relieved when weight is transferred to the toes; the result is that walking is difficult and running is impossible. Movement of the ankle without bearing weight is painless.

Treatment is based on reducing weight-bearing activity and by increasing the shock absorption of footwear and the foot. Supporting a high arch with an orthotic insert will increase the ability of the foot to handle loads.

MEDIAL TIBIAL STRESS SYNDROME

Also known as shin splints, medial tibial stress syndrome is another overuse injury that affects the lower leg. Shin splints have been cited as the most common cause of leg pain in a report from a Swedish sports medicine clinic.[1] The name medial tibial stress syndrome describes the position and nature of the pain. Pain develops on the medial (inside) aspect of the shin (tibia), usually along the lower two-thirds of it (see Photo 19.2). Although the condition is more common in runners, pain appears in jumping and ballis-

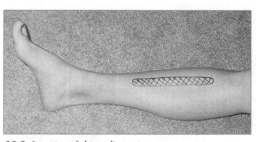

19.2 Location of shin-splint pain

tic activity as well. Early in the development, the pain is noted at the beginning of exercise and may even improve with exercise, only to recur after the workout.

Although the etiology of shin splints includes many theories, overuse plays a role in development of the attendant pain. As with all overuse injuries, both intrinsic and extrinsic factors are responsible for the development of shin splints. Among the intrinsic causes are anatomical factors such as excessive pronation.[2] Extrinsic factors include harsh running surfaces, poorly cushioned footwear, and poorly conceived training plans that rapidly increase volume.

Two particular anatomical variables that predispose an athlete to developing shin splints are strong or inflexible calf muscles and pronation of the foot. If the calf muscles are disproportionately stronger than the muscles in the rest of the lower leg, the imbalance pulls on the tibia. Weak muscles do not pull on the tibia enough, which causes the bone to absorb most of the shock. The tissue layer that adheres tightly to the bone is called periosteum. Pronation results in traction on the periosteum by the calf muscles, and the tension is transmitted to the bone. The result is pain if the bone does not have the chance to adapt, due either to sudden increases in training volume or to poor bone growth response, which is common in individuals who are calcium-deficient (because of eating disorders, for example).

Prevention of shin splints should be aimed at reversing anatomical anomalies and decreasing stress by providing cushioned footwear and insoles.[3] Other interventions such as heel pads, stretching, and various insoles have not proved to be effective.[4] Preventing excessive pronation through the use of arch-supporting insoles should also prevent shin splints.

Preseason conditioning may be the most effective measure in preventing overuse injuries, with a focus on undertaking specific training with a solid base of flexibility and strength.[5] Pay special attention to flexibility in the gastrocnemius and soleus muscles in the calf. Strengthening the ankle dorsiflexor muscles (the muscles responsible for tilting the foot up at the ankle) will help to balance the muscle forces on the tibia.[6]

The mainstay of treatment for medial tibial stress syndrome is removing the stress. This is accomplished through reduction in volume and intensity until walking is pain-free. During this period, fitness can be maintained through crosstraining. Pain can be managed with NSAIDs and ice massage. Also recommended is calcium supplementation of 1,000 mg/day for men and 1,500 mg/day for women.

After pain is gone, return to training at half the pre-injury volume and progress in 10–15 percent increases.

Conservative management should be effective in resolving pain. Be sure to stretch, strengthen, and correct anatomical malalignments. If pain continues, follow up with a physician.

MORTON'S NEUROMA

When I started speed skating, there was an employee at the local skate shop who claimed that in order for skates to fit well, they had to be tight. Everyone who started skating that summer had numerous foot problems, all related to skates that were too tight. What nobody told that skate salesman was that footwear should fit well and be snug but it should not be tight.

One of the problems associated with shoes that are too tight is the development of Morton's neuroma. Repetitive trauma to the nerves that run along the bottom of the foot will result in a painful irritation of the nerves between the metatarsal heads at the base of the toes (see Photo 19.3).

Compression of the nerves occurs during extension of the toes (toes pointed up) and

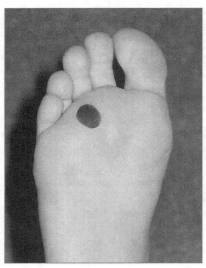

19.3 *Typical location of Morton's neuroma is between third and fourth toes*

pronation or when wearing tight shoes. This is a position that the feet are forced into with high-heeled shoes, but this position may also occur with any shoes that have a height differential between the heel and the toe. Extension of the toes is more common during running or stair climbing. Tight shoes not only cause physical compression but also result in decreased blood flow.

The pain in Morton's neuroma gradually worsens, and you may notice numbness of the toes when wearing certain footwear. Pain is better when you are barefoot or wearing comfortable shoes. Neuromas most commonly develop between the base of the middle and second smallest toes but can occur between any two toes. Direct pressure to the area or squeezing the toes together can elicit symptoms.

Treatment is aimed at reducing pressure on the bottom of the foot. Loosening laces, reducing activity, changing footwear, and placing a gauze "donut" under the neuroma are all helpful. To make a donut, roll a piece of gauze into a long cylinder, shape it into a ring, and tape it to the bottom of the foot. The center of the donut should be over the painful part of the foot (see Photo 19.4). If none of these treatments are effective, steroid injections and surgical excision are options.

PLANTAR FASCIITIS

Plantar fasciitis is one of the most common overuse injuries of the lower extremity.[7] The plantar fascia is a strong ligament that runs from the front of the calcaneus (heel bone) to the metatarsal heads (base of the toes) as shown in Photo 19.5. During normal walking, the ligament helps to support the weight of the body and provides support for the foot. The plantar fascia acts as a thick rubber band to absorb shock from weight bearing, and it supports the arch of the foot.

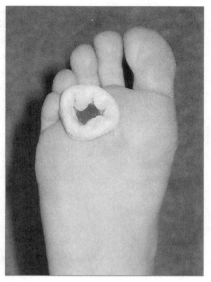

19.4 *A gauze donut will help decrease pain from Morton's neuroma between third and fourth toes*

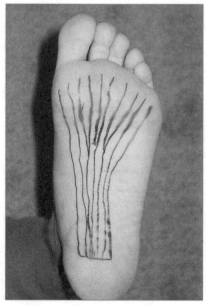

19.5 *Anatomical distribution of the plantar fascia*

Increased shock absorption from running (up to 250 times body weight with foot strike), increased force from high gears or low cadence cycling, or the combination of these factors with increased body weight can cause microscopic damage to develop at the point where the plantar fascia inserts into the calcaneus. Small amounts of damage can be repaired with rest and recovery, but when the damage is too great for the body to repair, plantar fasciitis develops. This microtrauma is usually felt as pain on the sole of the foot, just in front of the medial (inside) part of the calcaneus.

The pain of plantar fasciitis can be felt anywhere along the entire length of the plantar fascia. The pain is usually worse in the morning and improves with the first few steps. Because it is difficult to rest the foot, the pain can become chronic. The shearing and microtrauma to the plantar fascia and calcaneus can result in severe pain and extended healing time. The pain is frequently blamed on bony prominences that stick out from the calcaneus (heel spurs), but these spurs are unrelated to development of plantar fasciitis.[8]

In one study, conservative treatment of plantar fasciitis was 97 percent effective with either resolution of symptoms or return to activity without limitation.[9] The outcome was worse for patients who delayed treatment, had symptoms in both feet, or were overweight. Nonsurgical, conservative treatment consists of adjusting biomechanical abnormalities, stretching and strengthening, and correcting training errors.

Biomechanical correction

Excessive pronation, pes planus (flat feet), or pes cavus (high arches) frequently can lead to plantar fasciitis. Leg-length discrepancy and rotational malalignments of the leg bones also are predisposing factors that place stress on the plantar fascia.

Stress to the plantar fascia can be mitigated through the use of orthotics and shoe inserts to maintain proper alignment of the foot and cushion the plantar fascia. When the foot is loaded with body weight, the plantar fascia is under tension. Pronation and poor arch support do not allow the foot to aid in absorption of that stress, resulting in trauma to the plantar fascia. There are several ways to help the foot absorb the stress.

Arch taping is an inexpensive, effective method of supporting the plantar fascia. However, taping is not intended for long-term use and has been shown to lose effectiveness after twenty-four minutes.[10]

Over-the-counter arch supports can be found in sporting goods and running stores. These supply medial (inside of the foot) arch support and will last longer than taping. Arch supports can be used continuously to prevent recurrence in individuals who have poor intrinsic arch support. Choose the densest material available that is still comfortable to stand and walk on.

Heel cups cushion the calcaneus and are especially useful in the older athlete who has natural age-related thinning of the heel fat pad.[11] Although heel cups have not proved universally effective in the treatment of plantar fasciitis, athletes with the condition have less natural heel cushioning,[12] so using heel cups is a logical option.

Custom orthotics are expensive but should be tried if the other corrective measures fail to resolve symptoms or alignment problems.

Stretching

As in many overuse cases, lack of flexibility can precipitate injury. The Achilles tendon inserts into the calcaneus on the opposite end of the plantar fascia. If the Achilles tendon and the muscles that pull on it are tight, there is increased traction on the plantar fascia. Stretching the gastrocnemius and the soleus muscles is helpful.

The plantar fascia itself can be stretched to help reduce tension across it when weight is being loaded. Several stretches are effective. Rolling the foot over a fifteen-ounce can or a tennis ball will increase plantar fascia flexibility (see Photo 19.6). Another technique is the towel stretch, which involves holding a rolled-up towel under the front half of the foot and pulling the foot forward (see Photo 19.7). Cross-friction massage of the place where the plantar fascia inserts into the calcaneus can help decrease morning pain (see Photo 19.8).

Strengthening

Strengthening exercises are aimed at increasing the strength of the intrinsic muscles of the foot: abductor hallucis, flexor digitorum brevis, and abductor digiti minimi. All of these muscles arise from the same point as the plantar fascia.

Toe taps can be done anywhere; for an especially good use of time, do them while sitting at a desk or watching television. Keep the foot planted on the floor and raise all the toes in the air, then tap only the big toe on the floor. Next raise the big toe and tap the other toes on the floor (see Photo 19.9). Repeat with the other foot. Increase from ten to fifty taps a session.

Once you have mastered toe taps, move on to towel curls. Lay a towel on a smooth floor and place your foot on the towel. Move the towel toward you by curling it in

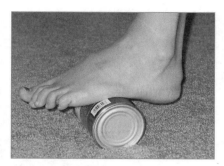

19.6 *Dynamic stretch*

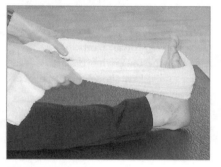

19.7 *Towel stretch*

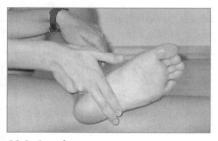

19.8 *Cross-friction massage*

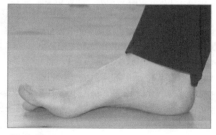

19.9 *Toe taps*

19.10 *Towel curls*

your toes (see Photo 19.10). Add a weight to the end of the towel for increased resistance. If you are really advanced, try picking up marbles or coins with your toes.

Training
Volume and intensity of training should be decreased until symptoms subside. Experts recommend decreasing the impact of exercise by switching surfaces or applying less force to the feet. For cyclists, this would mean using lower gears and avoiding hills. Runners may wish to switch to synthetic tracks.

Decreasing inflammation
Although the underlying problem of plantar fasciitis is an increased ratio of damage to repair, studies have shown the effectiveness of using ice and nonsteroidal anti-inflammatory medications to lessen pain.[13]

FOOT BIOMECHANICS AND ORTHOTICS
The foot contains twenty-six bones and numerous ligaments. The complex structure gives the foot flexibility for travel over uneven surfaces, it cushions during impact, and it provides a solid platform from which to launch a step.

A few of the many foot bones are worth describing in some detail (see Photo 19.11). The talus is the bone that articulates with the bones of the leg to form the ankle joint. The bone under the talus is the calcaneus, which is the bone that can be felt in the heel. The joint between the talus and the calcaneus is known as the subtalar joint. This joint is responsible for pronation.

During normal mechanics of walking, there are six to eight degrees of subtalar pronation (see Photo 19.12). The body weight is transmitted through the tibia to the talus, which is pushed down and to the inside of the foot, pressing the calcaneus forward and downward and rotating the foot into the pronated position. In the fully pronated position, the plantar fascia is stretched out, placing tension on the

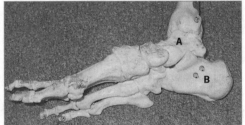

19.11 *Bones of the right foot, medial view (a) talus, (b) calcaneus*

point where the fascia inserts into the bone (see Photo 19.14). With overpronation, the tilt of the subtalar joint increases to ten to twelve degrees (see Photo 19.13).

Several anatomical factors increase pronation: leg-length discrepancy, calf muscle tightness or weakness, and ligament laxity. Excessive pronation is a culprit for many of

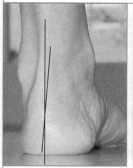
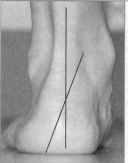
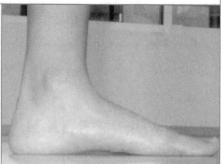

19.12 *Normal foot pronation*

19.13 *Pronation (Achilles tendon angle)*

19.14 *Foot rolls inward in overpronation*

the overuse injuries of the leg: medial tibial stress syndrome, Achilles tendonitis, plantar fasciitis, patellofemoral disorders, iliotibial band friction syndrome, and stress fractures.

The amount of pronation can be measured by using the angle formed by the intersection of two lines, one drawn through the lower leg and the other through the calcaneus. This is known as the Achilles tendon angle, this measures the tilt at the subtalar joint, where bones of the foot and ankle meet (see Photos 19.12 and 19.13). An excessive subtalar tilt can be limited by using footwear with a harder sole on the inside edge, as found on running shoes, or through use of orthotic arch supports. Several over-the-counter arch supports are available, or a podiatrist can make custom orthotics with foam, plaster, or computer analysis.[14]

The foot also can have excess motion along the axis of the foot. If you hold your heel steady with your hand, you can rotate the ball of the foot fifty degrees. For these joints to act as shock absorbers, the middle of the foot must be mobile. Rigid-sole shoes, such as cycling or mountain biking shoes, restrict this motion, which may be needed during an off-the-bike running session. The rotational movement of the foot must be provided by further tilt of the subtalar joint. Cushioned arch supports are therefore recommended for mountain biking shoes. Running shoes that have a groove for midfoot rotation should be used if uneven surfaces are encountered.

NOTES

1. S. Orava, J. Puranen. Athletes' leg pains. *British Journal of Sports Medicine* 1979, 12: 155–68.

2. D. E. Detmer. Chronic shin splints: Classification and management of medial tibial stress syndrome. *Sports Medicine* 1986, 3: 436–46.

3. M. P. Schwellnus, G. Jordan, T. D. Noakes. Prevention of common overuse injuries by the use of shock absorbing soles: A prospective study. *American Journal of Sports Medicine* 1990, 18: 636–41.

4. J. T. Andrish, J. A. Bergfeld, J. A. Walheim. A prospective study of the management of shin splints. *Journal of Bone and Joint Surgery* 1974, 56: 1697–1700.
   C. K. Bensel, R. N. Kish. Lower extremity disorders among men and women in Army basic training and effects of two types of boots. *Technical Report Natick* 1983 TR-83/026.

5. S. B. Thacker, J. Gilchrist, D. F. Stroup, C. D. Kimsey. The prevention of shin splints in sports: A systematic review of literature. *Medicine and Science in Sports and Exercise* January 2002, 34(1): 32–40.

6. C. J. Couture, K. A. Karlson. Tibial stress injuries. *The Physician and Sportsmedicine* June 2002, 30(6): 29–36.

7. J. E. Taunton, M. B. Ryan, D. B. Clement, D. C. McKenzie, D. R. Lloyd-Smith, B. D. Zumbo. A retrospective case-control analysis of 2002 running injuries. *British Journal of Sports Medicine* April 2002, 36(2): 95–101.

8. C. C. Young, D. S. Rutherford, M. W. Niedfeldt. Treatment of plantar fasciitis. *American Family Physician* 2001, 63: 467–74, 477–78.

9. M. Wolgin, C. Cook, C. Graham, D. Mauldin. Conservative treatment of plantar heel pain: Long-term follow-up. *Foot and Ankle International* March 1994, 15(3): 97–102.

10. Young et al. Treatment of plantar fasciitis.

11. J. M. Bedinghaus, M. W. Niedfeldt. Over-the-counter foot remedies. *American Family Physician* September 1, 2001, 64(5): 791–96.

12. W. C. Tsai, C. L. Wang, T. C. Hsu, F. J. Hsieh, F. T. Tang. The mechanical properties of the heel pad in unilateral plantar heel pain syndrome. *Foot and Ankle International* October 1999, 20(10): 663–68.

13. T. J. Chandler, W. B. Kibler. A biomechanical approach to the prevention, treatment and rehabilitation of plantar fasciitis. *Sports Medicine* May 1993, 15(5): 344–52.
B. L. Warren. Plantar fasciitis in runners: Treatment and prevention. *Sports Medicine* November 1990, 10(5): 338–45.

14. Nesbitt, L. Correcting overpronation: Help for faulty foot mechanics. *The Physician and Sportsmedicine* May 1999, 27(5): 95–96.

OTHER REFERENCES

Harries M., C. Williams, W. D. Stanish, L. J. Micheli. *Oxford Textbook of Sports Medicine.* 2d ed. Oxford: Oxford Medical Publications, 1998.

IV

PUTTING IT ALL TOGETHER

CASE
STUDIES

EXERCISE-INDUCED ASTHMA

Mark is a category road, mountain, and cyclo-cross racer. During the spring, he participates in collegiate road races, and during the summer, he can be found at road and mountain bike races. Every spring, Mark finds himself coughing for thirty minutes after a race, sometimes so hard that he tastes blood in the back of his mouth. The cough is dry and hacking and often leaves him short of breath after a race, but he finds that the cough improves as he "races himself into shape." While he was preparing for the collegiate season and training hard during the cold winter months in New England, the cough would leave Mark breathless while he was doing intervals. After consulting with his primary care doctor, he was started on albuterol and found that his exercise tolerance was improved during the colder months. That fall, after finding himself coughing again, he was started on cromolyn sodium with improvement of his symptoms after exercise. To his surprise, he also found that he was breathing better during races and hard efforts.

Mark was suffering from a classic case of exercise-induced asthma. The underlying problem is a constriction of the small airways in the lungs, resulting in a dry cough, wheeze, or sensation of shortness of breath. The condition affects nearly 10 percent of athletes, but it is often overlooked as a problem because the majority of symptoms aren't felt until after exercise. The notion that it goes away as the athlete gets into better shape comes in synchrony with warmer weather.

The medications to treat exercise-induced asthma are albuterol (Ventolin) and cromolyn (Intal). When taken before exercise, these can keep the constriction from becoming symptomatic.

After the problem was recognized and successfully treated, Mark rode to a top-ten national ranking in collegiate cyclo-cross.

REFLUX: EPIGASTRIC PAIN

Rob, a 30-year-old elite road racer, began to experience a burning feeling in the upper middle part of his abdomen when training hard. The pain was gnawing, was sometimes accompanied by nausea, sometimes by belching, but was the symptom Rob primarily felt. As the season progressed, the pain became worse, finally causing Rob to drop out of races because it worsened when he breathed. When his doctor questioned him, Rob admitted to occasionally having what he called the "verps," during which his mouth would fill with vomit. Rob was started on ranitidine (Zantac), his symptoms improved, and he returned to his previous level of performance.

Acid reflux occurs when stomach acid escapes the stomach and reaches the esophagus. Symptoms include a burning sensation, burping, an acid taste in the back of the mouth, and even regurgitation of stomach contents in the mouth.

The two strategies to prevent acid from hitting the esophagus are to keep the stomach contents in the stomach and to reduce the amount of acid the stomach makes. The first step involves maximizing gastric emptying by eating the right foods and starting exercise well nourished but not having a full stomach. (A timetable and feeding schedule can be found in Chapter 10.) In addition, foods such as caffeine, chocolate, and alcohol, which weaken the sphincter at the top of the stomach, should be avoided. The second step involves decreasing the amount of acid in the stomach. Tomatoes, citrus, and coffee should be limited, and an antacid such as ranitidine should be taken an hour before exercise.

REFLUX: SHORTNESS OF BREATH

Laura is a Category-II bicycle racer who posts excellent results when she is feeling well. Throughout last season, she felt she had difficulty breathing during certain hard events, especially on humid days. She saw her primary care physician, who started her on albuterol and cromolyn, but these produced no change in the frequency or severity of symptoms. Questioning during a consultation revealed that the episodes during races typically began with coughing or choking. An exercise test done under simulated race intensity indicated no significant change in her lungs. She was started on ranitidine (Zantac), which decreased the frequency and severity of her breathing problems during races.

Although she had no gastrointestinal symptoms of acid reflux during exercise, Laura's experience highlights an important yet frequently overlooked complication of acid reflux: breathing difficulties. Acid reflux is frequently blamed for asthma when people are taking maximum medications. Although research has not proved that reflux worsens exercise-induced asthma, it has been frequently implicated. If breathing difficulties are encountered during intense exercise (instead of after exercise as is expected with exercise-induced asthma) and are of a sudden onset, and only occur sporadically under particular conditions look to acid reflux as the culprit.

People often describe the choking/coughing sensation as worse during hot and humid weather, although the reason for this is unknown. As with all acid reflux, the primary treatment involves modifying diet, optimizing prerace nutrition, and taking ranitidine before intense exercise. Of course, it is important to rule out other problems such as pneumonia and bronchitis, for which the treatment is very different.

THE FEMALE ATHLETE TRIAD: TOO THIN, TOO TIRED, STRESS FRACTURE

Anna was a competitive swimmer before turning to cycling. As far back as she can remember, she has always been thin. Her coaches have always positively reinforced her thinness, and when she transitioned to cycling, her power-to-weight ratio was an ingredient in her early success. As cycling became harder, she wanted to improve on what she felt to be her advantage, her thinness. Eating was never a priority, and she felt that skimping on calories would be a benefit. Anna replaced her carbohydrate solution with water when riding. Climbing hills, usually an area of standout ability, became more difficult, and her endurance was less than she remembered. Feeling that perhaps weight gain was the problem, she cut back further on calories. Decreased energy intake did little to bolster her endurance problems. When Anna was brought to my attention, I found she had not had her menstrual period regularly for several years, and menstruated only when she was on birth control pills to regulate her period.

Although she remained thin, Anna switched to sources of energy with more calorie content from carbohydrates and has restarted birth control pills to regulate her period and maintain bone density. Anna realized that her athletic prowess does not hinge upon her weight but stems from her aerobic capacity and adequately fueled body. She is now focused on those factors so that she may continue training.

The female athlete triad represents one of the biggest health threats to female athletes, especially in aesthetic and endurance sports where thinness is considered to confer an advantage. The three problems involved are disordered eating, amenorrhea, and osteopenia (low bone density). In high-impact sports, osteoporosis frequently leads to stress fractures. Fortunately, Anna was involved in low-impact sports, and stress fractures were not an issue.

The key to treating the female athlete triad is first to recognize it. After that, treatment avenues include counseling for disordered eating and the thought processes behind it, oral contraceptives for hormonal regulation, and calcium supplementation to mitigate low bone density.

FATIGUE: TOO FEW CARBS, TOO LITTLE PROTEIN

After winning many in-line skating races, Allison felt her energy was dropping. She could no longer train at her optimal levels and was concerned about fatigue. Although she was still placing high in races, she had less ability to support her active lifestyle. She had a physical and reported no increase in her training schedule, her blood count was normal, there were no sleep disturbances, and her resting pulse was unchanged.

Questions about diet revealed some inadequacy. It is possible to be a vegetarian athlete, but endurance athletes need more protein than their strength-based counterparts. Allison began to keep a diet journal listing all of the food she ate over a week. The numbers in the columns for grams of carbohydrate and protein were lower than would be expected. Allison, who is a vegetarian for health reasons, became convinced that following a strict vegetarian diet was not the most healthful choice for her. She began to add lean animal protein to her diet in the form of fish and egg whites. After a few weeks, she felt better able to fuel her training sessions, and the feeling of constant fatigue disappeared.

The body stores energy as fat, glycogen, and muscle for fat, carbohydrate, and protein respectively. Fat provides the body with nine calories per gram; both protein and carbohydrate provide four calories per gram. Despite the same number of calories per gram, protein is a far less efficient fuel source.

If inadequate calories are consumed, the body searches for other sources of energy. Protein breakdown occurs as a last resort. When this happens, athletes often recall a taste or smell of ammonia from themselves during exercise. Occasionally, training partners smell ammonia too. This is a state of muscle breakdown, or catabolism, during which the body's glycogen stores are not being replenished and muscle growth does not occur.

When properly fueled with energy bars and carbohydrate drinks throughout the day, Allison was able to keep up with her energy requirements. Adding lean protein allowed her to reach her goal of consuming 1.2 grams per kilogram of body weight. Allison is continuing her training, feels better, and continues to be successful in racing and training.

SIDE PAIN: LOWER GI TROUBLE OR LIGAMENT STRETCH

Andy is a 30-year-old competitive cyclist, triathlete, and adventure racer who is plagued by frequent bouts of intense side pain. The side stitch frequently strikes without warning and subsides only after he stops all activity. Although the side pain comes on either side, it occurs more often on the left. Andy has tried numerous remedies without relief, including breathing exercises, synchronizing his feet and breathing, drinking pickle juice, increasing his fluid intake, and restricting all food and liquid during competition.

The cause of side pain has long been a mystery, but two theories prevail. The first is stretching of the ligaments that support the intestine, such as when there is too much fluid in the intestine. This can occur when a carbohydrate-electrolyte sports drink that is too concentrated causes a flux of water into the intestine; the flow not only impairs hydration but also causes the intestines to weigh more and tug at the ligaments supporting them. Too many carbohydrates also can cause intestinal bloating from the excess gas created by bacteria in the large intestine.

A second mechanism that causes side pain is decreased blood flow to the so-called watershed areas of the intestine. These areas of the intestine receive blood flow from the ends of two overlapping arterial supplies. When blood flow to the intestines is decreased, as during exercise, the decreased blood brings less oxygen than needed. The relative lack of oxygen during these times causes pain.

Evaluation of Andy's sports drink showed that his mixture was too concentrated. After he followed my recommendations about hydration and reflux (Chapters 5 and 10), his side pain decreased, and he was able to finish more races.

OVERTRAINING

Chris is a triathlete who felt that his hard training did not result in increased strength. He was training himself using a popular coaching book. In his mind, if some exercise is good, more must be better. When he had the time, he doubled his workouts. Not one to sit idle, he often added intensity to his rest days and did endurance rides in excess of six hours.

As his training increased, so did his need for sleep, but he was not sleeping well and had frequent sleep disruptions, waking in the middle of the night. He came to see me when he just couldn't shake his latest cold.

I insisted he take two weeks completely off from running, swimming, and cycling. After reviewing his training log, I cut out the endurance rides and replaced them with morning lipolysis rides. Moderate intensity was replaced with rest, and all intensity was done above the lactate threshold to maximize recovery by increasing secretion of growth hormone. Chris's increased rest led to better sleep and waking refreshed in the morning. He worked out intensely for three or four consecutive days, then took off completely for three or four rest days.

Chris not only felt better, but he also had extra time to spend with his family and friends. His performance improved, as did his overall level of happiness. By maximizing his recovery, he was able to complete harder workouts when he was supposed to go hard and rest completely on his off days. Additionally, he was able to spend his rest days socially. During the recovery days, he was able to maintain his calorie intake, although he occasionally fell behind on exercise days. Overall, Chris became a more well-rounded athlete by increasing rest and recovery and working harder on interval days.

COPING WITH INJURY

Eric, a 21-year-old student, was having a terrific season. After being introduced to cycling, he quickly ascended through the ranks to become one of the best regional riders in his category. High placement seemed to come easily for him and he pushed himself harder in his training. When his knee began to ache after rides, he tried ice and anti-inflammatory medications for the pain. Since his knee only hurt after rides, he would "ride through the pain." Soon, however, his knee began to bother him when walking.

Being sidelined from racing was devastating for Eric and he came very close to quitting the sport when he wasn't motivated to participate in rehab for his knee. Eric sat down with a pad of paper and completed the following exercises (see chapter 13).

Sidebar 20.1   No.2

List the reasons you participate in your primary sport.
Next, make a separate list explaining why the reasons in the first list are important to you.

Reason for participation	Importance
Opportunity to excel	Self-worth
Teamwork	Camaraderie
Fitness	Physical well-being
Love the riding	Fun and enjoyment

After creating this list, Eric realized why cycling was important to him. Not only did it provide him with a sense of accomplishment, but it was social and fun as well. Understanding the motivation for the sport made him realize how important it was to return, both for the physical and emotional rewards. After this revelation, Eric became significantly more motivated to participate in rehabilitation.

Eric knew that rehab wouldn't be easy. While he was stretching and strengthening his knee, his teammates kept racing and he became frustrated and jealous. Understanding that he had a long road of recovery ahead of him, he made a list of all his resources for support and rehabilitation.

After several weeks of rest and non-weight bearing exercise, Eric was glad to have the available resources to recovery. His physical therapist was able to introduce him to someone who was also undergoing rehabilitation for the same problem. Having someone else with whom to stretch and strengthen his knee made a big difference. Eric no longer had to deal with rehab alone and he even got some of the camaraderie from rehab that he enjoyed as part of a cycling team.

Eric soon realized that his season was over, however, and he suddenly found himself with extra time that he usually spent training. For the past year Eric had defined his successes and failures in life by his accomplishments on the bicycle. Eric lost a lot of his feelings of self-worth and sat down for a final exercise.

Although he enjoys cycling immensely, Eric realized that he could still enjoy life while not racing his bicycle. By using his mechanical skills and nurturing instincts, he was able to participate in racing as his team's mechanic and soigneur. He still derived enjoyment from his sport and was able to realize his potential as an individual by getting personal satisfaction from taking care of others.

Upon completion of his rehab, Eric returned to cycling and continued to race and enjoy it.

Using tools for psychological recovery are important to remaining motivated and participating in proper rehab from injury. Injury is not easy, but using tools that shift the focus from being an athlete, to why being an athlete is important to you can help you to achieve your goals and potential even during times when participation as an athlete is not practical.

Sidebar 20.2

Available resources in the event of injury or disappointing competition.

Girlfriend

Teammates

Physician

Physical Therapist

Coach

Family

Training Partner

Sidebar 20.3

Positive characteristics that are not related to sports.

Sense of humor

Motivated

Intelligent

Good mechanical skills

Nurturing

Hard working

INDEX

Abdominal muscles, 88, 176

Abdominal pain, 85

Abductor digiti minimi, 187

Abductor hallucis, 187

Above-neck symptoms, 123, 129

Acclimatization, 40–41, 99, 145, 146

Acetaminophen, 77, 78

Achilles tendon, 187, 189; angle of, 189 (photo)

Acid reflux, 79–83, 194; foods associated with, 80 (table); physiology of, 80–81; symptoms of, 89; treatment of, 81–84, 196

Adenosine triphosphate (ATP), 11, 13, 42

Adipocytes, 29

Adipose tissue, 14, 24, 29

Adrenalin, 94

Advil, 77

Aerobic exercise: fat and, 34; HGH and, 54; warm-up and, 63

Aerobic system, 59, 60, 64

Alanine, 14, 25

Albuterol, 70, 128; acid reflux and, 194; EIA and, 193

Aldosterone, 40

Alignment issues, leg, 168

Allegra, 71, 130

Allergic rhinitis, 129–30

Allergies, 72, 127, 129, 130

Alpha agonists, 128

Altitude tents, 6

Aluminosilicates, 90

Alveoli, 69

Ambien, sleep stages and, 101

Amenorrhea, 134, 136, 195

American College of Sports Medicine, WBGT index and, 142

American Psychiatric Association, eating disorders and, 133, 134

Amino acids, 14, 25, 96, 120; essential, 23, 23 (table), 26; free, 23; HGH and, 52; non-essential, 23, 23 (table), 119; peptide bonds and, 23; role of, 13, 24, 26, 27. *See also* Branched chain amino acids

Ammonia, tasting/smelling, 13, 26, 196

Amphetamines, 14

Anabolic, 24, 55, 95

Anaerobic exercise, 19, 59, 64; HGH and, 53, 54; lactate and, 54; warm-up and, 63

Analgesics, 127

Anaphylaxis, 129, 130–31

Androgenic, 55

Anesthesia, 77

Angiotensin, 40

Ankle: bones of, 188 (photo); overuse injuries of, 181–89

Ankle dorsiflexor muscles, 184

Anorexia athletica, 133, 138–39

Anorexia nervosa, 134, 135

Antacids, 83, 194

Anterior superior iliac spine, 161

Antibiotics, 76, 77

Anticholinergics, 128

Antihistamines, 130, 131

Anti-inflammatory medications, 197

Antioxidants, 32, 121–22, 147

Anxiety, 144

Arch supports, 166, 186, 189

Asthma, 130; acid reflux and, 194. *See also* Exercise-induced asthma

Atarax, 130

ATP. *See* Adenosine triphosphate

Attribution, 105–6, 107–8, 107 (table)

Bacitracin, 75, 76, 77

Back problems, 61

Bacteria, fighting, 77, 117, 118, 121, 127

Banned-substances list, 115, 128

Basal metabolic rate (BMR), 34, 141

BCAAs. *See* Branched chain amino acids

B cells, 116

Bellows effect, 145

Below-neck symptoms, 123

Benadryl, 130

Benzodiazepines, jet lag and, 101

Benzonatate, 128

Beta-carotene, 121

Bile, 89

Biomechanical problems, ix, 160–61, 166–67; correcting, 161, 186–87, 188–93; foot, 188–89

Bladder, emptying, 90

Bloating, 85, 88, 89, 196

Blood clotting, 24

Blood doping, 6

Blood flow, 87, 89

Blood pressure, 39, 95

Blood sugar, 11

BMR. *See* Basal metabolic rate

Body clocks, 100

Body fat, 29; amenorrhea and, 136

Body image, unhealthy concern about, 134

Body type, changes in, 135

Body water, 39, 40

Bone density, 136, 137, 181, 195

Bone loss, 133, 136–37, 138

Bones: ankle, 188 (photo); fatigued, 181; overuse of, 155, 156; partial collapse of, 181; weight-bearing exercise and, 137

Bonking, 14, 43, 97

Bowel, 88, 90

Bowlegs, 168; correcting, 169, 169 (photo)

Branched chain amino acids (BCAAs), 25, 35, 98; muscle glycogen and, 96

Breathing, 6, 71, 127; acid reflux and, 194; body water and, 40; pathology of, 69–70; physiology of, 69; relaxation and, 111; stomach and, 81

Bronchi, 69; constriction of, 70, 71, 72, 151

Bronchitis, acid reflux and, 194

Bronchodilators, 128

Bronchospasm, 128

Bulimia nervosa, 134, 135

Bursae, 156, 159

Bursitis, 155

Caffeine, 14, 34, 44; lipolysis and, 35

Calcaneus, 185, 188, 189; photo of, 188; stress fracture of, 183, 186

Calcium, 136; deficiency, 183; eating disorders and, 137, 138; flux, 144; hyperventilation and, 143; supplementation, 184, 195; Vitamin D and, 137

Calf muscles, 162, 171; stretching, 163–64; tightness in, 176, 188

Calories, 32, 33, 196

Camphor, 147

Carbohydrate solutions, 83, 123, 195

Carbohydrates, 23, 24; acid reflux and, 82; availability of, 30, 31, 34; bloodflow and, 87; complex, 12; consuming, 11, 16, 25, 43, 88, 195; energy in, 196; exercise and,

19; fatigue and, 195–96; glucogenesis and, 13–14; high glycemic, 19; hydration and, 43; intestinal blood flow and, 87; metabolism of, 11, 12; oxygen and, 12; simple, 12; storing, 11, 32

Carbo loading, 18–19

Carbon dioxide, 143, 144

Cardiac output (CO), 3, 4, 39

Carnitine palmitoyl system (CPT), 30, 31

Cartilage, 158

Casein protein, 35

Catabolism, 13, 25, 26, 53, 196; HGH and, 52; increase in, 24

Catecholamines, 94, 100, 101, 123, 129

Causality, stability/locus of, 107

Cellular responses, nonspecific, 115, 116

Central nervous system, overtraining and, 96

Cetirzine, 130

CH20, 11

CHARGE, 18–19

Chest pain, 79

Chilblain, 148

Chimney effect, 145

Chlamydia pneumonia, 119

Chlamydia trachomatis, 119

Chloride, 43

Chlorohexidine, 74

Cholesterol, 28–29, 30

Chromium picolinate, 35

Circadian rhythms, 100

Citric acid cycle, 13, 14, 15, 25

Clarinex, 130

Claritin, 71

Cleats, adjusting, 166 (photo), 169 (photo), 170 (photo), 174, 174 (photo)

Clothing: cold weather, 150–51; dry/wet, 145; hypothermia and, 150; layering, 71; sweat, 146

CO. *See* Cardiac output

Codeine, 128

Cognitive appraisal theory, 109

Cold: dressing for, 150–51; exposure to, 148

Collagen, 74; breakdown of, 173, 174, 175

Colloid, 75, 76, 77

Colon, 85; glucose and, 88; oral contraceptives and, 86

Common colds, 127–31

Competition, 105; GI symptoms and, 89 (table); reducing stress of, 110

Compression bandages, 157; photo of, 157

Conconi, Francesco, 7

Conconi test, 4, 7, 8; analysis/data from, 8 (fig.); protocol for, 7 (table)

Conduction, 141, 142, 148, 150, 151

Contractions, 3, 5, 62

Convection, 141, 142, 148, 150

Cooling mechanisms, 142

Cori cycle, 14

Corn syrup, 18

Corticosteroid, 117

Cortisol, 53, 54, 95, 121, 136

Coughs, productive/nonproductive, 127

Cough suppressants, 127, 128

Country mallow, 14

Coxsackie B virus, 119

CPT. *See* Carnitine palmitoyl system

Cramping, 85, 88; alleviating, 90; fructose and, 19; heat, 144; symptoms of, 89

Creatine, 35

Cromolyn: acid reflux and, 194; EIA and, 70, 193; sodium inhalers, 130

Cryotherapy, 156

Cushioned insoles, ITBFS and, 169

Cytokines, 122

Cytotec, 90

Debridement, 75, 78

Decongestants, 127, 128, 129, 130

Dehydration, 41, 71, 86, 128, 135, 142; acid reflux and, 80, 81; blood flow and, 87; eating disorders and, 137; fatigue and, 39; heat illness and, 143; high-protein diets and, 35; preventing, 90; problems caused by, 39; voluntary, 44

Depression, 96, 137

Desloratadine, 130

Dextromethorphan, 128

Diagnostic and Statistical Manual (DSM-IV), eating disorders and, 133

Diarrhea, 85, 87, 88, 90; fructose and, 19

Diet, ix, x, 18; acid reflux and, 194; eating disorders and, 135; exercise and, 34; fatigue and, 33; GI symptoms and, 89 (table); heat cramps and, 144; hypothermia and, 150; immunity and, 119–20; negative energy expenditure and, 32–34; proper, 98; vegetarian, 26, 195; weight loss and, 34

Dieting, 133, 135

Digestive enzymes, 89

Diphenhydramine, 130

Disordered eating. *See* Eating disorders

Dizziness, 144

DNA, 24, 119

Dressing, 75–78

Drinks: carbohydrate, 27, 196; carbohydrate-protein, 27; hypertonic, 44, 88; recovery, 123; replacement, 44; sports, 42, 98, 196. *See also* Fluids

Duodenum, 85

Duoderm Hydroactive, 76

Dynamic stretch, photo of, 187

Eating, 194; monitoring, 33; post-exercise, 16

Eating disorders, 109; calcium and, 137; diagnostic criteria for, 134, 135 (table); female athlete triad and, 195; hazards of, 133, 135–36, 135 (table), 139; men and, 134; performance and, 133, 134, 137, 139; protein and, 26; risk factors for, 134–35, 138 (table)

Edema, 74

EIA. *See* Exercise-induced asthma

Electrolyte concentration, 41

Electrolyte imbalance, 135, 143

Electromagnetic radiation, 146

Endurance, 60, 88, 97; decreasing, 129; glucose and, 18; increasing, x, 3, 61

Endurance exercise, 6, 61, 196, 197; energy for, 11; HGH and, 53; injuries and, 141; medical

issues associated with, ix; testosterone and, 56; weight loss and, 34

Energy, 59; glucose and, 13; muscle utilization of, 15; negative, 26; stores of, 23, 196

Energy balance; negative, 32, 136; training plans and, 31

Energy drain, hormonal secretion and, 136

Energy gels/bars, 11, 196

Enzymes, 89

Ephedrine, 14

Epigastric pain, 194

Epiglottis, 81

Epinephrine, 14, 94, 99, 123, 131; overtraining and, 95

Epithelium, 74

Ergogenic aids, 14

Esophagus, 79–80; acid reflux and, 80–81, 83, 194

Estrogen, 136–37

Ethylene vinyl acetate (EVA), 166

Evaporation, 141, 148, 150

Exercise, 116–17; acid reflux and, 80, 83; aerobic, 34, 54, 63; allergies and, 130; anabolic, 27; anaerobic, 19, 53, 54, 59, 63, 64; breathing and, 40; carbohydrates and, 19; chronic, 117; cold weather, 129; easy/moderate, 118; eating disorders and, 134; fat and, 29, 30; fueling, 12, 34; gastric emptying and, 81; GI symptoms of, 85; growth hormone and, 52–54; heart and, 3; HGH and, 53; immune system and, 116 (fig.), 119; maximal, 118; motility and, 87; pain-free, 174; plasma protein and, 41; protein dynamics in, 24–25; return to, 122–23, 129; science, ix, 5; sleep and, 100–101; testosterone and, 95; tolerance, 193; URIs and, 129; weight-bearing, 135, 137, 183; weight loss and, 34, 35. *See also* Endurance exercise; Resistance exercise

Exercise immunology, 115

Exercise-induced asthma (EIA), 81, 107, 128, 130; acid reflux and, 194; bronchi constriction and, 70; cold air and, 151; preventing, 64, 70–72; suffering from, 69–72; treatment of, 70, 193

Exercise physiologists, eating disorders and, 139

External rotators, 162, 164; stretching, 165, 165 (photo)

Eyes, protecting, 65, 146, 147

Failure, 108, 109

Fast-twitch muscle fibers, 5

Fat, 23, 137; aerobic exercise and, 34; availability of, 30; body, 29, 136; energy from, 15, 26, 31, 34, 196; harmful effects of, 30; intake, 29; monounsaturated, 30, 32, 35; polyunsaturated, 30; recognizing, 29–30; saturated, 26–27, 30, 35; storing, 29, 32; unsaturated, 30

Fatigue, 123, 195–96; anaerobic, 64; decreasing, 176, 195; dehydration and, 39; diet and, 33; eating disorders and, 138; extended, 97; female athletes and, 195; heat cramps and, 144; muscle, 181; overtraining and, 96; serotonin and, 98

Fatty acids, 14, 29, 30, 34; energy from, 31; HGH and, 52, 54; insulin and, 31; n-3 polyunsaturated, 121; trans-, 30

Female athlete triad, 133, 195

Femoral condyles, 158, 161, 168 (photo), 169

Femur, 158, 159, 160

Fexofenadine, 130

Fibrin, 74

Fibroblasts, 173

Fibula, 158

Figure-4 stretch, photo of, 164

Fish oil, 121

Fitness: cardiovascular, 4; improving, x, 59, 94, 96; loss of, 60

Flat feet, 160, 186

Flatulence, 85

Flexibility, 97, 158, 161, 162–65; decreasing, 61, 164; increasing, 61, 62, 164–65; maintaining, 151, 157

Flexor digitorum brevis, 187

Fluids, 42; adequate, 39; ingesting, 44, 89; replacing, 41. *See also* Drinks

Flu shots, 123

Food diaries, 33

Foods: acid reflux, 80 (table); checking labels on, 130–31; high glycemic, 17; less-processed, 16; low glycemic, 19; pre-exercise, 81

Foot, overuse injuries of, 181–89

Foot biomechanics, orthotics and, 188–89

Foot inserts, 175

Footwear, 156, 189

Forward-set position, 175; photo of, 176

Free radicals, 121, 147

Frostbite, 149–50

Frostnip, 148–50

Fructose, 16, 18, 43; cramping/diarrhea and, 19; glycogen and, 19

Gastric emptying, 41, 44, 81, 82, 194

Gastrocnemius, 184, 187; stretching, 163–64, 164 (photo)

Gastrointestinal tract (GI), 89–90; acid reflux and, 81; anatomy of, 79–80; blood flow to, 86–87; ischemia and, 86; liver and, 89; lower, 85–86; motility and, 87–89; upper, 79, 85

Gastrointestinal upset, 144, 196; acid reflux and, 194; blood flow and, 87; diet and, 89 (table); mechanical causes of, 87; preventing, 89, 90

Gauze, 78, 185; plain, 76; treated, 76–77; using, 74–75

Genu varum, 168; correcting, 169, 169 (photo)

Gerdy's tubercle, 167–68

GH-binding protein, 52

GI tract. *See* Gastrointestinal tract

Glucagon, 15, 26, 86

Glucocorticoids, 95

Glucogenesis, 13–14, 27

Gluconeogenesis, 14, 15

Glucose, 11; blood, 14, 19, 43; colon and, 88; endurance and, 18; energy and, 13; generating, 25; glucose-protein solutions and, 17; hydration and, 89; immune system and, 120–21; less-processed foods and, 12; levels, 16; liver glycogen and, 18; molecules, 82; motility and, 88; storing, 15; synthesis of, 13; tolerating, 88; transporting, 5

Glucose beverages, 88

Glucose polymers, 19, 82

Glucose-6–phosphate (G6P), 18

Glutamate, citric acid cycle and, 25

Glutamine, 121, 123; depletion of, 98, 120; immune system and, 23, 119–20; metabolization of, 98; supplementing, 120

Gluteus muscles, 63, 171, 176; photo of, 165, 172

Glycemic index, 11, 12, 31; of common foods, 12 (table)

Glycemic response, 19

Glycerol, 14, 29, 30

Glycogen, 24, 29, 43, 52; capitalizing, 19; depleting, 16, 18, 31; during exercise, 17; energy in, 196; estrogen and, 137; fructose and, 19; lack of, 137; liver, 14, 18, 43; muscle synthesis of, 16; post-exercise/pre-exercise, 17; reliance on, 30; replacing, 16, 17, 18, 19, 43; storing, 8, 14, 15, 17, 19, 97; synthesizing, 16, 17, 18. See also Muscle glycogen

Glycogenolysis, 14, 15

Glycogen synthase, 16, 17, 18

Glycogen window, 16–19

Glycolysis, anaerobic, 13

Goal setting, 110

Gonadotropin, 55

Granulation tissue, 74

Greater trochanter, 169

Growth hormone. See Human growth hormone

Guiafenasin, 128

Hamstrings, 63, 162, 176

Hamstring stretch, 163–64

Hay fever, 130

HDL. See High-density lipoproteins

Headaches, 144

Healing, 74, 78, 110, 112, 156, 158

Heart, function of, 3–4

Heartbeat, irregular, 119

Heart burn, 79

Heart muscle cells, death of, 119

Heart muscle fibers, contraction of, 3

Heart rate (HR), 3, 95, 123; endurance athletes and, 4; fatigue and, 97; maximum, 4, 34; monitors, 8; overreaching and, 97; over-training and, 101–2; power and, 97; resting, 97; threshold, 4, 6

Heart rate zones, 64, 98

Heat, 141, 142; strategies for, 144–46

Heat illness, 15, 71, 128, 143–44

Heat loss, 145; fat and, 29; injuries from, 141; preventing, 142, 144, 148, 150, 151

Heat sensation, scale of, 143 (table)

Heat stress, 29, 142, 146

Heat tetany, 143–44

Heel cups, 186

Heel pain, onset of, 183

Helmets, 65

Hexose monophosphate, 13

HGH. See Human growth hormone

High arches, 160, 189

High-carbohydrate diets, fatigue and, 33

High-density lipoproteins (HDL), 30

High-energy bonds, 13

High-fat diets, 33 (table); fatigue and, 33; HGH and, 54; long-term/short-term, 32

High-protein diets, dehydration and, 35

Hindfoot valgus, 168

Hip abductors, 162; strengthening, 162 (photo), 171 (photo)

Histamines, 71, 146

Hives, 71

Hormones, 4, 14, 51; antidiuretic, 40; balance of, 39; catabolic, 53; luteinizing, 55; oral contraceptives for, 195; overtraining and, 95; secreting, 136. See also Human growth hormone

HR. See Heart rate

Human growth hormone (HGH), 27; amino acids and, 52; catabolism and, 52; exercise and, 52–54; fatty acids and, 52, 54; gender and, 53; IGF-1 and, 53; overtraining and, 95; recovery and, 56; secretion of, 41, 51–52, 52 (table), 53, 197; sleep and, 101; testosterone and, 55; VO2max and, 52

Hydralazine, 130

Hydration, 40, 145; adequate, 39, 41, 42; carbohydrates and, 43; decongestants and,

130; effective, 44–45; factors affecting, 43–44; fluid loss and, 41; glucose and, 89; heat tetany and, 144; recommendations on, 41–43, 196

Hydrogenated oils, 30

Hydrolysis, 30

Hyperventilation, calcium and, 143

Hypobaric chambers, 6

Hyponatremia, 42

Hypothalamus, 55, 141; heat tetany and, 143

Hypothermia, 150

Hypotonic carbohydrate-electrolyte solution, 88

Ibuprofen, 77, 78, 147, 157

Ice, 156–57, 197

IgA, 115, 118, 121

IGF-1. *See* Insulin-like growth factor

Ileum, 85

Iliotibial band (ITB), 159, 160, 162, 168, 170; flexibility of, 165, 171; irritation of, 169; photo of, 168; stretching, 165 (photo), 171; tightness in, 176

Iliotibial band friction syndrome (ITBFS), 167–72, 176, 189

Illness: environmental, 141–52; preventing, 115; stress and, 108

Imagery, 111, 112

Immune responses, 115, 116

Immune suppression, 98, 121, 122, 129, 136

Immune system, 115–16; exercise and, 116 (fig.), 119; glucose and, 120–21; glutamine and, 23; innate, 117–18

Immunity: diet and, 119–20; innate/adaptive, 115, 116; vitamins and, 121–22

Imodium, 90

Indomethacin, 147

Infections, 76, 78, 116, 122. *See also* Upper respiratory tract infections

Infertility, 136

Inflammation, 74, 119, 173, 188

Inhalers, 71 (photo), 130

Injuries: acute, 156; causes for, 107; cold, 141, 148–50; coping with, 105, 197–98; envi-

ronmental, 141–51; motivation and, 108; overuse, ix–x, 155–76, 181–89; pathophysiology of, 173; preventing, 59–60, 61; resources during, 108; self-worth and, 109; stress and, 108–9, 110; warning signs of, 141

Insulation, 151

Insulin, 15, 16, 17, 27; absence of, 34; fatty acid and, 31; suppression, 31

Insulin-like growth factor (IGF-1), 26, 52, 53

Insulin response, 11, 17, 31

Intal, EIA and, 193

Intensity, 59, 98, 188; recovery and, 51; submaximal, 5; volume and, 95

Internal rotation, preventing, 169 (photo)

International Olympic Committee (IOC), 71; banned substances and, 70, 115, 127

Intervals, 197; anaerobic, 64; EIA and, 193; exhaustion from, 97; testosterone and, 56

Intestines, 85; blood flow to, 86; motility of, 87; oral contraceptives and, 86

Iodine, 74

Ipratropium, 128

Ironman, 41, 133

Irrigation, high-pressure/low-pressure, 75

Ischemia, 86

Isoleucine, 96

Isometric exercise, 176

ITB. *See* Iliotibial band

ITBFS. *See* Iliotibial band friction syndrome

Jejunum, 85

Jet lag, 101

Joints, stretching, 156

Knee: bones of, 158 (photo); muscles of, 159 (photo); overuse injuries of, 155–76

Knee cap, 158

Knee flexion, 161, 168 (photo), 173

Krebs cycle, 13

Lactate, 7, 13, 14, 15, 54

Lactate threshold (LT), 86, 110; anaerobic

metabolism and, 19; indication of, 8; VO₂max and, 7

Lactic acid, 4, 24, 64; overtraining and, 96; recycling of, 14

Lateral leg raises, 171

Lateral retinaculum, 160

LDL. *See* Low-density lipoproteins

Learned helplessness, 108

Leg-length discrepancy, 170, 170 (photo), 186, 188

LES. *See* Lower esophageal sphincter

Leucine, 96

Leukotriene inhibitors, EIA and, 70

Lidocaine, 77

Ligaments, 188; anterior cruciate, 159; flexibility of, 151; lateral collateral, 159; medial collateral, 159; posterior cruciate, 159; stretching, 196

Linear regression break-point analysis, 7

Lipase, 30

Lipids, 29, 30, 121

Lipolysis, 30, 31, 34, 52, 197; caffeine and, 35; HGH and, 54

Liver, 89

Loperamide, 90

Losing, failure and, 109

Low-density lipoproteins (LDL), 30

Lower esophageal sphincter (LES), acid reflux and, 80

LT. *See* Lactate threshold

Lungs, 4; warming, 71

Lymphocytes, 116, 120, 121

Lysine, 26

Maalox, 90

Macronutrients, 23

Macrophages, 74, 117, 120

Magnesium, 42

Ma huang, 14

Malalignments, 156, 181, 186

Maltodextrin, 43

Marathons, 85, 86; glutamine and, 120; sleep and, 99; URI and, 121

Massage, 99; friction, 176, 187, 187 (photo); ice, 157, 184; performance and, 98

Maximal oxygen uptake, factors limiting, 6–7

Maximum fat oxidation (fat_max), 34

McConnell method, 167

Meanings of consequences, 109

MED. *See* Minimal Erythema

Medial tibial stress syndrome, 183–84, 189

Medicine, patch kit, ix

Meditation, 111

Melatonin, 101

Menstrual periods, 88; missing, 133, 134, 136, 195; monitoring, 139; phases of, 136

Menthol, 147

Metabolism, 11, 12, 34, 98, 141; aerobic, 13; anaerobic, 19; at-rest, 39; carbohydrate, 14–15; glucose, 13; glycogen, 15; nitrogen balance and, 24; oxygen, 64

Metatarsal heads, 184, 185

Methione, 26

Methscopamine, 128

Microorganisms, 116, 119

Microtrauma, 159

Midfoot rotations, 189

Minimal Erythema (MED), 147

Misoprostal, 90

Mitochondria, 31

Monocytes, 117

Morton's neuroma, 156, 184–85, 184 (photo)

Motility, 87–89

Motivation, 105–6, 198; injuries and, 108; internal/external, 106, 107; negative, 107; participation and, 106; primary/secondary, 106

Motrin, 77

Moviegoers sign, 161

MRI, 182

Mucous membrane, 115

Mucus, 122

Muscle, 5; breakdown, 13, 17, 196; dysfunction, 159–60; energy in, 196; growth, 196; soreness, 122, 155; strain, 155; stretching, 156; viscosity, 63

Muscle glycogen, 14, 15, 18–19, 43; BCAAs and, 96; depletion of, 34; maximizing, 98; replacing, 16; synthesis of, 17

Muscle mass, 4, 55

Muscular imbalances, 156

Mylanta, 90

Myocarditis, 119

Napping, sleep and, 100

Nasal congestion, 122

Nasal spring dialator strips, 130

Nasal steroids, 130

Natural barriers, 115–16, 118–19

Natural killer (NK) cells, 117, 118, 121

Nausea, 79, 85, 89, 144; acid reflux and, 81, 194

Navicular, stress fracture of, 182

Neck check, 123, 129

Negative thoughts, 111

Neomycin, 76

Neosporin, 76

Neovascularization, 74

Nerves: compression of, 184; impulses of, 63; overuse of, 155, 156

Neuromas, 155, 184–85

Neurotensin, 86

Neutrophils, 74, 117, 118

Nitrogen: balance, 24, 28; loss, 25; retention, 55

NK cells. *See* Natural killer cells

Nonsteroidal anti-inflammatory drugs (NSAIDs), 90, 157, 172, 175; avoiding, 86; ITBFS and, 169; patellar tendonopathy and, 173; plantar fascitis and, 188; shin splints and, 184; stress fractures and, 182

Norepinephrine, 99

NSAIDs. *See* Nonsteroidal anti-inflammatory drugs

n-3 polyunsaturated fatty acids (PUFAs), 121

Numbness, 148

Nutrition, 85, 135, 138, 194; training, 33–34

Ointment, 75, 76, 77

Olive oil, 30

Open Window Theory, 122

OpSite, 76

Oral contraceptives, 86, 139, 195

Organizational psychology, 110

Orthotics, 156, 170, 175, 183, 186; custom, 186; foot biomechanics and, 188–89; ITBFS and, 169

Osmolality, higher/lower, 82

Osteopenia, 136, 195

Osteoporosis, 133, 136, 137, 195

Overloading, stress and, 108

Overpronation, 160, 188; photo of, 189

Overreaching, 93–94; heart rate and, 97; over-training and, 94

Oversupination, 160

Overtraining, 129, 196–98; detecting, 94 (table), 95–96, 97, 101–2; growth hormone and, 95; overreaching and, 94; prevention of, 95, 96–98, 102; syndromes of, 94–95

Overuse injuries, ix–x, 159, 161, 184–85; knee, 155–76; treatment of, 156–58

Oxygen, carbohydrates and, 12

Oxymetalazone, 128

Pain: abdominal, 85; chest, 79; epigastric, 194; heel, 183; management, 78, 197; side, 41, 85, 88, 90, 196

Parasympathetic syndrome, 94

Participation, reasons for, 106, 197

Patella, 158, 159, 160, 161, 167, 172; stretching and, 163

Patellar tendinitis, 173

Patellar tendonopathy, 172–76

Patellar tendons, 172, 175; anatomy/location of, 172 (photo); pressuring, 175 (photo); strained, 173, 174

Patellofemoral disorders, 171, 189; managing, 160–61

Patellofemoral syndrome, 159, 161, 162, 173, 176

Pedal spindles, 169 (photo); aligning with, 175 (photo)

Pelvic drops, 171; photo of, 172

Peptide bonds, amino acids and, 23

Performance, 112, 113; aerobic, 64; altitude

training and, 55; decreasing, 94, 95, 96; eating disorders and, 133, 137, 138; icing and, 157; improving, 41, 51, 108, 110, 197; massage and, 99; muscle and, 5; physical problems and, 107; psychological considerations and, 138; recovery and, 51; sleep and, 99; successful, ix; training and, 93; warm-ups and, 63–64

Periosteum, 183

Peristalsis, 80, 87

Permeation efficiency factor, 145

Peroxide, 74

Pes cavus, 160, 166, 168, 169, 186

Pes planus, 160, 168, 186

Petroleum jelly, 151

Phagocytes, 116

Pharynx, 81

Phenylpropanolamine, 14, 128

Phosphocreatine system, 64

Physical parameters, x, 10

Physiology, ix, x, 52, 69, 80–81

Pickle juice, drinking, 196

Pigeon toes, 168, 169

Piriformis, flexibility of, 164–65

Plantar fascia, 185 (photo), 187

Plantar fascitis, 185–88, 189; arch taping for, 186 (photo)

Plasma, 24; protein, 41; volume, 39, 40, 41, 42. *See* Progressive muscle relaxation

Pneumonia, acid reflux and, 194

PNF. *See* Proprioceptive neuromuscular facilitation

Polymixin, 76

Polysporin, 76

Positive characteristics, 110, 198

Postnasal drip, 127, 128

Postural correction, 161

Potassium, 42–43, 45

Power, 63, 98; heart rate and, 97

Power monitors, 8

Power zones, 97, 123

Precooling, 145

Progesterone, 136

Progressive muscle relaxation (PMR), 111, 113

Prolactin, 117

Pronation, 183, 184, 188; excessive, 186, 189; increasing, 189; normal, 189 (photo)

Proprioceptive neuromuscular facilitation (PNF), 61–62; stretch, 163

Prostaglandins, 86, 90, 146

Protective gear, 64–65

Protein, 23, 120; animal, 123, 195; consuming, 24, 26, 27, 53, 56; dynamics, 24–25; eating disorders and, 26; endurance sports and, 35; energy in, 196; fatigue and, 195–96; lean, 196; maximizing building of, 27; muscle, 25, 34; overlooking, 25; plant-based, 26; RDA of, 25; sources of, 26–27; soy, 26; storing, 24; turnover, 25; vegetarians and, 26

Pseudoephedrine, 14, 128

Psoas muscle, 87

Psychological issues, 105, 107, 110, 113, 137–38

Puberty, changes during, 135

PUFAs. *See* n-3 polyunsaturated fatty acids

Pyruvate, 13, 14

Q-angle, 161, 166–67; decreasing, 166 (photo); increasing, 160, 166 (photo); photo of, 160

Quadriceps, 63, 159, 161, 171, 172; strengthening, 175; stretching, 170 (photo); tightness in, 176

Radiant heat, gain/loss, 145

Radiation, 141, 142, 148, 150

Range of motion, 63, 176

Ranitidine, 83, 194

Rapid eye movement (REM), 99–100, 101

Recommended daily allowance (RDA), 25

Recovery, 59, 113, 156; combined, 98; eating disorders and, 138; growth hormone and, 56; hydration and, 41; increasing, 43, 51, 197; intensity and, 51; passive, 98; performance and, 51; periods for, 93, 94; prolonged, 94; psychological, 198; rest and, 61; testosterone and, 56; time for, x

Reflex time, icing and, 157

Regurgitation, 79

Rehabilitation, 157, 158, 198; motivation for, 106–7; undergoing, 105, 197, 198

Relaxation techniques, 110–11

REM. *See* Rapid eye movement

Renin, 40

Repetitive movement, 59, 155

Resistance exercise: HGH and, 53–54; lactate and, 54; strength and, 63; testosterone and, 55; weight loss and, 34

Resources, 108, 109, 198

Rest, 97, 129, 196; complete, 98; increasing, 197; recovery and, 61

Rest, ice, compression, and elevation (RICE), 156, 157

Restoril, jet lag and, 101

Rewarming, frostnip/frostbite and, 149

Rhinitis, 127–28

Rhinoviruses, 127

Ribose, 13

RICE. *See* Rest, ice, compression, and elevation

Road rash, 73–78

Rotated toes, 169

RSR 11, 6

Rubs, 71, 151, 152

Saddles, adjusting, 167 (photo), 170 (photo)

Salicylate, 151

Saline, 75

Saliva, 71, 80, 115

Salt: fluid retention and, 44; solutions, chilled/flavored, 144

Sarna lotion, 147

Saturated fats, 30; protein and, 26–27; weight loss and, 35

Second Skin, 76

Seizures, 15

Self-talk, 111, 112

Self-worth, 109, 198

Serotonin, 96, 98

Set-back position, 176

Sexually transmitted diseases, 119

Shin guards, 65

Shin splints, 183–84; pain from, 183 (photo)

Shur-Clens, 74

Side pain, 41, 85, 88, 90, 196

Sigmoid, 87

Silvadene, 76

Silver sulfadiazine cream, 76

Sinusitis, 127–35

Sitting toe touch, photo of, 163

Skin, 149; protecting, 65, 76; regeneration of, 74

Skin cancer, UVR and, 147

Sleep: disrupted, 93, 94, 101, 109, 195, 197; exercise and, 100; importance of, 99–101; napping and, 100; performance and, 99; recovery/repair and, 99; slow-wave, 99; travel and, 100, 101

Slow-twitch muscle fibers, 5

Soap, 75

Sodium: heat cramps and, 144; supplementing, 42

Soleus, 184, 187; stretching, 163–64, 164 (photo)

Somatostatin, 52

Spacers, inserting, 166 (photo)

Specificity, 59

Spectrum of cold injury, 148–50

Speed, 73, 129

Speedometers, 8

Sphincters, acid reflux and, 81

Sponges, debridement with, 74, 75

Sports drinks, 98; carbohydrate-electrolyte, 196; sodium in, 42

Sports medicine, ix, 105

Sports nutritionists, eating disorders and, 139

Sprinting, 55, 63, 98

Squat/lunge technique, poor, 174 (photo)

Steroids, 130, 185

Stimulants, weight loss and, 35

Stomach, 80; breathing and, 81; lining, protecting, 90; viruses, 115

Strength: decreasing, 129; increasing, 51, 61, 63, 157, 186, 187–88, 196

Strength training, 63, 156, 171; importance of, 158, 161, 162

Stress, 138; dealing with, 108–9, 123, 181; infections and, 122; injuries and, 108–9; medical/psychological problems and, 109

Stress fractures, 133, 181–84, 189; etiology of, 181; factors associated with, 181 (table); female athletes and, 195; overuse and, 155, 156; susceptibility to, 137; treating, 182

Stretching, 156, 158, 162, 163–65, 170, 171, 184, 186, 196; described, 61–62, 187; figure-4, 164 (photo); hamstring, 163–64, 163 (photo); injury prevention and, 61; photo of, 62, 163, 164, 165, 170, 171, 187; static, 62

Stroke volume (SV), 3

Subtalar tilt, 188, 189

Sucrose, 19, 43

Sugars, 11, 31

Sunburn, 146, 147

Sunscreen, 147

Supinator, 166

Supplements, 42, 98, 120, 121, 184, 185; performance-enhancing, 51; testosterone, 51; weight loss and, 35

Support, resources for, 198

SV. See Stroke volume

Sweat: evaporation, 142; excessive, 94

Sweat loss, 41, 42, 45

Sympathetic syndrome, 94

Talus, 188; photo of, 188

TCA cycle, 13

T cells, 116, 117, 121

Tegaderm, 76

Telfa, 78

Temazepam, jet lag and, 101

Tendonitis, 155, 157, 173

Tendonopathy, 173, 174, 175

Tendonosis, 173, 175

Tendons, 159, 172; flexibility of, 151; overuse and, 155; relieving stress on, 176 (photo); ruptured, 173; strengthening, 158; torn, 173

Tensing: 112 (photo); relaxation and, 111

Tensor fasciae latae (TFL), 165

Testosterone: cortisol and, 95; exercise and, 56, 95; HGH and, 55; intervals and, 56; maximizing, 55–56; overtraining and, 95; recovery and, 56; resistance training and, 55; supplements, 51

Tetanus boosters, 77–78

TFL. See Tensor fasciae latae

Thermoregulation, 141–42

Thigh bone, 158

Thinness, 134, 135, 138, 195

Thought stoppage, 111–13

Thyroxine, 117

Tibia, 158, 183, 184; stress fracture of, 182, 182 (photo)

Tibial tuberosity, 161, 172, 174–75; photo of, 175

Tightness, 61, 62, 176, 188

Toe taps, photo of, 187

Towel curls, photo of, 188

Towel stretch, photo of, 187

Trabeculae, 136

Trachea, 81

Training, ix; altitude, 55; caloric restrictions and, 32; correcting errors in, 186; endurance, x, 6; extrinsic, 155; fitness and, 60; GI symptoms and, 89 (table); injury prevention and, 59–60; interruptions for, 105; maintaining, 63, 89; performance and, 55, 93; return to, 115, 122–23, 129; specialized, 60–61; volume/intensity of, 95, 136, 188. See also Overtraining; Strength training

Training logs, 182, 197

Training plans, 59, 94, 98, 195; energy balance and, 31; fatigue and, 97; phases of, 60–61, 63; science and, 5; sleep and, 102

Trans-fatty acids, 30

Travel: sleep deprivation and, 100, 101

Triathlons, 133

Triglycerides, 29, 30, 31

Trochanteric bursa, 169

Tryptophan, 96

2, 3–DPG, 6

Tylenol, 77
Type A behavior patterns, 105

Ultraviolet rays (UVR), 146, 147
U.S. Anti-doping Agency Restricted Substance Notification forms, 128
U.S. Olympic team, EIA and, 72
Unsaturated fat, chemical description of, 30
Upper respiratory tract infections (URI), 93, 115, 116; exercise and, 129; preventing, 123, 128–29; symptoms of, 119, 121, 123; treatment of, 127–28
Upset stomach, 79
URI. *See* Upper respiratory tract infection
Urine, 40, 44
Urticaria, 130–31
UVB, 146, 147
UVR. *See* Ultraviolet rays

Valine, 96
Vaseline Gauze, 76
Vasoactive intestinal peptide (VIP), 86
Vasoconstriction, 128, 148, 149, 175
Vasodilation, 148
Vastus lateralis, 159, 160
Vastus medialus oblicans (VMO), 159, 162; strengthening, 162 (photo), 167, 167 (photo); weakness of, 160
Vegetarians: diet of, 195; protein and, 26, 120
Ventilation, 4, 7–8
Ventolin, EIA and, 193
Verps, 194
VIP. *See* Vasoactive intestinal peptide
Viral replication, 119
Viruses, 123, 129
Visualization, 111, 112
Vitamin A (retinol), deficiency of, 121
Vitamin C (ascorbic acid), 71, 121, 123, 147; wound healing and, 77–78
Vitamin D: calcium and, 137; eating disorders and, 138
Vitamin E (tocopherol), 121, 123

Vitamins, 29; immunity and, 121–22
VMO. *See* Vastus medialus oblicans
VO₂max, 14, 15, 34, 39, 81, 86, 87, 98, 121; acclimatization and, 40–41, 146; determining, 6; endurance training and, 6; enzyme increases and, 5; factors affecting, 6; HGH and, 52; lactic acid and, 4; LT and, 7
Volume, 95, 136, 188; decreasing, 98; increasing, 59; intensity and, 95
Vomiting, 144, 194

Warm-up, 100; aerobic, 64; EIA and, 64, 70; performance and, 63–64
Water-Pik, 75
Water vapor transfer, 145
WBGT index. *See* Wet bulb-globe thermometer
Weight-bearing exercise, 183; bone and, 137; eating disorders and, 135
Weight gain, 123, 135
Weight loss, 133; chromium picolinate and, 35; diet and, 34; eating disorders and, 135, 138, 139; exercise and, 34, 35; rapid, 123; scientific look at, 31–35; stimulants/supplements and, 35
Wet bulb-globe thermometer (WBGT) index, 142; risks/recommendations associated with, 143 (table)
White blood cells, 117
Wind-chill index, 148, 149 (table)
Wind speed, 145, 148
Wounds: cleaning/dressing, 73, 74, 75–78; healing, 74, 77–78

Xeroform, 76

Yoga, 111

Zantac, 83, 194
Zeitgebers (time givers), 100
Zinc, 77, 122, 123
Zolpidem, sleep stages and, 101
Zones of insulation, 142, 145, 150
Zyrtec, 71, 130

ABOUT THE AUTHOR

Michael J. Ross, M.D. holds degrees from Tufts University and Mount Sinai School of Medicine. He began his career in cycling medicine as the race physician for the First Union Cycling series and U.S. Pro Championships in Philadelphia. Since then, he has started providing medical care and training for endurance athletes through his company Bike Doc Training, LLC. He has consulted with numerous professional athletes and USA Cycling Coaches Association.

He is a board-certified Emergency Physician, USA Cycling certified coach, avid road, mountain and cyclo-cross rider. He has written articles for medical journals, *VeloNews*, and USA Cycling.

Dr. Ross lives in Newton, Massachusetts with his wife Wendy and his son Benjamin. He can be visited on the internet at www.bikedoctraining.com or emailed at Michael@bikedoctraining.com.